Lean Six Sigma Pocket Toolbook

A Quick Reference Guide to Nearly 100 Tools for Improving Process Quality, Speed, and Complexity

Michael L. George

David Rowlands

Mark Price

John Maxey

with contributions from

Paul Jaminet *Kimberly Watson-Hemphill* *Chuck Cox*

McGraw Hill Education (India) Private Limited
CHENNAI

McGraw Hill Education Offices
Chennai New York St Louis San Francisco Auckland Bogotá Caracas
Kuala Lumpur Lisbon London Madrid Mexico City Milan Montreal
San Juan Santiago Singapore Sydney Tokyo Toronto

McGraw Hill Education (India) Private Limited

McGraw Hill Education (India) Edition 2016

RLBCRRBQRQCRZ

Reprinted in India by arrangement with McGraw-Hill Global Education Holdings, LLC, New York

Sales territories: India, Pakistan, Nepal, Bangladesh, Sri Lanka and Bhutan

ISBN-13: 978-93-5260-352-7
ISBN-10: 93-5260-352-4

Published by McGraw Hill Education (India) Private Limited,
444/1, Sri Ekambara Naicker Industrial Estate, Alapakkam, Porur, Chennai 600 116, Tamil Nadu, India, and printed at Rajkamal Electric Press, Kundli, Sonepat, Haryana

Visit us at: www.mheducation.co.in

Contents

CHAPTER 1

Using DMAIC to Improve Speed, Quality, and Cost

DMAIC (pronounced "Duh-MAY-ick") is a structured problem-solving methodology widely used in business. The letters are an acronym for the five phases of Six Sigma improvement: **Define-Measure-Analyze-Improve-Control**. These phases lead a team logically from defining a problem through implementing solutions linked to underlying causes, and establishing best practices to make sure the solutions stay in place.

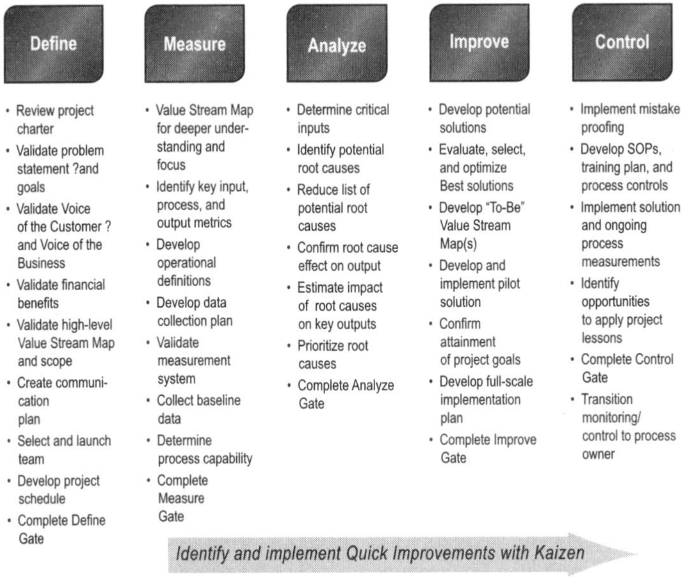

When to use DMAIC

The structure of DMAIC encourages creative thinking *within boundaries* such as keeping the basic process, product, or service. If your process is so badly broken that you need to start over from scratch or if you're designing a new product, service, or process, use Design for Lean Six Sigma (DMEDI), not covered in this book.

Selecting DMAIC projects

This book assumes that most readers will work on DMAIC projects selected for them by managers or sponsors. (If this is not the case and you are involved in the project selection process, *see* p. 26 at the end of this chapter for a quick overview.

Implementation Options for DMAIC

There are two primary options for implementing DMAIC:

1) Project-team approach

- Black Belts deployed full-time to projects
- Team members work on the project part-time—work on the project is interspersed with regular work
- Full involvement by all team members in all phases of DMAIC
- Duration can be 1 to 4 months depending on scope (some go longer; shorter is better because you can realize gains more quickly)

2) Kaizen approach

- Rapid (1 week or less), intense progress through all of DMAIC except full-scale implementation
- Preparatory work on Define, and sometimes on Measure, done by a subgroup (team leader and a Black Belt, for instance)
- Rest of the work done by the full group during several days or a week when they work ONLY on the project (participants are pulled off their regular jobs)

The basic DMAIC steps (pp. 4 to 19) apply to both of these models. Additional guidance on conducting a Kaizen project is provided on pp. 20 to 25.

"Do we have to follow all of DMAIC?"

DMAIC is a valuable tool that helps people find permanent solutions to long-standing or tricky business problems. The basic framework works well in a wide variety of situations, but using DMAIC does involve time and expense. So you should weigh the costs of using DMAIC against the benefits and the costs of skipping some steps or jumping right into solutions. Two indicators that you should follow all of DMAIC:

1) **The problem is complex.** In complex problems, the causes and solutions are not obvious. To get at the root of a complex problem, you need to bring together people with different areas of knowledge or experience. You may have to gather lots of different data before you discover patterns that provide clues about the causes.

   If you have a simple problem (or one you think is simple), often an experienced person can gather and analyze data and find a solution without going through all of the DMAIC steps.

2) **The solution risks are high.** A key part of the DMAIC methodology is developing, testing, and refining solution ideas *before* you impose them on the workplace and on customers. So you should use DMAIC any time the risks of implementation are high, even if you think a solution is obvious. However, if you've stumbled on an obvious problem and the risks of implementing the solution are minor–meaning little disruption to the process, little or no impact on customers, little cost–go ahead and try it out (using proper "solution implementation" procedures, *see* Chapter 11).

For most projects, it's risky to skip any DMAIC steps. The logic that links the DMAIC phases is key to success. But we recognize that it is human nature to want to jump to solutions and quickly make the improvement.

If you think you have an obvious solution with minimal risks, you can try skipping some of the DMAIC steps. But before you do so, ask:

- What data do I have to show that this idea is the *best possible* solution?
- How do I know that the solution will really solve the targeted problem?
- What possible downsides are there to the solution idea?

If you can't provide data to support your answers to these questions, you need to work through all the DMAIC phases.

- If you want to skip steps, see p. 152 for guidelines on how to test obvious solutions
- If you encounter problems with an "obvious solution to a simple problem" and cannot prove *with data* that the situation has improved, be prepared to launch a full DMAIC project

Define

Purpose

To have the team and its sponsor reach agreement on the scope, goals, and financial and performance targets for the project

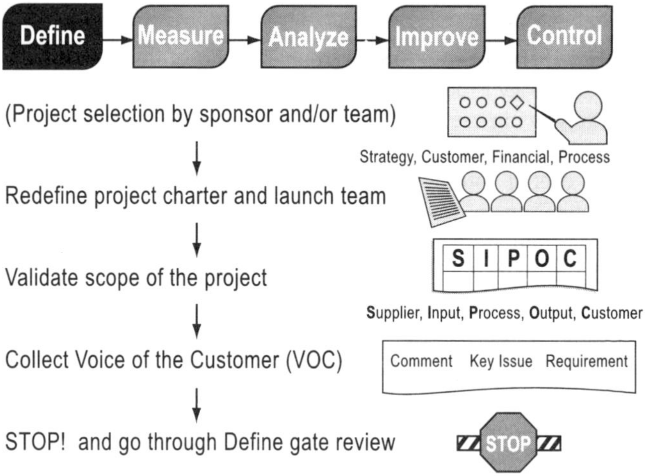

What you need before you start

- First draft of project charter from sponsor(s)
- Resource allocation (time of team members, initial budget)

Deliverables

1. A completed project charter (covering the problem statement, business impact, goals, scope, timeline, defined team)
2. Documentation showing what customers (internal and external) are or will be affected by this project and what their needs are
3. High-level process map(s), at least a SIPOC diagram, p. 38
4. Completed project plans. Requirements will vary by company but often include Gantt charts; stakeholder analysis; resistance analysis; risk analysis; action logs, responsibility assignments, and communication plans *(not covered in this book)*

5. Outcomes from the project launch meeting showing team consensus around project purpose, charter, deliverables, and team responsibilities

Key steps in Define

Note: Some companies have the full team do all of this work. Others have the Black Belts do some or all of the background work before bringing together the team. Do what makes sense for your situation.

1. **Review project charter.** Have your team discuss the draft charter from sponsors. Get answers to questions. Negotiate compromises or adjustments to scope, resources, timing, team membership as needed.

2. **Validate problem statement and goals.** Review existing data or other sources of information to confirm that the problem you've been given…
   - Exists
   - Is important to customers (collect the Voice of the Customer)
   - Is important to the business (collect Voice of the Business information)
   - Can reasonably be expected to be improved using Lean Six Sigma (DMAIC) methodologies

3. **Validate financial benefits.** Use existing data to calculate current costs, profits, margins, or other financial metrics relevant to your project. Estimate the financial impact if you achieve the project goal, and verify that it meets management expectations.

4. **Create/validate process map and scope.** Document the main steps of the process (with a SIPOC diagram, p. 38) to verify project scope; see if data exists to provide baseline measures on time, defects/errors, rework, etc., for a value stream map.

5. **Create communication plan.** Identify project participants and stakeholders (sponsors, customers, managers, process operators, etc.) and develop plans for keeping them informed about and/or involved in the project.

6. **Develop project plans (schedule, budget, milestones).**

7. **Complete the Define gate review.**

Gate review checklist for Define

A. An updated Project Charter

- **Problem Statement** detailing *when* the problem has been seen, *what* the problem is, the *magnitude* of the problem, and the *impact or consequence* of the problem (such as effect on customer Critical-to-Quality expectations). **Make sure the problem statement focuses on symptoms only** (not on causes or solutions).
- **Key stakeholders:** Who are they? How will they be involved in the project? How will progress be communicated to them?
- **Business Impact** reflecting expected financial benefits and assumptions.
- **Goal Statement** clearly identifying the key output metric (Y) to be improved.
- **Verification of Project Scope**: broad enough to achieve the project objectives yet narrow enough to be completed within the Project Plan timeframe.
- **High-level Project Plan** showing the targeted completion date for the project and intermediate milestones.
- **List of team members** representing key stakeholders, appropriate mix of skills, and knowledge (especially about the current process).

B. Documentation on your customer knowledge

- Primary external and internal customers identified
- Voice of the Customer gathered
- Customer needs evaluated for priority and importance (through Kano analysis, p. 64, for example)
- Ability to measure customer requirements

C. A high-level process map and/or SIPOC diagram (p. 38)

- High-level map showing major steps or activities (details will come in Measure)
- SIPOC map completed to identify key Suppliers, Inputs, Process boundaries, Outputs, Customers (should demonstrate that the process boundaries align with the project goals)
- Key process output variables (KPOVs) such as time, quality, and cost metrics (to show process links to project goals)

- Optional: Key data on time, delays, queues, defects, etc. (*see* p. 47)—if you don't gather these data here, you'll be collecting them in Measure

D. Detailed Project Management plans

- More detailed schedule of activities, especially for Measure (using a Gantt chart, for example)
- List of stakeholders who will be impacted by the project, and their expectations and concerns
- Communications Plan for the identified stakeholders and their concerns
- Risk management plans
- Identification of barriers/obstacles that could hinder the team (will likely require help from the Black Belt and sponsors to overcome these barriers)

Tips for Define

- If you have to spend longer than one to two days (full time) or one to two weeks (part time) in Define, that's an indication that the scope may be too broad or too vague. Talk to your manager or sponsor to see if you can rescope the project (choose a narrower topic), divide the project into phases, or adjust team membership to give you the knowledge/resources needed to complete the task.
- Speed up DMAIC by doing Define as mini-Kaizen event, where people come together for a half- or full-day session and complete all the required work (no disruptions allowed). Post documents on the wall as you work so you can update your sponsor at the end of the meeting.
- Do a thorough job of capturing customer needs as that can reveal important critical inputs (Xs).
- Make sure the team is well balanced. Try to include team members from areas both upstream and downstream from the process that's being studied.
  - If the project will require assistance from another area/specialty (such as Information Systems, finance, marketing) establish those links as early as possible. Ask representatives from that area to sit in on a team meeting and/or send a team member to meet with them one on one.

Measure

Purpose

To thoroughly understand the current state of the process and collect reliable data on process speed, quality, and costs that you will use to expose the underlying causes of problems

Deliverables

- Fully developed current-state value stream map
- Reliable data on critical inputs (Xs) and critical outputs (Ys) to be used for analyzing defects, variation, process flow, and speed
- Baseline measures of process capability, including process Sigma Quality Level, and lead time
- Refined definitions of improvement goals
- A capable measurement system
- Revised project charter (if data interpretation warrants a change)

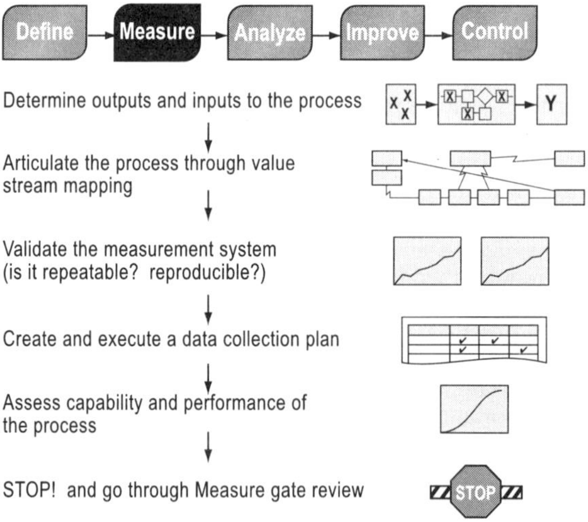

Key steps in Measure

1. **Create/validate a value stream map to confirm current process flow.** Use a basic process map (p. 39) or deployment flowchart (p. 43) to get started. Add defect, time, and other process data to generate a value stream map (p. 45).

2. **Identify the outputs, inputs, and process variables relevant to your project.** You want to collect data that relates to your project goals and targeted customers.

3. **Create a data collection plan including operational definitions for all measures.**

4. **Create a data analysis plan.** Verify what types of tools can be used for the type of data you will collect. (*See* p. 72.) Modify your data collection plan as needed.

5. **Use Measurement System Analysis and Gage R&R** (p. 87), or other procedure to ensure accurate, consistent, reliable data.
   - If using measurement instruments, be sure to calibrate them if it hasn't been done recently
   - Make sure Operational Definitions (p. 76) of all metrics are commonly used and applied by all data collectors

6. **Collect data to establish baselines.**
7. **Update value stream map with data.**

8. **Use Little's Law (p. 202) to calculate lead time.**

9. **Perform process capability evaluation (p. 138).**

10. **Make quick-hit improvements** if warranted by data analysis and risk analysis so you can get partial benefits now (be sure you are in a position to measure and show improvement), then continue with project.
    - Use a Kaizen approach or, minimally, follow guidelines on implementing obvious solutions (p. 152)
    - If solution ideas pop up but the risks are high or unknown, keep track of the ideas for potential implementation but continue with your DMAIC project

11. **Prepare for Measure gate review.**

Gate review checklist for Measure

A. Detailed value stream map (VSM)

- Documentation of people who were involved in creating the value stream map (should include representative operators, technical experts, supervisors, perhaps customers and selected suppliers)

- Map showing the main process steps relevant to the project scope, along with the inventories/work in process, lead times, queues, customer demand (takt) rate, and cycle times for those steps
- Supplier and customer loops clearly identified; output and inputs clearly understood

B. Data and Metrics

- Lists of key process output variables (KPOVs) and key process and input variables (KPIVs) identified and checked for consistency against the SIPOC diagram
- Indications of how KPOVs are tied to Critical-to-Quality customer requirements (CTQs)
- Notations on which KPOVs are selected as the primary improvement focus
- Operational Definitions (p. 76) and data collection plans (p. 72) that were created, tested, and implemented for all metrics
- Documentation of measurement system analysis (p. 87) or its equivalent performed to ensure accuracy, consistency, and reliability of data
- Notes on problems or challenges with data collection and how they were addressed
- Notes on ANY assumptions that were made
- Copies or printouts of completed data collection forms

C. Capability Analysis

- Time-ordered data collected on process outputs, charted on a control chart (p. 122), and analyzed for special and common causes (p. 133)
- Baseline capability (p. 135) calculations for key output metrics (Ys)
- Product/service specifications framed in terms of external customer requirements or internal performance expectations (note any assumptions made)
- Documentation on reliability of the capability estimates (is the measurement process stable, and does it have the expected distribution?)

- Project goals reframed in terms of shifting the mean, reducing variation, or both

D. Updated project charter and plans

- Project charter, financial benefits, and schedule timeline updated to reflect new knowledge
- Project risks re-evaluated
- Documentation of issues/concerns that may impact project success
- Team recommendation on whether it makes business sense to continue with project
- Detailed plans for Analyze, including anything that requires sponsor approval (changes in scope, budget, timing, resources)

E. Quick improvements

Actions recommended for immediate implementation, such as:

- Non-value-added process steps, sources of special cause variation that can be eliminated to improve process time and/or capability
- Required resources (budget, training, time) for implementation

Tips for Measure

- **Be sure to check your measurement system.** You'll end up wasting a lot of time and effort if you get unreliable data. Use Measurement System Analysis (p. 87) or Gage R&R (p. 88).
- Be sure your team understands the difference between lead time, takt rate (customer demand rate), and process capacity—these are commonly confused.
- Build your value stream map manually. Include pictures of tools, templates, documents or other devices used at each step in the process. This help the team members to "see" what is really going on in the process.

Analyze

Purpose

To pinpoint and verify causes affecting the key input and output variables tied to project goals. ("Finding the critical Xs")

Deliverables

- Documentation of potential causes considered in your analysis
- Data charts and other analyses that show the link between the targeted input and process (Xs) variables and critical output (Y)
- Identification of value-add and non-value-add work
- Calculation of process cycle efficiency

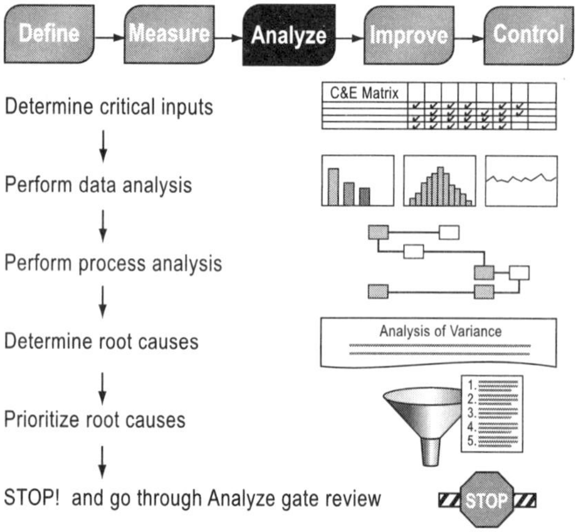

Key steps in Analyze

1. **Conduct value analysis.** Identify value-add, non-value-add and business non-value-add steps (*see* definitions on p. 50).
2. **Calculate Process Cycle Efficiency (PCE).** Compare to world-class benchmarks to help determine how much improvement is needed.
3. **Analyze the process flow.** Identify bottleneck points and constraints in a process, fallout and rework points, and assess their impact on the process throughput and its ability to meet customer demands and CTQs.

4. **Analyze data collected in Measure.**
5. **Generate theories to explain potential causes.** Use brainstorming, FMEA, C&E diagrams or matrices, and other tools to come up with potential causes of the observed effects. (*See* Chapter 8.)
6. **Narrow the search.** Use brainstorming, selection, and prioritization techniques (Pareto charts, hypothesis testing, etc.) to narrow the search for root causes and significant cause-and-effect relationships.
7. **Collect additional data to verify root causes.** Use scatter plots or more sophisticated statistical tools (such as hypothesis testing, ANOVA, or regression) to verify significant relationships.
8. **Prepare for Analyze gate review.**

Gate review checklist for Analyze

A. Process Analysis

- Calculations of Process Cycle Efficiency
- Where process flow problems exist

B. Root Cause Analysis

- Documentation of the range of potential Key Process Input Variables (KPIVs) that were considered (such as cause-and-effect diagrams, p. 146; FMEA, p. 270)
- Documentation of how the list of potential causes was narrowed (stratification, multivoting, Pareto analysis, etc.)
- Statistical analyses and/or data charts that confirm or refute a cause-and-effect relationship and indicate the strength of the relationship (scatter plot, design of experiment results, regression calculations, ANOVA, component of variation, lead time calculations showing how much improvement is possible by elimination of NVA activities, etc.)
- Documentation of which root causes will be targeted for action in Improve (include criteria used for selection)

C. Updated charter and project plans

- Team recommendations on potential changes in team membership considering what may happen in Improve (expertise and skills needed, work areas affected, etc.)
- Revisions/updates to project plans for Improve, such as time and resource commitments needed to complete the project

- Team analysis of project status (still on track? still appropriate to focus on original goals?)
- Team analysis of current risks and potential for acceleration
- Plans for the Improve phase

Tips for Analyze

- If you identify a quick-hit improvement opportunity, implement using a Kaizen approach. Get partial benefits now, then continue with project.
- Be critical about your own data collection—the data must help you understand the causes of the problem you're investigating. Avoid "paralysis by analysis": wasting valuable project time by collecting data that don't move the project forward.
- This is a good time in a project to celebrate team success for finding the critical Xs and implementing some quick hits!

Improve

Purpose

To learn from pilots of the selected solution(s) and execute full-scale implementation

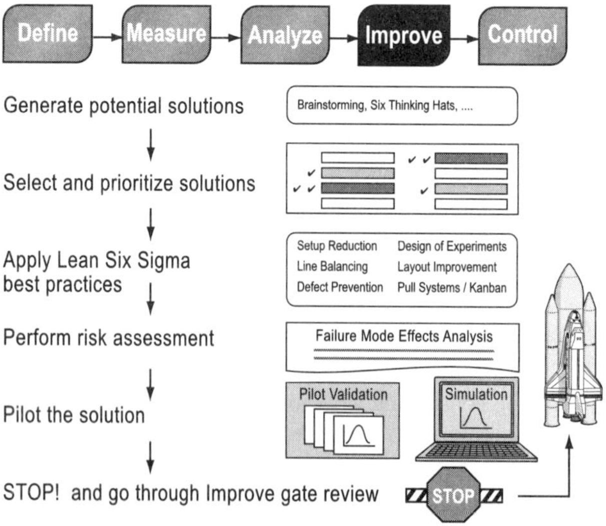

Deliverables

- For a quality-improvement project: Tested, robust solutions shown to affect the proven causes (Xs) that affect the critical output (Y)
- For a Lean project: Documentation on results of the chosen Lean best practice or solution applied (5S, Pull system, Four step rapid set up, etc.)
- An improved process that is stable, predictable and meets customer requirements

Key steps in Improve

1. **Develop potential solutions.** Use the confirmed cause-and-effect relationship (from Analyze) to identify a wide range of potential solutions. This is one step where pushing for creativity is highly desired.
2. **Evaluate, select, and optimize best solutions.** Flesh out the solution ideas, develop criteria and evaluate the alternatives, document the results (*see* criteria development, p. 256; solution matrix, p. 258; Pugh matrix, p. 265). Be open to altering or combining options to optimize the final selections. If necessary, perform designed experiments (p. 185) to find optimal settings for combinations of factors.
3. **Develop "To Be" value stream map.** Revise the existing VSM to reflect what the process will look like after changes are made. Include estimates of time savings, improved quality, and so on.
4. **Develop and implement pilot solution.** Write up the tasks to be performed in the pilot solution. Train pilot participants. Document results of pilot along with ideas for improvements.
5. **Confirm attainment of project goals.** Compare results to baseline.
6. **Develop and execute full-scale implementation plan.**
7. **Prepare for Improve gate review.**

Gate review checklist for Improve

A. Solution development and selection

- Documentation on alternative solutions considered
- Data displays, statistical analysis, or documentation on other tools used to develop the solutions

- List of weighted criteria used to evaluate solution; solution matrix or other display summarizing the evaluation results (should include benefit, effort, cost, ease and timing of implementation, resource requirements, etc.)
- List of concerns raised by process participants and the process owner, and notes on how those concerns have been or will be addressed

B. Pilot testing

- Documentation (including "to be" value stream map) of the redesigned process with changes in process flow highlighted
- Documentation on communication with process participants, customers, and owners (as appropriate)
- Data display, statistical analyses or other documentation showing the results of pilot test or simulation
- Documentation of what was learned from the pilot test and plans for improvement during full-scale implementation
- Documentation confirming that the pilot solution can achieve project goals (include before/after charts, hypothesis tests, etc.)

C. Full-scale implementation

- Documentation of plans you used for full-scale implementation
- Risk management plans (for avoiding, reducing, or mitigating risks)
- Plans for addressing regulatory (e.g., OSHA), legal, fiscal, or other business requirements
- Documentation of results from full-scale implementation (especially data showing stable performance)

D. Updated charter and project plans

- Updated project charter, financial benefits, and schedule

Tips for Improve

- Caution: Be on the alert for "scope creep" during Improve–the tendency to go beyond the defined boundaries of the project. Keep your team focused on the scope of your charter.

Control

Purpose

To complete project work and hand off improved process to process owner, with procedures for maintaining the gains

Deliverables

- Documented plan to transition improved process back to process owner, participants and sponsor
- Before and after data on process metrics
- Operational, training, feedback, and control documents (updated process maps and instructions, control charts and plans, training documentation, visual process controls)
- A system for monitoring the implemented solution (Process Control Plan), along with specific metrics to be used for regular process auditing
- Completed project documentation, including lessons learned, and recommendations for further actions or opportunities

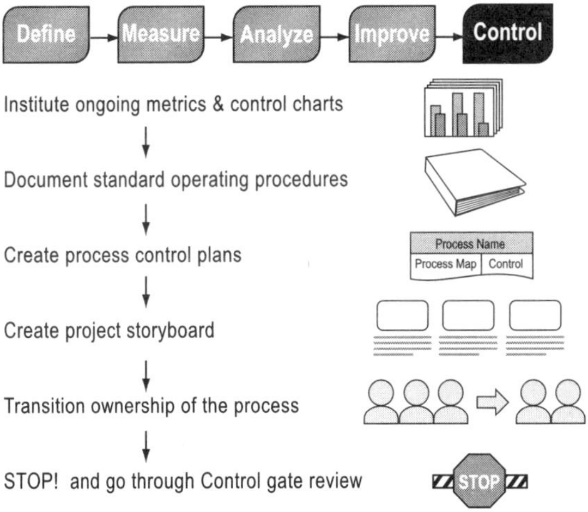

Key steps in Control

1. **Develop supporting methods and documentation** to sustain full-scale implementation.

2. **Launch implementation.**
3. **Lock in performance gains.** Use mistake-proofing or other measures to prevent people from performing work in old ways.
4. **Monitor implementation.** Use observation, interaction, and data collection and charting; make additional improvements as appropriate.
5. **Develop Process Control Plans and hand off control to process owner.**
6. **Audit the results.** Confirm measures of improvements and assign dollar figures where appropriate. Give audit plan to company's auditing group.
7. **Finalize project:**
   - Document ideas about where your company could apply the methods and lessons learned from this project
   - Hold the Control Gate Review
   - Communicate project methods and results to others in the organization
   - Celebrate project completion
8. **Validate performance and financial results** several months after project completion.

Gate review checklist for Control

A. Full-scale Implementation results

- Data charts and other before/after documentation showing that the realized gains are in line with the project charter
- Process Control Plan

B. Documentation and measures prepared for sustainability

- Essential documentation of the improved process, including key procedures and process maps
- Procedures to be used to monitor process performance and continued effectiveness of the solution
- Control charts, capability analysis, and other data displays showing current performance and verifying gains
- Documentation of procedures (mistake-proofing, automated process controls) used to lock in gains

C. Evidence of buy-in, sharing and celebrating

- Testimonials or documentation showing that:
  - The appropriate people have evaluated and signed off on the changes
  - The process owner has taken over responsibility for managing continuing operations
  - The project work has been shared with the work area and company at large (using a project database, bulletin boards, etc.)
- Summary of lessons learned throughout the project
- List of issues/opportunities that were not addressed in this project (to be considered as candidates for future projects)
- Identification of opportunities to use the methods from this project in other projects
- Plans for celebrating the hard work and successful efforts

Tips for Control

- **Set up a realistic transition plan** that will occur over a series of meetings, training events, and progress checks scheduled between the team and the process participants (avoid blind handoffs of implementation plans).
- **Schedule a validation check 6 to 12 months after the control gate review.** Be sure the project sponsor and local controller / finance representative is present to validate that the results are in place and stable!
- **Never anticipate perfection!** Something always goes wrong. Develop a rapid response plan to address unanticipated failures via FMEA (p. 270). Identify who will be part of the "rapid response team" when a problem arises. Get permission from sponsor to use personnel should the need arise.
- **Develop tools that are easy for process participants to reference and use.** It's hard to keep paying attention to how a process operates, so you need to make it as easy as possible for people to monitor the work automatically.
- **Work out the kinks before transferring responsibility for managing the new process.** Handing off (to the sponsor or process owner) a process that is still being worked on will compromise success.

Kaizen DMAIC

Kaizen is a method for accelerating the pace of process improvement in any setting. It evolved in the application of Lean methods in manufacturing settings, but has since been adapted to the broader DMAIC framework.

Characteristics of a Kaizen approach

The term Kaizen is used for any intensive project where employees are pulled off their regular jobs.

- Team works 3 to 5 days full time (vs. typical team approach of spreading project work over 3 to 6 months)
- Resources dedicated
  - Participants spend 100% of their time on the project during the Kaizen event
  - Participants should be treated as if they are on vacation from their regular responsibilities
  - Project sponsor, event leader, and participants must work together to make arrangements to have work covered
  - The handling of emails, voicemails, etc., is minimized (if not outright forbidden) during project time
- Project is well-defined going in
  - There is not time to redefine the purpose or scope, so the boundaries must be well defined ahead of time
- Basic data already gathered (by a Black Belt or Team Leader)
- Implementation is immediate!
  - Bias for action (will act when 70% to 80% confident vs. 95% confident as in typical DMAIC projects)
  - Implementation is completed as much as possible during the week of the event
  - Doing something now that is "roughly right" is OK (vs. the typical DMAIC approach of waiting until solutions have been refined)
  - Items that cannot be finished during the Kaizen event are to be completed within 20 days
- Management makes support areas (maintenance, information technology, human resources, marketing, etc.) available during the Kaizen event

When to use Kaizen

- When obvious waste sources have been identified
- When the scope and boundaries of a problem are clearly defined and understood
- When implementation risk is minimal
- When results are needed immediately
- In the early stages of deployment to gain momentum and build credibility of the DMAIC problem-solving approach
- When opportunities to eliminate obvious sources of instability and waste have been identified through process mapping, work area tour, data collection, etc.

How to conduct a Kaizen DMAIC

A. DEFINE (Prep Week)

- **Clearly define the Kaizen objective.**
- **Select a Kaizen leader**, usually an area leader, group leader or someone close to process activities (not management) to be the Kaizen team leader.
  - Make sure the Kaizen team leader or facilitator is involved in project selection and scoping.
- **Select and notify participants.** Optimum is 6 to 8 team members, including at least 2 people who work directly in the project area (process staff), and 1 who supervises or leads the project area (supervisor). In order of importance, complete the team as follows:
  - People from the direct upstream process
  - People from the direct downstream process
  - People from areas that directly support the process being studied, such as information technology, finance, purchasing, engineering
  - Management staff of the project area, such as a division manager, operations manager, engineering manager, etc.
  - Other functions that may have useful insights (HR, sales and marketing, corporate functions, or other divisions)
- **Prepare training and materials** (if needed). Tailor training to the focus of the project. Make copies of training manuals for team use. Make poster-size worksheets for the Kaizen workshop.

- **Assemble background information** including existing data on the problem, customers, etc.
- **Complete logistics planning**–meeting rooms, workplace tours, meals, lodging if people are coming from out of town, supplies needed, etc.
- **Arrange for coverage during participants' absence from their workplace and/or during disruptions to workplace**. In manufacturing, build some WIP to cover for Kaizen-related production stoppages. (Ex: a team may want to implement a new setup reduction process and will require the machine to be down to try new techniques.) In service situations, arrange for temp staff, job-sharing, or other means to make sure service to customers is not disrupted (much like you would if the person were going on vacation).
- **Arrange for management/sponsor participation**. Plan for top manager to launch team with motivational, appreciative kick-off. Sponsors should check in at the end of each day to provide guidance and approval.
- **Contact departments/functions whose support you'll need during the week.**
  - Information technology (prep them for potential software/programming needs and ideas)
  - Facilities management (rooms needed, potential support if work layouts will be changed, etc.)

B. MEASURE (Prep Week and Monday of Event)

- Validate the value stream map of the process. Complete a resource flow layout for all operations or tasks if necessary (people, paper, material, machines, information).
- Carefully observe then collect needed metrics for tasks or steps in the selected process.
  - The Kaizen leader should determine whether it would help to gather preliminary data during the Prep Week

C. ANALYZE (Tuesday-Wednesday)

- Quickly validate root causes and identify sources of waste
- Review waste elimination techniques then brainstorm process improvements for eliminating non-value-added tasks and reducing variation

Typical Plan for Kaizen

Prep	BB and sponsor DEFINE project, select Kaizen leader (usually group leader), ID participants. BB and leader assemble background material, prep training, secure logistics.
Mon	(Often start midday.) BB and Kaizen leader brief team on Define decisions. Deliver training if needed. Resolve questions about charter. Begin MEASURE by creating/validating value stream map (including process observation).
Tues	MEASURE continues until all data collected, move into ANALYZE as soon as possible to identify and verify root causes.
Wed	By Wed. afternoon should be in IMPROVE, working on solutions (developing criteria, evaluating alternatives, conducting pilot).
Thurs	Finish IMPROVE and move into CONTROL (develop new documentation, develop plans for full-scale implementation).
Fri	Usually by midday, team is prepared to present results to management. Get approval for plans, resolve questions.
Follow up	BB, Kaizen leader, and process owners (as appropriate) help guide full-scale implementation and monitoring of solutions. Adjustments made as necessary

D. IMPROVE (Wednesday-Thursday)

- Create action item list to accomplish improvements
- Implement process improvements, train employees then test, fine-tune, and ensure the process is capable

E. CONTROL (Thursday-Friday)

- Create Standard Operating Procedures to document and sustain improvements
- Present results to management team, complete follow-up, develop plan to monitor results over time

Management/sponsor involvement in the Kaizen Event

1. Kickoff

- Plan for top manager to launch team with motivational, appreciative kickoff.

2. *Mid-Week Review Meeting:*

- Purpose: To review with local management team the analysis findings and the proposed Kaizen activities for implementation; to address any obstacles impacting the team's implementation plan; to gain understanding and agreement from management to proceed with proposed Kaizen implementation.
- Responsibility for conducting the meeting: Kaizen project team leader.
- Timing: For projects beginning Monday afternoon this meeting will occur early Wednesday afternoon typically between 1:00 p.m. and 2:30 p.m.
- Duration: 30 minutes for each project team.
- Attendees: Kaizen project team leader, team sponsor, management or the work area/facility.
- Agenda:
  - Full group reviews Kaizen project scope, goals, and objectives
  - Team leader summarizes the Kaizen analysis findings and conclusions
  - Team leader presents improvement activities and steps developed by the Kaizen project team
  - Full group discusses and resolves anticipated or real obstacles to improvement, and any issues or obstacles identified by management
  - Sponsors and management endorse continuation of the Kaizen event with agreed-on modifications

3. *Final Presentation*

- Purpose: To inform sponsors and local management of workshop findings and outcomes
- Kaizen team leader and members present findings and results
  - Tell how the team progressed through each phase of DMAIC
  - Include data charts, process maps, etc., of before/after results
  - Document what is needed to maintain the gains
  - Document open action items and responsibilities for getting them done
- Sponsors and management should congratulate team members for successes and thank them for their dedicated team work

Tips on using a Kaizen DMAIC

- If you're the Kaizen team leader or facilitator, "walk the process" the week before the Kaizen.
- Have an experienced Kaizen or improvement expert facilitate the session.
- Use any appropriate improvement tools in your toolbox—as long as they can be successfully employed in the time given!
- Use daily goal sheet at end of every day to do a 10-minute review with your sponsor—what you did today, what is planned for tomorrow.
- Post charts and plans; make everything visible.
- Run the process backwards (starting from the output and working backwards) to help generate ideas for improvement.
- Prepare some form of Kaizen team recognition (hats, shirts, certificates printed, etc.).
- Be creative in your use of a Kaizen philosophy. For example, many traditional projects start off with a 1- or 2-day mini-Kaizen where the team works through all of Define and perhaps gets started on Measure. Subsequent intensive sessions can replace shorter weekly or biweekly meetings.

Quick Take

Project selection

Most team members do not join an improvement project until after the problem has been identified. But if you are asked to participate in selecting and defining projects, here is a quick overview.

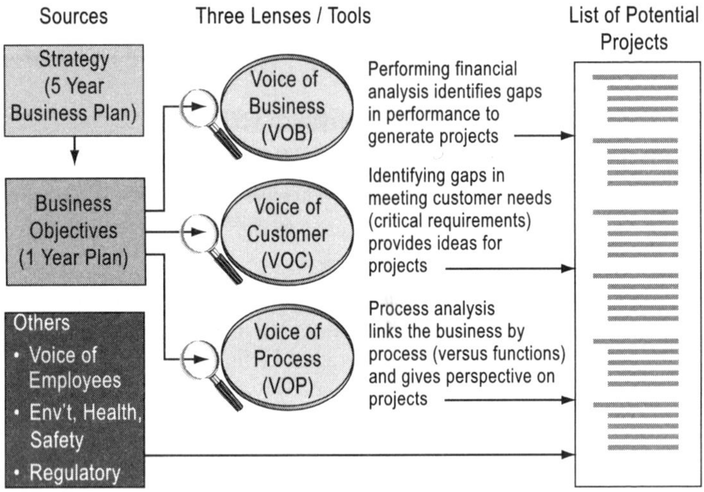

Reprinted courtesy of Alcan.

- Target areas are usually identified by looking at what's important to the business (the "value levers" such as cost, profit, revenue, customer segments, etc.) and gathering ideas from diverse sources (customer/marketing information, process data, employee opinions, regulatory changes, etc.).
- The project selection process starts by screening the ideas based on just a few critical criteria to make the list more manageable. Each remaining idea is assigned to someone who will do more investigation and prepare a draft charter that provides more details about potential costs, benefits, scope, etc. These draft charters are then evaluated against more rigorous criteria to select the best opportunities.
- Deciding which of the best candidate projects to implement first involves a strategic decision about what is most important to the company and its customers.

Chapter 2
Working With Ideas

Purpose of these tools

Most of the value in a team's work lies in the ideas and insights generated during a project. The tools in this section will help your team generate, organize, and process ideas.

Note: There are many good resources available to teams on generating and working with "language data." We've included three that are used universally not only for their own sake but as part of many other tools that appear in this book. We encourage teams to investigate creativity tools and additional methods for decision making.

Deciding which tool to use

- **Brainstorming**, below, basic guidelines for holding an idea-generating discussion. All teams will need this.
- **Affinity diagram**, p. 30, a way to organize a large set of ideas. Very helpful for any team after a brainstorming session, when analyzing customer comments, etc.
- **Multivoting**, p. 31, a method for identifying priorities or narrowing down alternatives. Helpful when you have more ideas than your team can reasonably handle.

Brainstorming

Purpose

To provide a group with a wide range of ideas around any topic

Why use brainstorming

- Brainstorming produces many ideas or solutions in a short time
- Brainstorming stimulates the creative thinking process
- Brainstorming helps make sure that all group members' ideas are considered

When to use brainstorming

Use brainstorming whenever your group wants to make sure a range of ideas are considered, including…

- Completing elements in a project charter
- Identifying customers to include in research
- Identifying potential causes to investigate
- Identifying types of data to collect
- Identifying solution ideas

How to brainstorm

1. Review the problem definition
2. Clarify the goal/question and provide any relevant information
3. Give everyone a few minutes of silence to think about the question and individually write down some ideas
    - For ease of consolidation later, have people write down their ideas on self-stick notes or cards (one idea per note or card)
    - Encourage creativity; no idea is too outrageous for brainstorming
4. Gather ideas
    - Do a round robin, where people state one idea at a time, or do an open "popcorn," where anyone can speak up at any time.
    - Capture every idea…
        - If ideas are written on self-stick notes, post them on the wall, board, or flip chart
        - Alternatively, have each person read one idea aloud so a scribe can write it on a flip chart posted where everyone can see it
        - If doing cause analysis, post the ideas on a blank cause-and-effect diagram (this helps make sure all categories are considered)

- Do not allow discussion until after all ideas are gathered; allow only questions of clarification. ("By 'important' do you mean to us or to our customers?")
- OK for people to write down or add new ideas sparked during the sharing session. Make sure the new idea is captured on both the flip chart and on a self-stick note.
- Continue until everyone is out of ideas.

5. Consolidate similar ideas and discuss the complete set of ideas. Use other tools as appropriate:
   - To find patterns, use affinity diagrams (p. 30), or cause-and-effect diagrams (p. 146)
   - To narrow down or prioritize items, use Multivoting, p. 31

Brainstorming DOs and DON'Ts

DO...

- Go for quantity (not necessarily quality) in the early rounds
- Allow individuals to complete their thoughts
- Build on existing ideas
- Be brief when stating an idea
- Organize, categorize, and evaluate only after the brainstorming session
- Keep the self-stick notes even if you transcribe ideas onto a flip chart (the self-stick notes can be reused for creating an affinity diagram)

DON'T...

- Criticize ideas (do not allow "idea assassins")
- Make judgments as ideas are being offered
- Paraphrase an individual's idea when scribing
- Allow any one person to dominate the session

Affinity diagrams

Purpose

To organize facts, opinions and issues into natural groups to help diagnose a complex situation or find themes

Why use an affinity diagram

- To help organize a lot of ideas
- To help identify central themes in a set of ideas
- When information about a problem is not well organized
- When a breakthrough is needed beyond traditional thinking

When to use affinity diagrams

- Use to organize ideas from a brainstorming session in any phase of DMAIC
- Use to find themes and messages in customer statements gleaned from interviews, surveys, or focus groups

How to create an affinity diagram

1. Gather ideas from brainstorming session, or customer need statements from interview transcripts, surveys, etc.
2. Write ideas on cards or self-stick notes (one idea per card; stay as close to original language as possible).
3. Post self-stick notes randomly on a board or flip chart; if using cards, place them randomly on a table top.
4. Allow people to SILENTLY start grouping the cards or notes.
    - It's OK to move notes or cards that someone else has already moved. If you cannot agree on where an idea belongs, write a duplicate note and put it in both groups
    - Silence is critical!–don't let the talkers sway the non-talkers
5. When the clustering is done, create a "header" label (on a note or card) for each group.
    - Work through the groups one at a time
    - Ask participants to interpret what they see
    - Ask them to suggest a label or key theme for that group

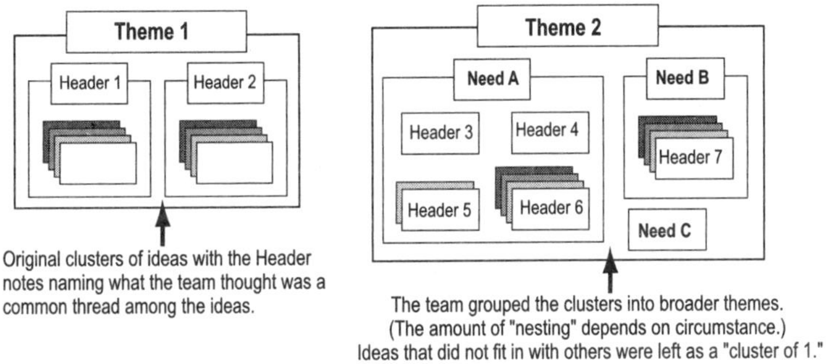

- Write the theme on a larger self-stick note or card (the "Header") and place it at the top of a cluster
- Continue until you've labeled all clusters

6. OPTIONAL: Do a second round of clustering if desired. Clip together all the cards or notes from each cluster with only the Header labels showing. Then move the Headers into groups. Create "Master" header labels for the larger clusters.

7. Complete the diagram and discuss the results.
   - How will the patterns you've found influence your actions?
   - If you're working with customer need statements, move into developing requirements based on those needs. May want to separate the needs based on the Kano Model categories (p. 66) before starting.

Quick Take

Multivoting

Highlights

A quick technique for identifying priorities or at least narrowing down the options from a list of ideas

To use multivoting...

Prework: This method assumes you have an existing list of ideas or options. Eliminate duplicates and combine related ideas before continuing.

1. Number every idea or option being considered
2. Write each idea on a flip chart or whiteboard visible to all participants

3. Decide how many votes each person will have
   - Rule of thumb: Participants should be able to cast multiple votes equal to about 1/3 of the total number of items on the list (Ex: 33 items on the list = 11 votes per person)
4. Cast votes
   - Decide if people can cast more than one vote for an item or if they must split their votes between items.
   - Easiest method: Give everyone a marker and have them go to the flip chart or whiteboard and mark their votes.
   - Confidential method: Have people write down on a slip of paper the numbers of the items they are voting for. Collect the slips and mark the votes on the flip chart or whiteboard.
5. Count votes
   - Tally the votes and record the totals next to each item
6. Decide on a course of action
   - Identify the top vote-getters
   - Eliminate from consideration all ideas with few or no votes
   - OPTIONAL: If the list of top vote-getters is still too large for your purposes, do a second round of multivoting using only those top vote getters. (Ex: First round of votes on a list of 33 items identified 12 top vote-getters; do a second round on those top 12, this time giving only 4 votes each)

Solution Alternatives
(highest possible score = 8)

Idea Scores

Idea Scores	Totals
Idea A: 8, 8, 6, 7, 8, 2	6/39
Idea B: 6, 5, 4, 7, 3	5/25
Idea C: 3, 2, 2, 1	4/8

CHAPTER 3

Value Stream Mapping and Process Flow Tools

Purpose of these tools

- Visually documents a process (including key data as captured on a value stream map)
- Provides fact-based process description as basis for understanding current problems (poor flow, rework loops, delays, etc.) and opportunities
- Enables teams to quickly see improvement opportunities within the process and begin defining critical Xs (underlying causes)
- Helps team see how a process should work (future state) once they eliminate waste
- Helps communicate inside and outside the organization

Deciding which tool to use

- **Tips on process mapping**, p. 34, gives practical tips for generating a useful process map. Review as needed.
- **Process observation**, p. 36, gives tips for going out to watch what really goes on in a process. Always a good idea at the beginning of a process improvement project, even if you think your team members already have a lot of process knowledge.
- **SIPOC**, p. 38, is a simple diagram for identifying the basic elements of a process (boundaries, supplier inputs, process inputs, steps, customers and outputs). Most teams will want to do a SIPOC diagram at the beginning of their project to capture a high-level view of targeted operations (helps communicate with sponsors and others). SIPOC is a good tool for translating customer requirements into output requirements and identifying related Key Process Output Variables (KPOVs).
- **Process mapping steps**, p. 39, covers the elements of creating a flowchart.
- **Transportation diagrams, spaghetti/workflow diagrams,** p. 42, are specialized maps that show unique ways to depict different aspects of workflow. Skim through to see if they could help your project.

- **Swim-lane (deployment) flowcharts,** p. 43, are especially useful when the process being studied goes across three or more functions. Very often there are discontinuities in the process during the hand-offs between functions. Effective at showing the many handoffs, transports, queues and rework loops in a process.
- **Value stream map,** p. 45, is a "process map with data"–a tool for capturing process data (on WIP, setup time, processing time/unit, error rates, idle time, etc.) as well as flow. The foundation for Lean improvement methods. Mandatory tool for all teams whose mission is to speed up the process and eliminate non-value-add cost. (*See also* the complexity value stream map on p. 243)
- **Value-add/non-value-add analysis,** p. 49, gives guidelines for identifying which work in a process your customers value and which they do not value. Every project that involves process improvement should establish before and after levels of value-add and non-value-add cost.
- **Time Value Map,** p. 52, and **Value-add Chart (task time or takt time chart)**, p. 53, are visual tools for emphasizing how process time is divided between value-add and non-value-add work. Particularly recommended for teams whose members are new to thinking in VA/NVA terms.

Quick Take

Process mapping

Key principles

- **Documentation is no substitute for observation.** You MUST walk the process and talk to the staff to find out what really goes on day to day. Do this even if you're studying a work area you think you already know!
- **A flowchart is a means, not an end.** Don't get so wrapped up in creating the perfect flowchart that you delay the value-add work on a project. Only go to a level of detail that is helpful for the project.
- **Boundaries of what to map should come from your project charter**. If boundaries are not spelled out, check with your sponsor(s).

- **Involve a cross-representation of those who work in the process to create the map.** No one person will have all the process knowledge you need.
- **Process maps are meant to be used**. If your maps sit on a shelf or are stuck in one person's computer, they aren't doing you much good. Establish practices that make them living documents; refer to them in all team meetings, use in training and re-training; update with each process change, etc.

Recommended process maps

- Process study should include at a minimum…
  - SIPOC diagram
  - Basic value stream map with value-add vs. non-value-add identification; add other project-critical metrics as applicable
  - Process observation
- If you work in transactional processes, you may find the swim-lane/functional deployment format more informative because it emphasizes the handoffs between people or groups
- If your project will focus on improving the workplace, use a workflow diagram to get a visual map of the workspaces

Decide on level/breadth of the flowchart…

High-level view: Depicts the major elements and their interactions. Should show the role of feedback and information flow. Useful early in a project to identify boundaries and scope. (Not useful during improvement because of lack of detail.)

Low-level view: Depicts specific actions, workflow, rework loops, etc., in a process. Useful for a process of limited scope; too cumbersome when all you need is a view of the overall flow.

Select current (as-is) vs. ideal (should-be or future) vs. updated (to-be) versions

Current/as-is: Captures the process as it works today. Most projects should include a current map of the project.

- If the problems are so severe that a major process redesign is required, create an ideal/future map instead

Ideal/future/should-be: Created by asking "What would we do if we didn't have any of the restrictions we have today? What would we do if we could start from scratch?" Helps teams see the work in a new way and generate creative ideas about how to do the work better or faster.

- Stretch your team's imagination by quickly constructing a future state map that contains only the value-added steps. The comparison of current reality to this "Ideal" future will generate a lot of improvement ideas.
- Should-be maps *must* be consistent with the goals set down in a team's charter.

Updated/to-be: Describes the new process flow after changes are implemented. Do a to-be chart as part of solution planning or when designing or redesigning a process.

Tips

- If you are guiding another team, try to get a mental image of how the work should flow at the end of the project. That can help you focus on the gap between where you need to be and the current state.

Quick Take

Process observation

Highlights

- Observing a process in action gives team members a deep understanding of reality and can spark ideas about improvement opportunities and solutions
- Observation works best if you plan what you want to do and how you will capture and use the insights people gain

To observe a process...

1. Clarify the purpose of observation.
   - Is this a general walkthrough or is there a specific purpose (Ex: observing handoffs at a specific step)

2. Identify observers.
   - If possible, include both experienced and novice process operators/staff

3. Prepare an observation form and train observers.
   - Create a form to capture process data or general impressions
   - Train all observers in how to use the form; hold practice runs to make sure everyone is using the form in the same way

4. Prepare staff in the workplace.
   - Well in advance of the observation session, alert people in the affected work area about the timing and purpose of the observation
   - Get permission from a process owner, supervisor, or manager; make sure it's OK to conduct the observation session and talk to process operators/staff

5. Walk the process; carry out your observations plans.

6. Have observers summarize lessons learned and present them to whole team. Discuss the results.
   - Try to determine the "best repeatable time." Then have your team discuss how to make "best repeatable" the standard for every step in the process.

Example Process Observation Form

(focus here is on process flow and timing)

Process Observed: ______________________ Date: _______ Time: __________

Step	Description	Worker	Distance from last step (in ft.)	Task time	Wait time	WIP	Observations
Totals:							

Tips

- If one purpose of the observation is to measure lead time, try to schedule multiple sessions so that you can capture the variation.
- It is also a good idea to make multiple observations for WIP and items in queue.
- Make sure all your timing measurements are coordinated. If, for example, observers are working in parallel at different points the process, make sure they all start and end their timing devices at the same time. Later, at a team meeting, you can piece together the data for the entire process without worrying that the measures won't line up.

Quick Take

SIPOC

Highlights

- A process snapshot that captures information critical to a project
- SIPOC diagrams help a team and its sponsor(s) agree on project boundaries and scope
- A SIPOC helps teams verify that process inputs match outputs of the upstream process and inputs/expectations of downstream process(es)

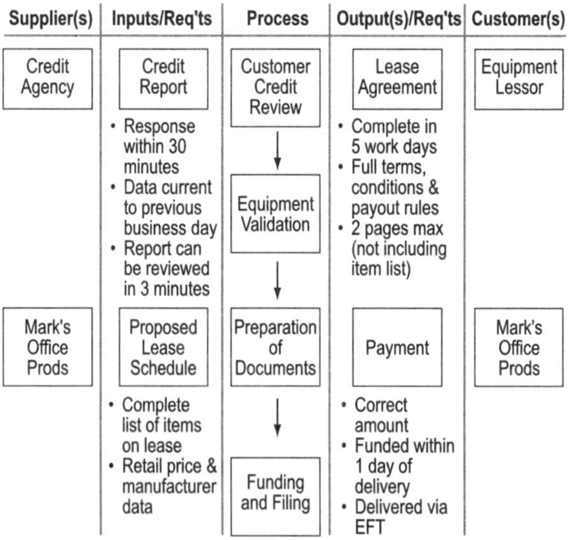

To create a SIPOC diagram...

Note: You can vary the sequence of these activities. Often it works best to identify the process steps you're concerned with because that defines boundaries, then move on to Outputs/Customers, and back to Suppliers/Inputs. But do them in any order that makes sense for your project.

1. Identify process boundaries and key activities
   - Keep at a high level, with perhaps 6 activities at most
2. Identify the key outputs (Ys) and customers of those outputs
   - Brainstorm outputs and customers
   - If you have a lot of different outputs and customers, focus on a critical few
3. Identify inputs (Xs) and suppliers
   - Brainstorm inputs and suppliers
   - If you have a lot of different inputs and suppliers, focus on a critical few
4. Identify critical-to-quality requirements for the inputs, process steps, and outputs
   - Remember, you'll have to verify this later with data collection

Tips

- Be very specific about where the process starts and ends. This should align with the scope of your project.

Quick Take

Process mapping steps

Highlights

- The basic steps for creating a process map are the same no matter what type of map you're creating.
- Strive for a level of detail that is useful to your project—no more, no less. Too much detail will bog you down; too little will make the flowchart useless.

To create a process map...

1. Review the process being studied and its boundaries as defined for your project.
2. Identify the type of chart you want to create.
3. Have participants identify the steps in the process. Write each step on a self-stick note or card using the appropriate symbol (*see* p. 49).
   - For "as-is" charts, include rework loops, delays, etc.
   - For "should-be" charts, include only the work as you want it to flow.
4. Working as a team, arrange the steps in order (by posting the self-stick notes on a blank flip chart, whiteboard, or table)

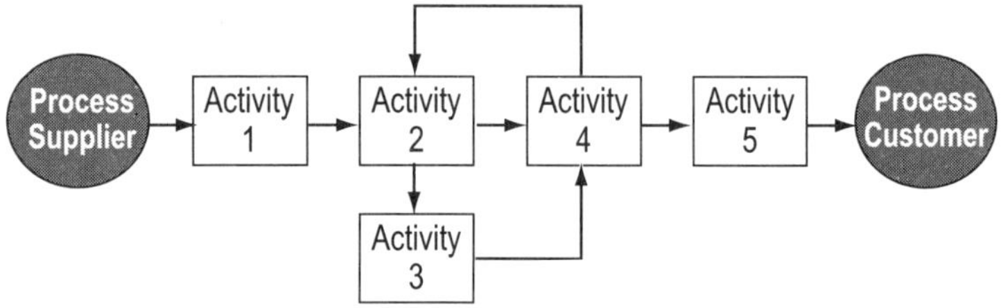

   - Eliminate duplicates; combine similar ideas and agree on wording.
   - Determine and maintain a consistent level of detail as you go.
   - Keep the process flow moving in one direction, usually left-to-right or top-to-bottom. Only go in the reverse direction if a decision calls for repetition of a step. This helps people keep clear about the sequence of events, which can get confusing if you allow "time" to flow both backwards and forwards.
   - If steps continue from one wall to another or over an obstacle (such as a picture on the wall), attach the connected steps with string and tape.
5. Discuss the results. Does it match reality as you know it? Adjust as needed.
   - If you discover you have forgotten a step, move the self-stick notes to the right and insert the new step (this is why it helps to work with self-stick notes that can be easily rearranged).

6. When done, number the tasks sequentially through the most direct route, then number off-line tasks.
7. Transfer completed map to paper or computer.
   - Be sure to date the map and provide names of those involved in the mapping process.

Tips

- Walk the process forward to understand what happens, then backward pretending to be a customer–ask questions that a customer would ask such as, "Why do you do things that way? Would it be possible to do this other thing that would help me?"
- "Go to the Gemba" (the place where the work occurs). Always do as much of the mapping where reality is. Videotape if possible.
- Draw first drafts manually using self-stick notes and markers. Transfer to computerized drawing only after the team agrees on a version.
- If your map does not have enough space to list all the information, use numbered reference sheets as attachments.
- Always date a process map.
- Maintain version control; decide who is authorized to update the chart (which is equal to changing the process) and under what conditions.
- A lot of ideas will come up when you start creating a flowchart. To keep focused on your primary task, create a "Parking Lot" where you can capture important ideas that are not directly linked to the flowcharting exercise. Parking Lot topics usually include (1) improvement ideas; (2) assumptions; (3) questions; (4) additional observations; and (5) out-of-scope issues and ideas.
- Concentrate on the process, not the tools and symbols.
- Step back and talk about what metrics could be used to measure process effectiveness, efficiency, and customer satisfaction. Take notes.

Quick Take

Transportation and spaghetti (workflow) diagrams

Highlights

- Diagrams that depict the physical flow of work or material in a process
- Used to improve the physical layout of a workspace (office, factory, warehouse) or a work form

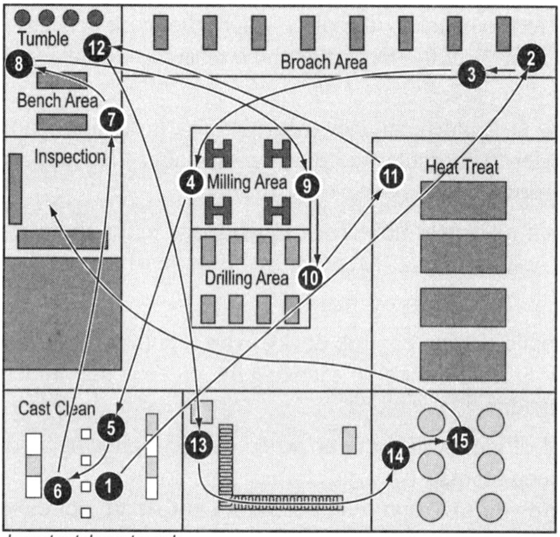

Layout not drawn to scale

To create a workflow diagram...

1. Find or create a diagram of the workspace (or obtain a hard copy of a form or worksheet if that is the target of improvement).
2. Work from an existing flowchart of the process steps or brainstorm a list of steps.
3. Mark where the first step of the process happens, draw an arrow from there to where the second step happens, etc. Continue until you have mapped all process steps.
4. Discuss the final diagram with an aim towards improving the workflow.
   - If the lines crisscross, experiment with workspace arrange-

ments to create a cleaner flow (ideally, work will never backtrack)

- If lines repeatedly come back to one location, see if the work performed there can be combined and performed at the same time (again, to prevent backtracking)

Tips

- Spaghetti diagrams can be used to depict the flow of information, material, or people.
- Handoffs add significant delays and queue times. So if you see a lot of crisscrossing lines, investigate ways to reduce handoffs and simplify the layout.

Quick Take

Swim-lane (deployment) flowcharts

Highlights

- A flowchart that emphasizes the "who" in "who does what"
- Makes it easy to study handoffs between people and/or work groups in a process
- Especially useful with administrative (service) processes

To create a swim-lane or deployment flowchart...

Review the basic flowcharting steps. The difference here is that you need to identify WHO does the work, not just what gets done.

1. Identify the different people or job functions involved in the process. List them down the left side or across the top of a flip chart or whiteboard.
2. Brainstorm the steps in the process and write them on self-stick notes.
3. Work through each step in order, placing the notes in the appropriate swim-lane.
    - Use conventional flowcharting symbols if appropriate.

4. Use the result to spark discussions on how to improve workflow.
   - The ideal is to have each person or work function touch the form or other item only once.
   - Look for reasons behind repeated handoffs back and forth between individuals or work functions. Try to combine or resequence work so one person can complete all their tasks at one time.
   - If missing or incomplete information is the source of back-and-forth handoffs, try to error- or mistake-proof the process (*see* p. 233) so work cannot move on to the next process task or step unless it's complete to that point.

Swim-lane Flowchart

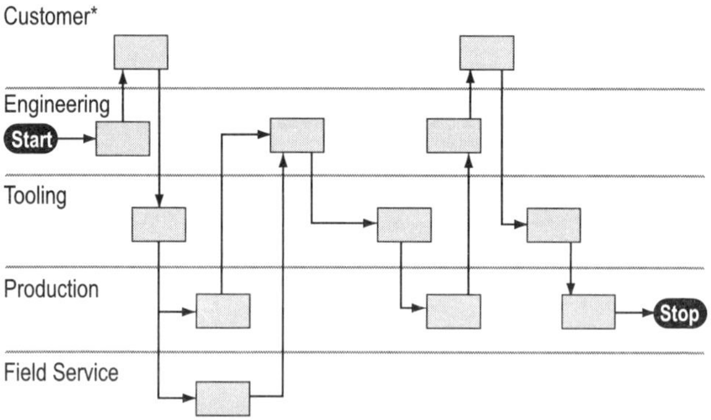

**Top lane is always the designated customer*

Tips

- Place the people or functions most heavily involved in the top swim-lane if steps flow across the page or in left-most swim-lane if steps flow down the page. Place those with less interaction in the lowest or right-most swim-lanes.
- Task symbols with more than one exit *(excluding those leading to multiple input/output/document symbols)* usually indicate that a decision block is required or the activity/task has not been broken down to the appropriate level.
- Communication paths are especially important in processes with a lot of handoffs. Use dotted lines to reflect informal lines of communication (those that occur outside the formal process) if there is evidence that the informal link has an impact on the process.

Quick Take

Value stream maps (basic)

Purpose

To capture all key flows (of work, information, materials) in a process and important process metrics

Why use a value stream map

- More complicated to construct than other flowcharts, but much more useful for identifying and quantifying waste (especially in time and costs)

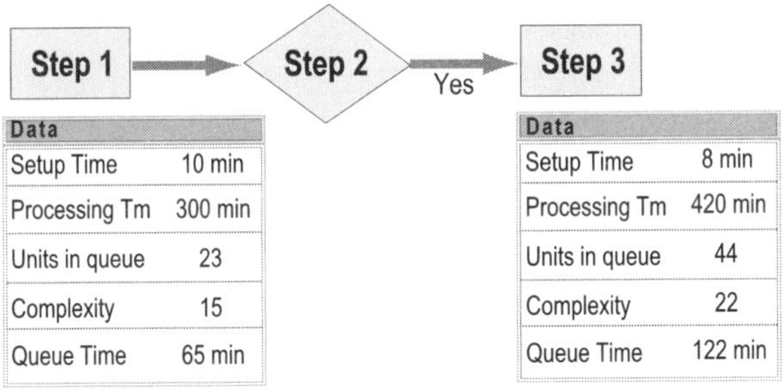

When to use a value stream map

- Use at the business (strategic) level by management teams and deployment champions for opportunity and project identification.
  - Maps at this level are owned by the business unit leaders (management teams, deployment champions)

- Create an "as-is" version at the project (tactical) level in Define and Measure to identify and visualize the improvement opportunities. Create a future version ("should-be") in Improve or Control.
  - Maps at this level are created and initially owned by improvement teams and transitioned to process owners during the DMAIC Control Phase
- If your team has to assess the impact of multiple products or services, *see* Chapter 10 on Complexity (p. 241).

How to create a value stream map

Prework: Create SIPOC and top-down or swim-lane flowcharts as appropriate to identify scope, key metrics, and basic process steps.

1. **Determine what individual product, service, or family you will map.** If there are multiple options use a Product/Service Family Grid (p. 242) to identify the family. Choose one that meets as many of these criteria as possible:
   - Has a common flow (all products/services in the family use essentially the same steps)
   - Has high volume and cost
   - Meets industry or other segmentation criteria important to the company
   - Has the biggest impact on customers or the customer segment of choice

2. **Draw the process flow**
   - Review process mapping symbols (*see* p. 49)
   - Begin at the end of the process with what's delivered to the customer and work upstream
   - Identify the main activities
   - Place the activities in sequence on the map

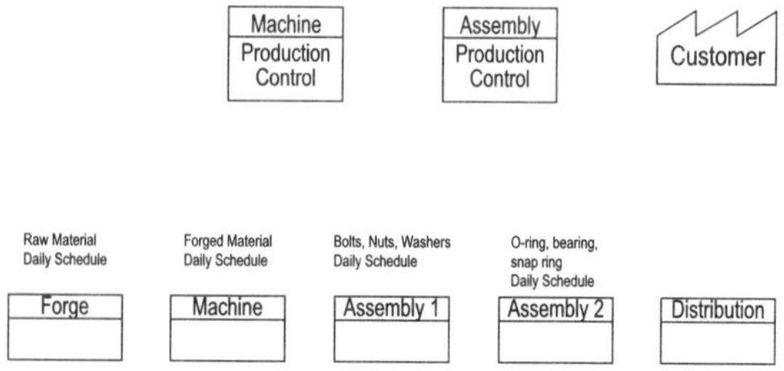

3. **Add the material flow**
   - Show the movement of all material
   - Group together material with the same flow
   - Map all subprocesses
   - Include any incoming inspection, and material and process testing activities
   - Add supplier(s) at beginning of process
   - See symbols, p. 49

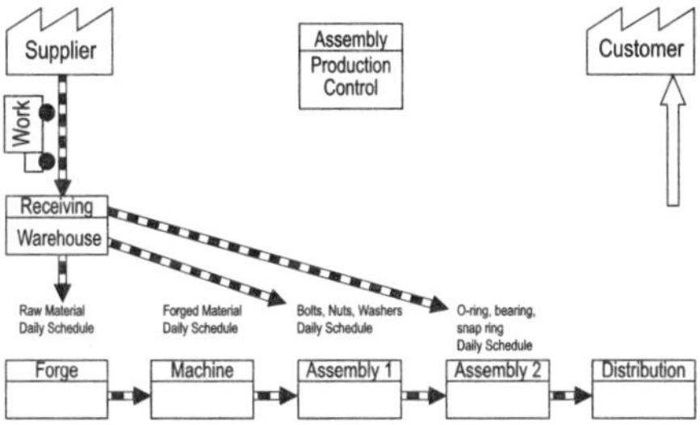

4. Add the information flow

- Map the information flow between activities
- For manufacturing areas:
  - Document the production orders associated with the parts through the process
  - Document the scheduling system and tracking of the parts as they move through the process
- Document how the process communicates with the customer and supplier
- Document how information is gathered (electronic, manual, "go look," etc.)

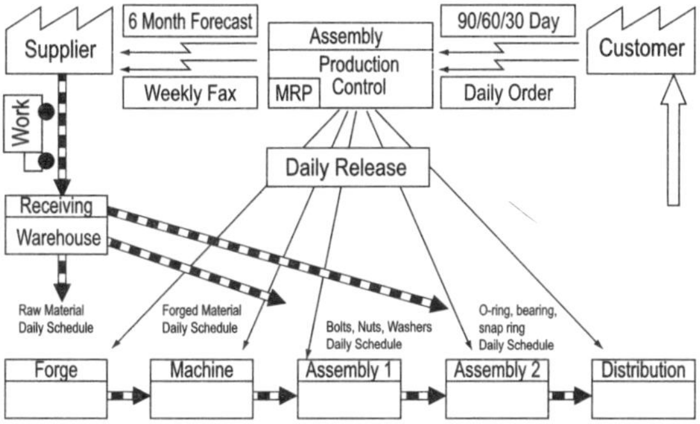

5. Collect process data and connect it to the boxes on the chart

- Walk the process to observe reality
- For each step, gather the following data:
  - Trigger – what starts the step
  - Setup time and Processing time/unit
  - Takt rate (rate of customer demand)
  - Percent defective and/or scrap rate (in mfg.)
  - Number of people

  - Downtime % (includes any time that people cannot reach full productivity because machines, computers, materials, information, etc., is not available when needed)
  - WIP downstream and upstream
  - Cost of links to IT, warehouse(s), etc.
  - Batch size

6. **Add process and lead time data to the chart**
   - Include delays (queue times), processing (value-add) time, setup time, etc.

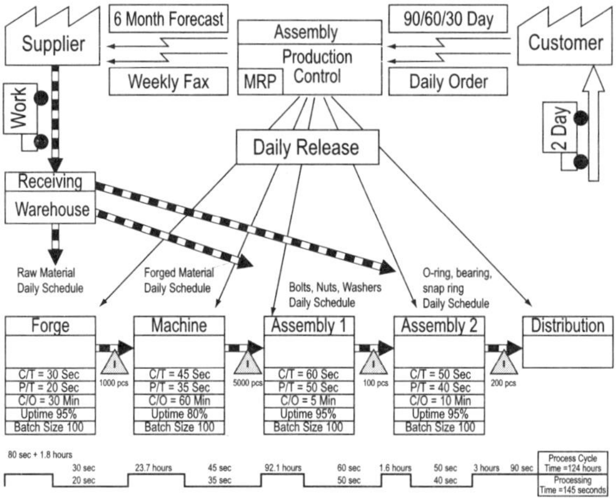

7. **Verify the Map**

   Have non-team members who know the process review the flow and data. Check with suppliers and customers as well (interface points). Make changes as needed then check the final results with people who work on the process.

Tips

- As you create the VSM, tape copies of tools, templates, reference tables, spec sheets, job instructions, etc. to the wall next to the growing chart. This will help the team to see everything going on in the process.
- Constructing the basic process flow first is a timesaver. If you try to piece the VSM together step by step it will take longer and you will go too deep, too fast on specific steps.
- Use the same unit of time (sec, min, hr, days, wk) for cycle times, takt times, and work times.

Quick Take

Flowchart and value stream symbols

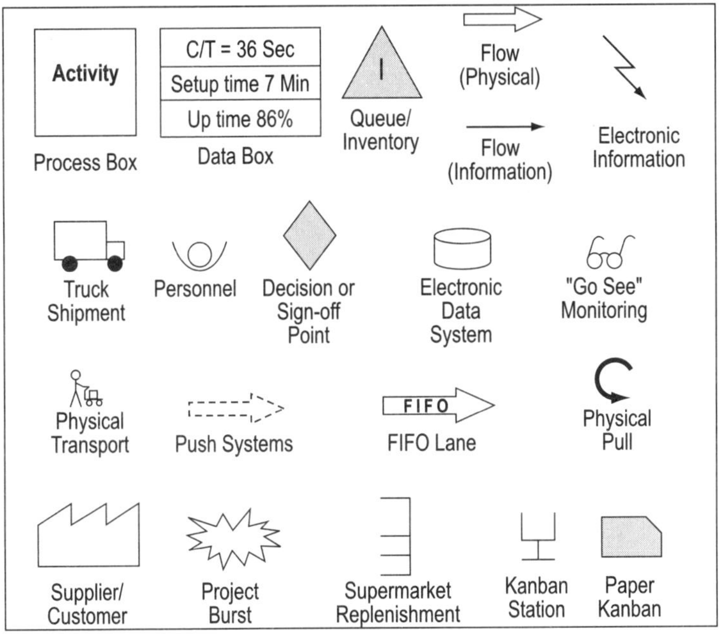

Quick Take

Value-add (VA) vs. non-value-add (NVA) analysis

Highlights

- Used to distinguish process steps that customers are willing to pay for from those they are not
- The objective of VA/NVA analysis is to:
  - Identify and eliminate the hidden costs that do not add value for the customer
  - Reduce unnecessary process complexity, and thus errors
  - Reduce the process lead time; improve PCE
  - Increase capacity by better utilizing resources

To perform a value analysis...

1. Classify each process step as value-added (also known as "customer value-add"), business non-value-add (sometimes called "required waste"), and non-value-add. *See descriptions below.*
2. Add up the time spent in each category. Use a Time Value Map (p. 52) or Value-add Chart (p. 53) to display the results.
3. Decide what to do next.
   - Value-add tasks should be optimized and standardized
   - Business non-value-add tasks should be checked with the customer and, where possible, minimized or eliminated
   - Non-value-add activities should be eliminated

Value classifications

1. **Value-Added (VA),** also called **Customer Value-Add (CVA):** Any activity in a process that is essential to deliver the service or product to the customer
   - Must be performed to meet customer needs
   - Adds form or feature to the service
   - Enhances service quality, enables on-time or more competitive delivery, or has a positive impact on price competition
   - Customers would be willing to pay for this work if they knew you were doing it
   - *Tip: If it's not clear whether a task is value-added to your customers, imagine what would happen if you STOP doing it. Would your external or end customer complain? If yes, then it's likely value-add.*
2. **Business Non-Value-Added (BNVA):** Activities that are required by the business to execute VA work but add no real value from a customer standpoint
   - Usually includes work that:
     - Reduces financial risk
     - Supports financial reporting requirements
     - Aids in execution of value-add work
     - Is required by law or regulation

     Ex: Order entry/processing; purchasing, product development; sales/marketing; IRS/OSHA/EPA reporting
   - *Tip: Pick an activity. If you STOP doing it now, would your internal customers complain? If yes, then it is probably business non-value-add.*

3. **Non-Value-Added (NVA)** or **waste:** Activities that add no value from the customer's perspective and are not required for financial, legal, or other business reasons
   - The types of NVA work are endless. They include:
     - handling beyond what is minimally required to move work from value-add to value-add activity (includes inspection, transportation, moving/storing materials/paperwork, counting, storing, retrieving)
     - rework needed to fix errors
     - duplicative work (supervision or monitoring of work, multiple signatures, proofing, checking of calculations, inspection)
     - waiting, idle time, delays
     - Overproduction (producing too much too soon)
     - Unnecessary motion by process staff
     - Overprocessing (too many steps to complete a job or exceeding customer requirements)
   - *Tip: Pick an activity. If you STOP doing it now would any customer (internal or external) know the difference? If not, the work is probably non-value-add.*

Tips

- Many non-value-add costs are "quantized"—that is, you cannot eliminate the cost until the source is COMPLETELY eliminated. Ex: it costs just as much to run a warehouse that's 10% full as one that's 100% full. But if you can reduce lead time such that you can close down the warehouse, costs take a "quantum" jump down. Be alert for quantized costs in your process and work to eliminate the sources.

Quick Take

Time value maps

Highlights

- A visual depiction of value-add and non-value-add time in a process
- Gives better impression of overall cycle time than Value-add chart (*see* next page)

Purchase Order Request—Observed Time

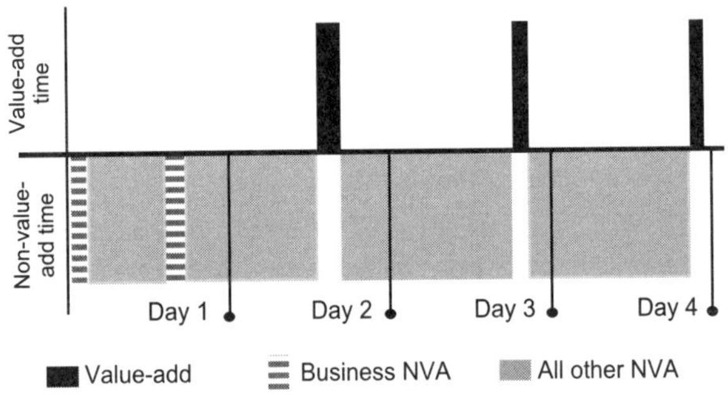

To create a time value map...

1. Determine process cycle time
2. Determine queue times (delays) between steps and the value-add time needed to perform each task
3. Draw a timeline and divide into units equal to the total process time
4. Place steps and delays along the timeline in the order in which they happen; use segments proportional to the times
   - VA steps go above the line
   - Non-value-add goes below the line (think about using different colors for emphasis)
   - The white space between boxes indicates queue or delay time
7. Draw in feedback loops and label yield percentages
8. Summarize time use
   - Activity vs. non-activity times
   - Value-add vs. non-value-add times

Quick Take

Value-add chart (task time or takt time chart)

Highlights

- A visual depiction of value-add and non-value-add time in a process
- Does more to illustrate balance of time between process steps; weaker on overall cycle time (compare to time value map on previous page)
- Does not visually emphasize wasted time as strongly as a time value map does but makes it easier to compare steps to each other

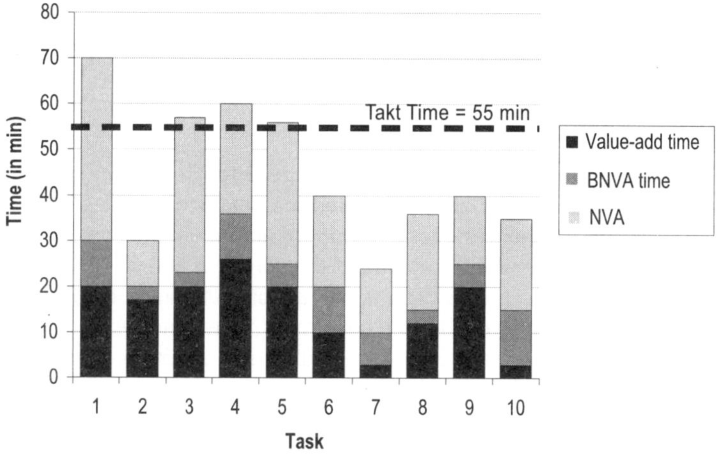

To create a value-add chart...

1. Follow instructions in the value-add analysis (p. 49) to classify process work as customer value-add (VA), business non-value-add (BNVA), or other non-value-add
2. For each step in the process, collect data on how much time is spent on each type of work
3. Visually display the results in a bar chart like that shown here

4. Calculate takt time
   - The takt time is the amount of available work time divided by the customer demand during that time period.

     Ex:

     8 available hours = 480 min
     60 customer orders to be filled
     takt time = 480/60 = 8 min
     (you should complete an order every 8 minutes to satisfy customer demand)
5. Act on the result by brainstorming ways to:
   - Eliminate NVA activities
   - Improve VA activities
   - Reduce BNVA activities

Tips

- Any VA step that takes longer than the takt rate is considered a time trap (*see* p. 203) and must be improved. The goal is to level the times across steps so no step is longer or slower than any other step.
- Divide the total time by takt time to get a rough estimate of the minimum number of staff required to operate the process. In the chart shown here, the total amount of time spent in all 10 steps is about 445 minutes. If this company had 10 people working in the process, that equals about 44.5 minutes worth of work per employee. But the takt time is 55 minutes. As a rule of thumb, workloads at each step should equal about one takt. In this situation, they could reduce staff to 8 or 9 people (so each employee has about 55 minutes worth of work).

CHAPTER 4

Voice of the Customer (VOC)

Purpose of these tools

- To figure out what customers care about
- To set priorities and goals consistent with customer needs
- To determine what customer needs you can profitably meet

Deciding which tool to use

Customer segmentation, p. 56, principles for identifying subsets of customers who may have differing needs or requirements. Especially useful for any team dealing with a moderate to large customer base.

Types and sources of customer data, p. 58, a list of typical customer data your organization may already have or can get. Use to prompt your own thinking before a VOC effort.

Collecting VOC:

Interviews, p. 59, guidance on conducting professional interviews with customers. Recommended for any team that wants to develop a deep understanding of customer needs and how customers use the product or service

Point-of-use observation, p. 60, guidance for what to do if you can visit a customer's workplace or observe the point of contact between the customer and your product/service. Use to gain greater insight or confirm interview results.

Focus groups, p. 61, guidance on how to structure focus groups. More efficient than doing separate interviews but still time intensive. Use as needed.

Surveys, p. 62, guidance on conducting surveys. Best used to confirm or quantify theories developed after other customer contact. Also can be used to identify most important issues to research. Good for gathering quantitative information.

Kano analysis, p. 64, a technique that helps you understand varying levels of value that customers place on different features of your product or service.

Developing critical-to-quality requirements, p. 67, instructions for converting customer need statements into product or service requirements. Use when your mission is to deliver products/services that better meet customer needs.

Tips

- With any direct customer contact (interviews, customer observation, focus groups), the stakes are high. Since you will deal with customers face to face, you must leave a good impression. Be organized, be professional. And make sure you follow up or customers will feel their time was wasted.
- Work with your sales or marketing department to identify and coordinate contact with customers. If multiple people from different departments all contact customers separately, your customers may view you as incompetent.
- If you're working on a design project, we recommend you investigate the many sophisticated VOC methods usually linked to Design for Lean Six Sigma or DMEDI approaches (such as the House of Quality).
- Dealing with customers can be tricky. Get help from experts, if available.

Quick Take

Customer segmentation

Highlights

- All customers are not created equal, and do not create equal value for the organization
- Customer segmentation is a way to identify and focus on the subgroups of customers who generate the highest value from the product, service, or process being designed or improved

Customer	Internal or External?	Segments/Description	Priority
Consumers with Children	External	• Senior citizens (>65) • Families, parents 16 to 24 yrs old • Families, parents 25 to 40 yrs old • Single parents, all ages	Low Low High Low
Children	External	• Children 7 to 12 yrs of age • Children < 7 and > 12 yrs of age	High Low

To use customer segmentation...

1. Identify the output (product or service) being studied
2. Brainstorm to identify the customers of that output
3. Identify the segmentation characteristics that you think may influence how a customer or group responds to your company and its products or services
   - Focus on just a few characteristics
4. Develop profiles of the segments you will seek out for your projects

   Ex: high-volume vs. low-volume, West Coast vs. Midwest vs. Southeast customers
5. Include representatives from each segment in whatever customer contact you initiate (interviews, surveys, focus groups, etc.)
6. Document the results
   - In any subsequent data analysis, do separate charts for each segment to see if there are different patterns

Product/Service	Customers	Potential Segments

Examples of segmentation criteria

Economic: Revenue, profit, loyalty, frequency of purchase, company size, cost of doing business with them, strategic goals

Descriptive: Geographic location, demographics, product or service feature that interests them most, industry

Attitudinal: Price, value, service

Quick Take

Sources of customer data

- **Existing company sales information:** Product/service sales, product/service returns or refunds, sales preferences, contract cancellations, customer referrals, closure rates of sales calls, DSO
- **Customer contact points (listening posts):** product/service complaint or compliment mechanisms (hotlines, website links); any customer-facing staff (customer service reps, sales reps, billing/accounting staff)
- **Research:**

  Direct: Interviews, surveys, focus groups, point-of-use observation

  Indirect (market trends): Market share changes, industry experts, market watchers

Choosing a contact method

Type of Contact	Choose if you want to get...
Face-to-face interviews	Unique perspectives Senior-level participation Ability to pursue unexpected lines of questioning In-depth understanding of the customer experience Insights that may lead to innovation
Focus groups	Information from customers with similar product and service needs Mid- to lower-level participation Information from many people for a single segment
Telephone interviews	Information from customers who are widely dispersed geographically Information on basic or simple issues Quick turnaround of information collection A lot of data at a low cost
Surveys	Quantifiable and statistically meaningful responses Information from many customers Confirmation of theories you've developed based on other forms of customer contact

Quick Take

Collecting VOC: Interviews

Purpose

To learn about a specific customer's point of view on service issues, product/service attributes, and performance indicators/measures

Why use interviews

- Establishes communication with *individual* customers (vs. groups of customers)
- Allows flexibility and probing of customer needs
- Customers feel "listened to"

When to use interviews

- At the beginning of a project: to learn what is important to customers (which supports the development of hypotheses about customer expectations)
- In the middle of a project: to clarify points or to better understand why a particular issue is important to customers, to get ideas and suggestions, or to test ideas with customers
- At the end of a project: to clarify findings, to validate improvement

How to do customer interviews

1. **Be clear about the purpose of the interviews.** What role will the interviews play in the project? How will you use the information afterwards?
2. **Prepare a list of questions.**
3. **Decide on interview method (face-to-face, phone).**
4. **Decide how many interviewers and interviewees will be present.**
5. **Do practice interviews internally** to refine the script, questions and interview process.
6. **Contact customers and arrange interviews.** Send out a confirmation letter or email stating the purpose of the interview and providing a list of general topics to be covered (no need to

share specific questions unless you think it will help customers prepare).

7. **Decide how you will collect data from the interviews.** If you plan to record them (audiotape, computer audio programs) make sure you tell customers and get their permission to do so.
8. **Conduct interviews.**
9. **Transcribe notes and continue with data analysis.**

Tips

- When analyzing the transcripts, highlight statements related to different questions or issues with different colors (Ex: highlight statements related to "reactions to current service" in blue and "ideas for future services" in red)

Quick Take

Collecting VOC: Point-of-use observation

Highlights

- The key is to watch how your customers use your product or service at their location or at any point where they interact with your company (Ex: bank lobby, retail store)
- High-impact technique for experiencing what it's like for a customer doing business with your company, and generating insights for improving products, services, or processes

To do customer observation…

1. **Be clear about the purpose of the observation.** What role will the observation play in the project? How will you use the information afterwards?
2. **Decide when and how you will observe** customers (in their workplace, in a retail situation, etc.).
3. **Develop and test an observation form** for collecting the data you desire.
4. **If going to the customer's workplace, contact them and arrange the time.** (*See also* customer interviews, p. 59, if you plan to simultaneously conduct interviews.)

5. **Train observers** to make sure everyone will follow the same procedures and leave a good impression with customers.
6. **Conduct the observation.**
   - ALWAYS do a pilot with a few low-risk customers and tweak your methodology
7. **Continue with data analysis.**
8. **Include follow-up contact with customers** (thank-you note, copies of observations, updates on changes made as a result of their contributions).

Quick Take

Collecting VOC: Focus groups

Purpose

To get feedback on existing products or services or on proposed ideas from the point of view of a group of customers

Why use focus groups

- Allows for more creativity and open-ended answers than surveys but isn't as time-consuming as interviews
- Allows participants to play off each other's ideas
- Lets you observe people interacting with physical items (products, prototypes, marketing materials, etc.), which you can't get from surveys

When to use focus groups

- To clarify and define customer needs (Define/Measure)
- To gain insights into the prioritization of needs (Define, Measure, or Improve)
- To test concepts and get feedback (Improve)
- As prework for a survey or interviews to identify topics of critical interest to customers
- As follow-up to customer interviews as a way to verify lessons or information learned

How to conduct a focus group

1. Identify the number and target size of focus groups
   - Time and expense will limit the number you can do (but you must do more than one!)
   - Each group usually has 7 to 13 participants
2. Identify participants
   - Your options are to mix representatives of different customer segments, or focus on a specific segment or on people known to have an interest in the topic
3. Develop questions
   - Do a pilot to test the ease of gathering and analyzing data
4. Conduct the focus groups
   - This is harder than it may seem. If no one within your organization has experience with focus groups, consider hiring outside help.
5. After the focus group, transcribe customer comments
6. Select appropriate follow-up action
   - Create an affinity diagram of selected customer statements to find themes in customer comments
   - Use customer statements to develop product/service requirement statements

Collecting VOC: Surveys

Purpose

To get quantitative data across an entire segment or group of segments on customer reactions to a product, service, or attribute

Why use surveys

- To efficiently gather a considerable amount of information from a large population
- To conduct analysis that will result in data with statistical validity and integrity (interviews and focus groups generate *qualitative* data only)

When to use surveys

- When you need or want to contact many customers to get quantitative information
- As prework for interviews or focus groups to identify target areas for more in-depth investigation
- As follow-up to interviews or focus group to quantify relationships or patterns identified

How to conduct a survey

1. Develop survey objectives.
2. Determine the required sample size (*see* p. 85).
3. Write draft questions and determine measurement scales.
    - Identify the specific information you need to collect
    - Numerical scales are easier to record and compare (such as rating items from 1 to 5 in importance) but qualitative scales are sometimes more appropriate ("not at all interested" to "very interested")
4. Determine how to code surveys so data can remain anonymous (if appropriate).
5. Design the survey.
6. Confirm that getting answers to the individual questions will meet your objectives (adjust, if not).
7. Conduct a pilot test.
8. Finalize the survey.
9. Send out survey (mail, fax, email attachment) to selected customers. Include a means for them to respond–SASE, return fax number, email reply. Or post on your website and give participants instructions on how to access the survey.
10. Compile and analyze the results.

Tips

- As with other forms of customer contact, work with your sales or marketing department to identify and coordinate contact with customers.
- Include a "not applicable" category where relevant so you aren't forcing customers to give you bad data.

Kano analysis

Purpose

To better understand what value your customers place on the features of your product or service, which can reduce the risk of providing products or services that over-emphasize features of little importance or that miss critical-to-quality features/attributes.

Why use Kano analysis

- Good "first cut" technique to evaluate relative importance of customer requirements
- Allows you to identify segments by the type or level of quality that customers expect
- Helps determine if there are requirements that:
  - were not explicitly stated by customers
  - were included in previous offerings and are still valued by the customer
- To help shape your VOC data-gathering plans

When to use Kano analysis

- Use in Define or Measure to understand scope and importance of project goals
- Use in Improve to help redesign a product, service, or process
- Use after interviews or focus groups to confirm that some needs spoken by the customer are truly critical requirements that will affect customer satisfaction or purchasing decisions

How to use Kano analysis

1. Collect VOC data through as many different means as you can
   - You cannot identify all customer needs through any single method
2. Identify known or presumed customer needs/requirements
3. For each **potential need**, ask the customer to assess:
   - How would they feel if the need WAS addressed? (Positive)
   - How would they feel if the need WAS NOT addressed? (Negative)

- The customer has four choices in response to each question:
  1. I'd like it
  2. It is normally that way (that feature is expected)
  3. I don't care
  4. I wouldn't like it

  Based on the answers to the "positive" and "negative" questions, use the table to determine the type of need

		Answers to Negative Questions			
		Like	**Normal**	**Don't Care**	**Don't Like**
Answers to Positive Questions	**Like**		Delighter	Delighter	Satisfier
	Normal				Dissatisfier
	Don't Care				Dissatisfier
	Don't Like				

4. Based on customer responses, classify each need as a dissatisfier, satisfier, or delighter (*see* definitions on next page)

5. Incorporate this information into product or service development efforts
   - You MUST deal with any basic requirements (dissatisfiers) that your product or service does not already deliver. If you don't do a good job on these, it doesn't matter how well you do on other features or options.
   - Do conjoint analysis or use another technique to evaluate how much of the "satisfiers" you can afford to include in your product/service.
   - If you already have delighters in your product or service, strengthen support for them. If you do not yet have delighters, work with management to launch a design or redesign effort to incorporate the new features you've identified (*after* you've dealt with dissatisfiers and satisfiers).

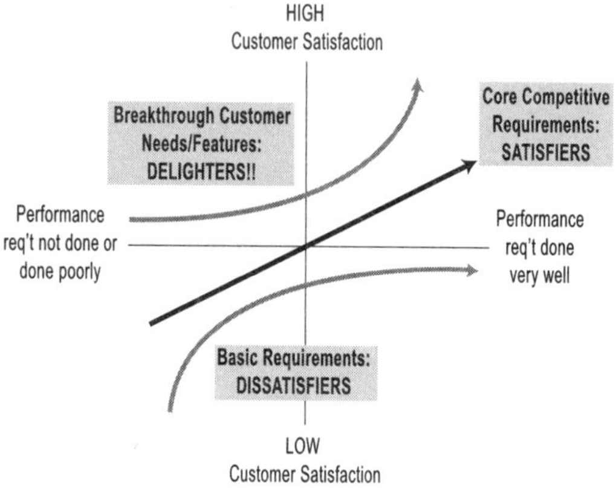

Definitions of Kano levels

- **Dissatisfiers – Basic requirements:** Expected features or characteristics of a product or service. If these needs are not fulfilled, the customer will be extremely dissatisfied. **Satisfying basic requirements is the entry point for getting into a market.**
  - Customers will seldom name basic requirements when asked what's important to them, because they take these features for granted (Ex: we expect every car to have a steering wheel). Because basic requirements are unspoken, don't rely on interviews or surveys to identify them. Review past product/service designs and observe customers in action to see what features they use all the time.

- **Satisfiers – Performance requirements:** Standard characteristics that increase or decrease satisfaction by their degree (cost/price, ease of use, speed). **Satisfying performance requirements will allow you to remain in the market.**
  - Customers will usually name features that are performance requirements when asked what's important to them.

- **Delighters – Excitement requirements:** Unexpected features or characteristics that impress customers and earn you extra credit. **Satisfying excitement requirements opens the opportunity to excel, to be World Class.**
  - Because these are often innovations that do not appear yet in the marketplace, customers will rarely tell you about delighters.

Tips

- Delighters often appear when someone recognizes a need that customers themselves aren't aware of and links it to a technology that no one has thought of applying to that need. Since customers can't articulate the need, you're most likely to identify them through observation or interviews or focus groups with diverse people (early adapters, industry trend experts, process experts). Include engineers or technology/delivery-method specialists on your team to expose them to the customer experience.

Tools for Identifying Customer needs

Likely Satisfiers (known to and voiced by customers)	Likely Dissatisfiers (known to but not voiced by customers)	Likely Delighters (customers unaware of needs or solutions)
• Surveys via mail, phone, e-mail, other • Face-to-face, phone interviews • Market research • Focus groups, clinics • Existing company Information • Competitor ads & marketing efforts	• One-on-one interviews • Functional requirements • Review industry standards trade literature, regulatory req'ts. • Review internal data on unhappy customers: – Switches to competitor – Refunds – Complaints • Personal experience	• Carefully planned focus groups • Watch customers • Look for frustrations and delighters • Reduction of time-consuming activities • Self-evident operability • "Painstorming" • Innovations/ Breakthroughs

Quick Take

Developing critical-to-quality requirements

Highlights

- Customer comments on what they want or need are often too vague to be acted on by the team
- This process can help you make the transition from vague statement to precise functional requirement
- This process will strengthen your ability to provide products or services that meet or exceed customer needs

To develop critical-to-quality requirements...

1. Gather VOC data relevant to the product, service, or other output you're studying.

2. Identify relevant statements in transcripts of customer comments and copy them onto slips of paper or self-stick notes. Focus on statements that relate to why a customer would or would not buy your product/service.
3. Use Affinity diagrams (p. 30) or Tree Diagrams (not covered in this book) to sort ideas and find themes.
4. Start with the themes or representative comments and probe for *why* the customer feels that way. Do follow-up with customers to clarify their statements. Be as specific as possible when identifying the why.
5. Conduct further customer contact as needed to establish quantifiable targets and tolerance (specification limits) associated with the need. (How do customers define "timely"? "comfortable"? "well-organized"? "friendly"?)
6. When you've completed the work, step back and examine all the requirements as a set. It's possible that customers simply didn't mention something key during your data collection. Have you covered all key aspects of your product or service? Fill in gaps as needed.

Voice of the Customer	**The "Why"** (After clarification)	**Critical Customer Requirement**
"I hate dealing with your company."	Products are not delivered on time	10 day lead time (± 1 day)

Good customer requirements:

- Are specific and easily measured
- Are related directly to an attribute of the product or service
- Don't have alternatives and don't bias the design toward a particular approach or technology
- Describe what the need is, not how it will be met

CHAPTER 5

Data Collection

Purpose of these tools

To help you collect reliable data that are relevant to the key questions you need to answer for your project

Deciding which tool to use

- **Types of data,** p. 70 to 71, discusses the types of data you may encounter, and how data type influences what analysis methods or tools you can and cannot use. Review as needed.
- **Data collection planning,** pp. 72 to 77, includes discussion of the measurement selection matrix (p. 74); stratification (p. 75); operational definitions (p. 76); and cautions on using existing data (p. 77). Use whenever you collect data.
- **Checksheets,** pp. 78 to 81, includes illustrations of different checksheets: basic (p. 79); frequency plot checksheet (p. 80); traveler (p 80); location (p 81). Review as needed.
- **Sampling,** pp. 81 to 86, discusses the basics (p. 81); factors in sample selection (p. 83), population and process sampling (p. 84), and determining minimum sample sizes (p. 85). Review recommended for all teams since almost all data collection involves sampling.
- **Measurement System Analysis (including Gage R&R)**, pp. 87 to 99, covers the kind of data you need to collect (p. 89), and interpretation of the charts typically generated by MSA software programs (pp. 90 to 95); includes tips on checking bias (p. 95), stability (p. 97), and discriminatory power (p. 99). Recommended for all teams.
- **Kappa calculations (MSA for attribute data),** pp. 100 to 103, is recommended whenever you're collecting attribute data.

Quick Take

Types of data

1. Continuous

Any variable measured on a continuum or scale that can be infinitely divided.

There are more powerful statistical tools for interpreting continuous data, so it is generally preferred over discrete/attribute data.

Ex: Lead time, cost or price, duration of call, and any physical dimensions or characteristics (height, weight, density, temperature)

2. Discrete (also called Attribute)

All types of data other than continuous. Includes:

- **Count:** Ex: counts of errors.
- **Binary data:** Data that can have only one of two values. Ex: On-time delivery (yes/no); Acceptable product (pass/fail).
- **Attribute–Nominal:** The "data" are names or labels. There is no intrinsic reason to arrange in any particular order or make a statement about any quantitative differences between them.

  Ex: In a company: Dept A, Dept B, Dept C

  Ex: In a shop: Machine 1, Machine 2, Machine 3

  Ex: Types of transport: boat, train, plane
- **Attribute–Ordinal:** The names or labels represent some value inherent in the object or item (so there is an obvious order to the labels).

  Ex: On product performance: excellent, very good, good, fair, poor

  Ex: Salsa taste test: mild, hot, very hot, makes me suffer

  Ex: Customer survey: strongly agree, agree, disagree, strongly disagree

  Note: Though ordinal scales have a defined sequence, they do not imply anything about the *degree* of difference between the labels (that is, we can't assume that "excellent" is twice as good as "very good") or about which labels are good and which are bad (for some people a salsa that "makes me suffer" is a good thing, for others a bad thing)

Quick Take

Input vs. output data

Output measures

Referred to as Y data. Output metrics quantify the overall performance of the process, including:

- How well **customer needs** and requirements were met (typically **quality** and **speed** requirements), *and*
- How well **business needs** and requirements were met (typically **cost** and **speed** requirements)

Output measures provide the best overall barometer of process performance.

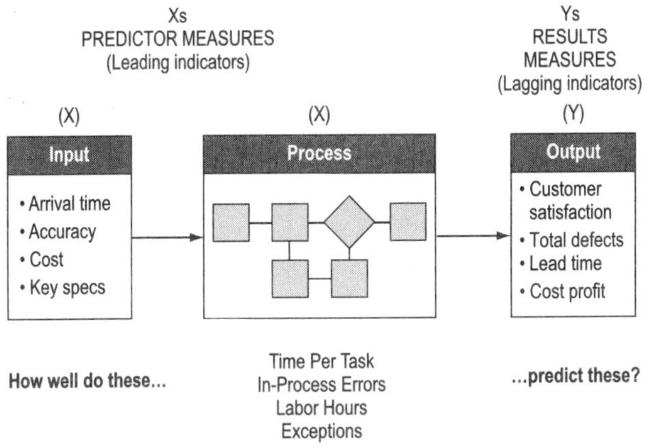

Process measures

One type of X variables in data. Measures quality, speed and cost performance at key points in the process. Some process measures will be subsets of output measures. For example, time per step (a process measure) adds up to process lead time (an output measure).

Input measures

The other type of X variables in data. Measures quality, speed and cost performance of information or items coming into the process. Usually, input measures will focus on effectiveness (does the input meet the needs of the process?).

Tips on using input and output data

- The goal is to find Xs (Process and Input Measures) that are leading indicators of your critical output (Y)
  - That means the Xs will give you an early warning about potential problems with the Y
  - Such Xs are also key to finding root causes (the focus of the Analyze phase) and to catching problems before they become serious (Control phase)
- Use your SIPOC diagram and subprocess maps to help achieve a balance of both input and output measures
- Generally, you'll want to collect data on output measures at the start of your project to establish baselines
- Begin collecting data on at least one process and/or input measure early in the project to help generate initial data for Analyze

Quick Take

Data collection planning

Highlights

A good collection plan helps ensure data will be useful (measuring the right things) and statistically valid (measuring things right)

To create a data collection plan...

1. Decide what data to collect

- If trying to assess process baseline, determine what metrics best represent overall performance of the product, service, or process
- Find a balance of input (X) factors and output (Y) metrics (*see* p. 71)
- Use a measurement selection matrix (p. 74) to help you make the decision
- Try to identify continuous variables and avoid discrete (attribute) variables where possible since continuous data often convey more useful information

Data Collection Plan

Metric	Stratification factors	Operational definition	Sample size	Source and location	Collection method	Who will collect data

How will data be used?	How will data be displayed?
Examples: • Identification of largest contributors • Checking normality • Identifying sigma level and variation • Root cause analysis • Correlation analysis	Examples: • Pareto chart • Histogram • Control chart • Scatter diagrams

2. Decide on stratification factors

- See p. 75 for details on identifying stratification factors

3. Develop operational definitions

- *See* p. 76 for details on creating operational definitions

4. Determine the needed sample size

- *See* p. 81 for details on sampling

5. Identify source/location of data

- Decide if you can use existing data or if you need new data (*see* p. 77 for details)

6. Develop data collection forms/checksheets

- *See* pp. 78 to 81

7. Decide who will collect data

Selection of the data collectors usually based on...

- Familiarity with the process
- Availability/impact on job
  - Rule of Thumb: Develop a data collection process that people can complete in 15 minutes or less a day. That increases the odds it will get done regularly and correctly.
- Avoiding potential bias: Don't want a situation where data collectors will be reluctant to label something as a "defect" or unacceptable output
- Appreciation of the benefits of data collection: Will the data help the collector?

8. Train data collectors

- Ask data collectors for advice on the checksheet design.
- Pilot the data collection procedures. Have collectors practice using the data collection form and applying operational definitions. Resolve any conflicts or differences in use.
- Explain how data will be tabulated (this will help the collectors see the consequences of not following the standard procedures).

9. Do ground work for analysis

- Decide who will compile the data and how
- Prepare a spreadsheet to compile the data
- Consider what you'll have to do with the data (sorting, graphing, calculations) and make sure the data will be in a form you can use for those purposes

10. Execute your data collection plan

Quick Take

Measurement selection matrix

OUTPUT MEASURES

CUSTOMER REQUIREMENTS	Delivery ≤30 Min. from order	% of pizzas that match order at delivery point	% of pizzas that match order before delivery	# of complaints about consistency	≤110° at delivery point	# of customer complaints about quality
on-time delivery	●	△	△	△	△	◍
right ingredients		●	●	◍		◍
the same product every time	△	△	△	●	◍	◍
hot	◍		△	◍	●	◍
not damaged	△		△	◍	△	◍

CONTRIBUTION: ● STRONG ◍ MODERATE △ WEAK

Highlights

Used to find the measures most strongly linked to customer needs

To create and use a measurement system matrix...

1. Collect VOC data (*see* Chapter 4) to identify critical-to-quality requirements. List down the side of a matrix.
2. Identify output measures (through brainstorming, data you're already collecting, process knowledge, SIPOC diagram, etc.) and list across the top of the matrix.
3. Work through the matrix and discuss as a team what relationship

a particular measure has to the corresponding requirement: strong, moderate, weak, or no relationship. Use numbers or symbols (as in the example shown here) to capture the team's consensus.

4. Review the final matrix. Develop plans for collecting data on the measures that are most strongly linked to the requirements.

Quick Take

Stratification factors

Highlights

Purpose is to collect descriptive information that will help you identify important patterns in the data (about root causes, patterns of use, etc.)

- Helps to focus the project on the critical few
- Speeds up the search for root causes
- Generates a deeper understanding of process factors

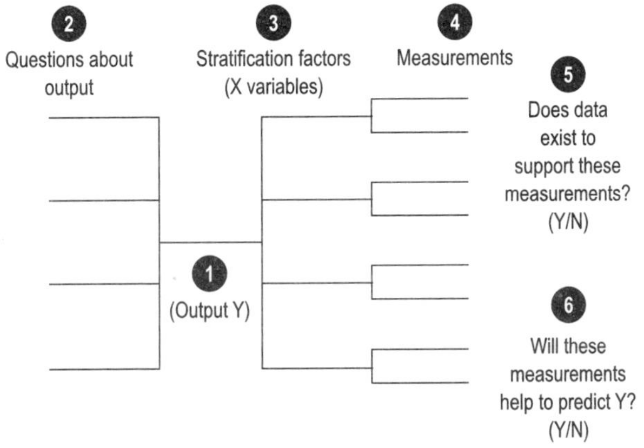

To identify stratification factors...

Your team can identify stratification by brainstorming a list of characteristics or factors you think may influence or be related to the problem or outcome you're studying. The method described here uses a modified tree diagram (shown above) to provide more structure to the process.

1. Identify an Output measure (Y), and enter it in the center point of the tree diagram.

2. List the key questions you have about that output.
3. Identify descriptive characteristics (the stratification factors) that define different subgroups of data you suspect may be relevant to your questions. These are the different ways you may want to "slice and dice" the data to uncover revealing patterns.
   - Ex: You suspect purchasing patterns may relate to size of the purchasing company, so you'll want to collect information about purchaser's size
   - Ex: You wonder if patterns of variation differ by time of day, so data will be labeled according to when it was collected
   - Ex: You wonder if delays are bigger on some days of the week than on other days, so data will be labeled by day of week
4. Create specific measurements for each subgroup or stratification factor.
5. Review each of the measurements (include the Y measure) and determine whether or not current data exists.
6. Discuss with the team whether or not current measurements will help to predict the output Y. If not, think of where to apply measurement systems so that they will help you to predict Y.

Quick Take

Operational definitions

Highlights

- Operational definitions are clear and precise instructions on how to take a particular measurement
- They help ensure common, consistent data collection and interpretation of results

To create operational definitions...

1. As a team, discuss the data you want to collect. Strive for a common understanding of the goal for collecting that data.
2. Precisely describe the data collection procedure.
   - What steps should data collectors use?
   - How should they take the measurement?
     Ex: If measuring transaction time in a bank, what is the trigger to "start the stopwatch"? When a customer gets in line? When he or she steps up to a teller?

Ex: If measuring the length of an item, how can you make sure that every data collector will put the ruler or caliper in the same position on the item?

Ex: What counts as a "scratch" on a product finish? What counts as an "error" on a form? (Misspellings? missing information? incorrect information?)

- What forms or instruments will data collectors have to help them? Specifically how are these forms or instruments to be used?
- How will the data be recorded? In what units?

3. Test the operational definition first with people involved in Step 2 above and then again with people not involved in the procedure, and compare results. Does everyone from both groups get the same result when counting or measuring the same things? Refine the measurement description as needed until you get consistent results.

Tips

- Develop visual guides to help people take the measurements correctly–such as photos with notes on what is to be measured or counted (and *how*), "good" vs. "bad" standard examples, etc.

Cautions on using existing data

Using existing data lets you take advantage of archived data or current measures to learn about the output, process or input. **Collecting new data** means recording new observations (it may involve looking at an existing metric but with new operational definitions).

Using existing data is quicker and cheaper than gathering new data, but there are some strong cautions:

- The data must be in a form you can use
- Either the data must be relatively recent or you must be able to show that conditions have not changed significantly since they were collected
- You should know when and how the data were collected (and that it was done in a way consistent with the questions you want to answer)

- You should be confident that the data were collected using procedures consistent with your operational definition
- They must be truly representative of the process, group, measurement system
- There must be sufficient data to make your conclusions valid

If any of these conditions are not met, you should strongly think about collecting new data.

Tips

- It's seldom wise to use old data only. Existing data is best used to establish historical patterns and to supplement new data.

Making a checksheet

Highlights

- Design a new checksheet every time you collect data (tailored to that situation)
- Having standard forms makes it easy to collect reliable, useful data
  - Enables faster capture and compiling of data
  - Ensures consistent data from different people
  - Captures essential descriptors (stratification factors) that otherwise might be overlooked or forgotten

To create and use a checksheet…

1. Select specific data and factors to be included
2. Determine time period to be covered by the form
   - Day, week, shift, quarter, etc.
3. Construct the form
   - Review different formats on the following pages and pick one that best fits your needs
   - Include a space for identifying the data collector by name or initials

- Include reason/comment columns
- Use full dates (month, date, year)
- Use explanatory title
- Decide how precise the measurement must be (seconds vs. minutes vs. hours; microns vs. millimeters) and indicate it on the form
  – Rule of thumb: smaller increments give better precision, but don't go beyond what is reasonable for the item being measured (Ex: don't measure in seconds a cycle time that last weeks–stick to hours)

4. Pilot test the form design and make changes as needed
   - If the "Other" column gets too many entries, you may be missing out on important categories of information. Examine entries classified as "Other" to see if there are new categories you could add to the checksheet.
   - Make changes before you begin the actual data collection trial

Quick Take

Basic checksheets

	Week				
Defect	1	2	3	4	Total
Incorrect SSN	|		|	|	3
Incorrect Address		|			1
Incorrect Work History	|			|	2
Incorrect Salary History	||	|	|||	||	8

- Easy to make and use
- Simply list the problems you're tracking and leave space to allow marks whenever someone finds that problem
- The example shown here also includes a time element

Quick Take

Frequency plot checksheet

- Easy to do by hand while a process is operating
- Automatically shows distribution of items or events along a scale or ordered quantity
- Helps detect unusual patterns in a population or detect multiple populations
- Gives visual picture of average and range without any further analysis

Repair shop output rate (Jul 1 – Jul 19)

Date	Completed repairs
1	
2	x x x x x x x
3	x x x x x
4	x x x x x
5	x x x x
6	x x
7	x x x
8	x
9	x x x x x x
10	x x x x
11	x x x x
12	x x x x
13	x
14	x x x
15	
16	x x x x x x
17	x x x x x
18	x x x x x x x x
19	x x x x

Quick Take

Traveler checksheet

- A checksheet that travels with a work item (product, form, etc.). At each process step, the operator enters the appropriate data.
- Good way to collect data on process lead time.
- Add columns as needed for other data, such as value-add time, delays, defects, work-in-process, etc.
- Put spaces for tracking information (a unique identifier for the job or part) at the top of the form

Traveler Checksheet
Six Sigma Pizza Order

Order # 3256-879 Date June 24, 2010

Order Type: ☒ Conventional ☐ Low Fat ☐ Other

Dollar Amount: $27.25

Customer Location ☐ NW ☐ W ☒ SW ☐ E

Process Step	Time Begun; Time Completed	Defects Found
Order Taking	13:30; 13:42	
Order Preparation	13:49; 14:03	//
Delivery	14:22; 14:37	

- Decide how the form will follow the work item (Ex: physically attached to paperwork or product, email alerts)

Quick Take

Location checksheet (concentration diagram)

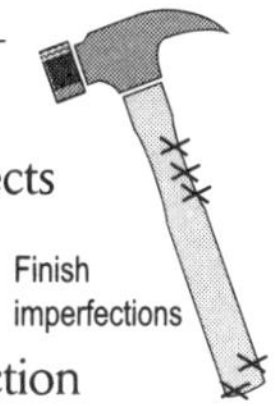

- Data collection sheet based on a physical representation of a product, workplace, or form
- Data collectors enter marks where predefined defects occur
- Allows you to pinpoint areas prone to defects or problems (and therefore focuses further data collection efforts)

Quick Take

Sampling basics

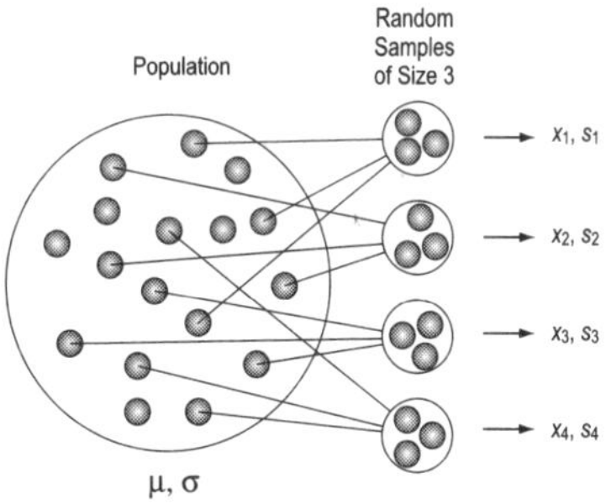

Sampling is taking data on one or more subsets of a larger group in order to make decisions about the whole group.

The trade-off is faster data collection (because you only have to sample) vs. some uncertainty about what is really going on with the whole group

The table to the right shows standard notations

	Population (= parameter)	**Sampling** (= statistic)
Count of items	N	n
Mean	μ	$\bar{X}$
Mean estimator	$\hat{\mu}$	$\bar{X}$
Median	$\tilde{\mu}$	$\tilde{X}$
Std. Deviation	σ	s
Std. Dev. estimator	$\hat{\sigma}$	s

Note: Technically, the Xbar symbols should be written with lower-case letters, but (except for statistics books) are more often seen with capitals, so that is the convention used in this book

μ = the Greek letter "mu" σ = the Greek letter "sigma"

— a straight line is called a "bar" and denotes an average	~ the curvy-line tilde (pronounced til-dah) denotes a median	^ a carat (or hat) denotes an estimator

Types of sampling: process vs. population

Population – Drawing from a fixed group with definable boundaries. No time element.

Ex: Customers, complaints, items in warehouse

Process – Sampling from a changing flow of items moving through the business. Has a time element.

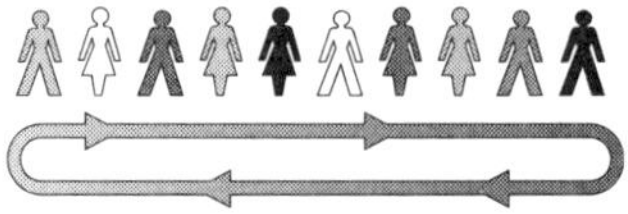

Ex: New customers per week, hourly complaint volume, items received/shipped by day

Why it matters whether you have process or population samples

- **There are different tools for analyzing population data than for process data,** so you must be clear about what kind of data you're gathering.
- **Most traditional statistical training focuses on sampling from populations**, where you have a nonchanging set of items or events from which it's relatively easy to select a representative sample. **In contrast, quality and business process improvement tends to focus more often on processes**, where change is a constant.
- **Process data give more information (on trends, for example) than population data**, so are preferred in most cases. Process sampling techniques are also the foundation of process monitoring and control.

Sampling terms

Sampling event – The act of extracting items from the population or process to measure.

Subgroup – The number of consecutive units extracted for measurement in each sampling event. (A "subgroup" can be just one item, but is usually two or more.)

Sampling Frequency – The number of times a day or week a sample is taken (Ex: twice per day, once per week). Applies only to process sampling.

Quick Take

Factors in sample selection

A number of factors affect the size and number of samples you must collect:

- **Situation:** Whether it is an existing set of items that will not change (a **population**) or a set that is continually changing (**process**)
- **Data type:** Continuous or attribute
- **Objectives:** What you'll do with results
- **Familiarity:** How much prior knowledge you have about the situation (such as historical data on process performance, knowledge of various customer segments, etc.)
- **Certainty:** How much "confidence" you need in your conclusions

Understanding bias

The big pitfall in sampling is bias—selecting a sample that does NOT really represent the whole. Typical sources of bias include:

- Self-selection (Ex: asking customers to call in to a phone number rather than randomly calling them)
- Self-exclusion (Ex: some types of customers will be less motivated to respond than others)
- Missing key representatives
- Ignoring nonconformances (things that don't match expectations)
- Grouping

Two worst ways to choose samples

- **Judgment:** choosing a sample based on someone's knowledge of the process, assuming that it will be "representative." Judgment guarantees a bias, and should be avoided.
- **Convenience:** sampling the items that are easiest to measure or at times that are most convenient. (Ex: collecting VOC data from people you know, or when you go for coffee).

Two best ways to choose samples

- **Random**: Best method for Population situations. Use a random number table or random function in Excel or other software, or draw numbers from a hat that will tell you which items from the population to select.
- **Systematic**: Most practical and unbiased in a Process situation. "Systematic" means that we select every nth unit. The risk of bias comes when the selection of the sample matches a pattern in the process.

Quick Take

Stable process (and population) sampling

Highlights

- A stable process is one that has only common cause variation (*see* Chapter 7). That means the same factors are always present and you don't need to worry about missing special causes that may come or go.
- In essence, a stable process is the same as a population.

To sample from a stable process...

1. **Develop an initial profile of the data**
   - Population size (N)
   - Stratification factors: If you elect to conduct a stratified sample, you need to know the size of each subset or stratum
   - Precision: how tightly (within what range of error) you want your measurement to describe the result
   - Estimate of the variation:
     - For **continuous data**, estimate the standard deviation of the variable being measured
     - For **discrete data**, estimate P, the proportion of the population that has the characteristic in question
2. **Develop a sampling strategy**
   - Random or systematic?

- How will you draw the samples? Who will do it?
- How will you guard against bias? (*see* p. 95)
  - You want the sample to be very representative but there is a cost in terms of time, effort, and dollars
  - The goal is to avoid differences between the items represented in the sample and those not in the sample

3. Determine the minimum sample size (see p. 85)

4. Adjust as needed to determine actual sample size

Tip

- By definition an unstable process is unpredictable. Making inferences about a population based on a sample of an unstable process is ill-advised. Establish stability before making inferences.

Quick Take

Formulas for determining minimum sample size (population or stable process)

Continuous data

$$n = \left(\frac{1.96s}{\Delta}\right)^2$$

n = minimum sample size

1.96 = constant representing a 95% confidence interval *(note: this factor is valid when sample size is estimated to be 30 or greater–for smaller sample sizes, increase the constant based on the t distribution)*

s = estimate of standard deviation data

Δ = the difference (level of precision desired from the sample) you're trying to detect, in the same units as "s"

Note: if the minimum estimated sample size is less than 30, use 30 as he sample size.

If you're using Minitab, it can calculate the sample size. Open Minitab, go to **Stat > Power and Sample Size >** then choose either…

a) 1-Sample t, if sample comes from a normally distributed data set and you want a relatively small sample (less than 25)

b) 1-Sample Z, if you are not sure about the distribution of your data set and a sample size greater than 30 is acceptable

You must tell Minitab what difference (Δ, delta) you are trying to detect and what power (the probability of detecting the difference) you are comfortable with (typically not less than 0.9) before a sample size can be calculated. For additional details refer to Minitab Help.

Discrete data sample size

$$n = \left(\frac{1.96}{\Delta}\right)^2 P(1 - P)$$

n = minimum sample size

P = estimate of the proportion of the population or process that is defective

Δ = level of precision desired from the sample (express as a decimal or percentage, the same unit as P)

- 1.96 = constant representing a 95% confidence interval
- The highest value of P(1 – P) is 0.25, which is equal to P = 0.5

Again, Minitab can calculate the sample size. Open Minitab, go to **Stat > Power and Sample Size >** then choose either…

- 1 Proportion (comparing a proportion against a fixed standard)
- 2 Proportions (comparing 2 proportions)

For small populations

Changes in the minimum sample size are required for small populations. If n/N is greater than 0.05, the sample size can be adjusted to:

$$n_{finite} = \frac{n}{1 + \left(\frac{n}{N}\right)}$$

The proportion formula should be used only when: $nP \geq 5$ or when $n(1\text{-}P) \geq 5$

Both sample size formulas assume a 95% confidence interval and a small sample size (n) compared to the entire population size (N).

Measurement System Analysis (MSA) and Gage R&R Overview

Purpose

To determine if a measurement system can generate accurate data, and if the accuracy is adequate to achieve your objectives

Why use MSA

- To make sure that the differences in the data are due to actual differences in what is being measured and not to variation in measurement methods
- NOTE: Experience shows that 30% to 50% of measurement systems are not capable of accurately or precisely measuring the desired metric

Types of MSA

Gage R&R (next page)

Bias Analysis (*see* p. 95)

Stability Analysis (*see* p. 97)

Discrimination Analysis (*see* p. 99)

Kappa Analysis (*see* p.100)

Components of measurement error

Measurements need to be "precise" and "accurate." Accuracy and precision are different, independent properties:

- Data may be accurate (reflect the true values of the property) but not precise (measurement units do not have enough discriminatory power)
- Vice versa, data can be precise yet *inaccurate* (they are precisely measuring something that does not reflect the true values)
- Sometimes data can be *neither* accurate nor precise
- Obviously, the goal is to have data that are both precise and accurate

From a statistical viewpoint, there are four desirable characteristics that relate to precision and accuracy of continuous data:

1) No systematic differences between the measurement values we get and the "true value" (lack of **bias**, *see* p. 95)
2) The ability to get the same result if we take the same measurement repeatedly or if different people take the same measurement (**Gage R&R**, *see* p. 87)
3) The ability of the system to produce the same results in the future that it did in the past (**stability**, *see* p. 97)
4) The ability of the system to detect meaningful differences (good **discrimination**, *see* p. 99)

(Another desirable characteristic, linearity–the ability to get consistent results from measurement devices and procedures across a wide range of uses–is not as often an issue and is not covered in this book.)

NOTE: **Having uncalibrated measurement devices can affect all of these factors.** Calibration is not covered in this book since it varies considerably depending on the device. Be sure to follow established procedures to calibrate any devices used in data collection.

Gage R&R: Collecting the data

Highlights

Gage R&R involves evaluating the **repeatability** and **reproducibility** of a measurement system.

- **Repeatability** refers to the inherent variability of the measurement system. It is the variation that occurs when successive measurements are made under the same conditions:
  - Same person
  - Same thing being measured
  - Same characteristic
  - Same instrument
  - Same set-up
  - Same environmental conditions
- **Reproducibility** is the variation in the average of the measurements made by different operators using the same measuring

instrument and technique when measuring the identical characteristic on the same part or same process.

Different person
Same part
Same characteristic
Same instrument
Same setup
Same environmental conditions

To use Gage R&R...

1. Identify the elements of your measurement system (equipment, operators or data collectors, parts/materials/process, and other factors).
   - Check that any measuring instruments have a discrimination that is equal to or less than 1/10 of the expected process variation/specification range
2. Select the items to include in the Gage R&R test. Be sure to represent the entire range of process variation. (Good and Bad over the entire specification plus slightly out of spec on both the high and low sides).
3. Select 2 or 3 operators to participate in the study.
4. Identify 5 to 10 items to be measured.
   - Make sure the items are marked for ease of data collection, but remain "blind"(unidentifiable) to the operators
5. Have each operator measure each item 2 to 3 times **in random sequence.**
6. Gather data and analyze. *See* pp. 90 to 95 for interpretation of typical plots generated by statistical software.

Tips

- In manufacturing you may want to start with one of the Automotive Industry Action Group (*see* www.AIAG.org) standards...
  - short form: 2 operators measuring 5 items 2 times (= 20 measurements total)
  - long form: 3 operators measuring 10 items 3 times (= 90 measurements total)

- Be there for the study–NOT as a participant, but as an observer. Watch for unplanned influences.
- Randomize the items continuously during the study to prevent operator bias from influencing the test.
- When checking a given measurement system for the first time, let the process run as it normally would (no pre-training, no adjustment of equipment or instruments, no special items).

Interpreting Gage R&R Results

Background

In most cases, the data you gather for an MSA or Gage R&R study will be entered in a software program. What follows are examples of the types of output you're likely to see, along with guidance on what to look for.

Basic terminology

Gage R&R = Gage system's *Repeatability* (how likely it is that the same person using the same method will get the same measurement) and *Reproducibility* (how likely it is that different people using the same method/tools will get the same measurement)

Measures the variability in the response minus the variation due to differences in parts. This takes into account variability due to the gage, the operators, and the operator by part interaction.

Repeatability: "Within the gage"–amount of difference that a single data collector/inspector got when measuring the same thing over and over again. Also called "test/retest error."

Reproducibility: Amount of difference that occurred when different people measured the same item. Calso called "between operator" error.

Part-to-Part: An estimate of the variation between the parts being measured.

Components of variation

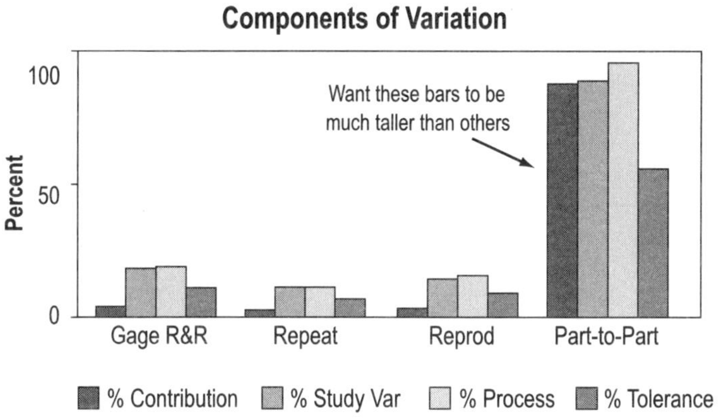

What you're looking for:

- You want the part-to-part bars to be much taller than the others because that means most of the variation is from true differences in the items being measured.
- If the Gage R&R, Repeat, and Reprod bars are tall, that means the measurement system is unreliable. (Repeat + Reprod = Gage R&R)
- Focus on the %Study Var bars—This is the amount of variation (expressed as a percentage) attributed to measurement error. Specifically, the calculation divides the standard deviation of the gage component by the total observed standard deviation then multiplies by 100. Common standards (such as AIAG) for %Study Var are:

  Less than 10% is good—it means little variation is due to your measurement system; most of it is true variation

  10% – 30% may be acceptable depending on the application (30% is maximum acceptable for any process improvement effort)

  More than 30% unacceptable (your measurement system is too unpredictable)

Repeatability

Repeatability is checked by using Range Graph of the Gage R&R control charts. This chart shows the variation in the measurements made by each operator on each part.

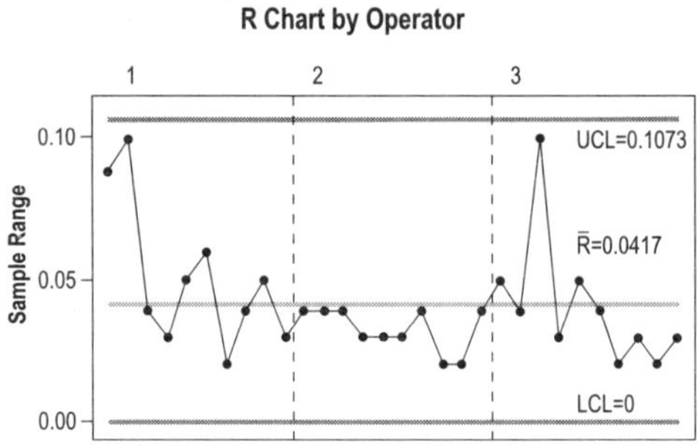

If chart is "in control" the gage and operator are "repeatable"

What you're looking for

- Is the range chart in control? (Review control chart guidelines, pp. 122 to 134)
- Any points that fall above the UCL need to be investigated
- If the difference between the largest value and the smallest value of the same part does not exceed the UCL, then that gage and operator may be considered Repeatable (depends on the application)

Reproducibility

Reproducibility is graphically represented by looking for significant differences between the patterns of data generated by each operator measuring the same items.

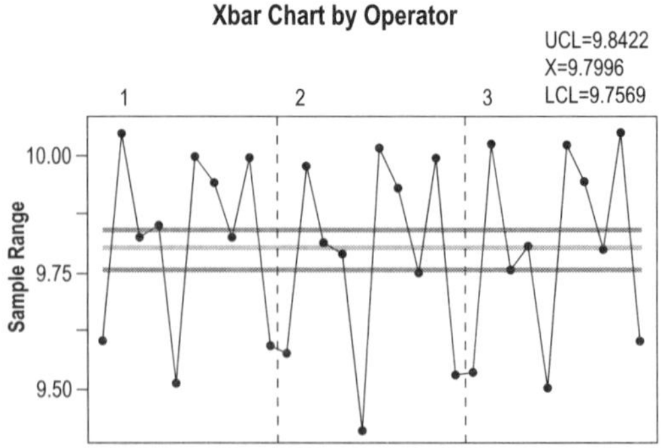

Want chart to be "out of control"—that means the gage variance is much smaller than the differences in the items being measured

- Compare all the "Xbar chart by Operator" for all data collectors/operators used in the study
- Remember: the range chart determines the Xbar upper and lower control limits

What you're looking for:

- This is one instance where you *want* the points to consistently go outside the upper and lower control limits (LCL, UCL). The control limits are determined by gage variance and these plots should show that gage variance is much smaller than variability within the parts.

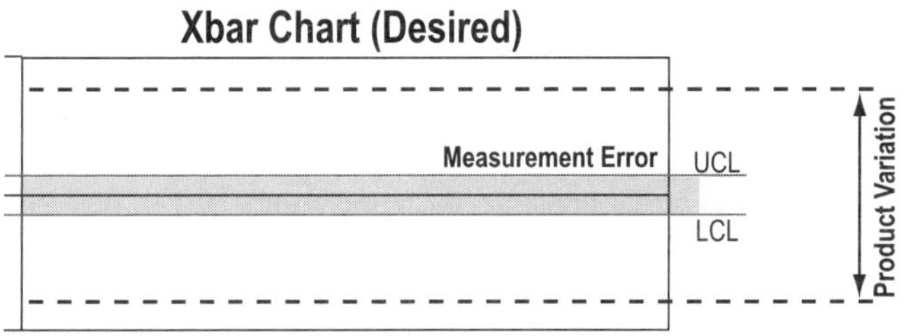

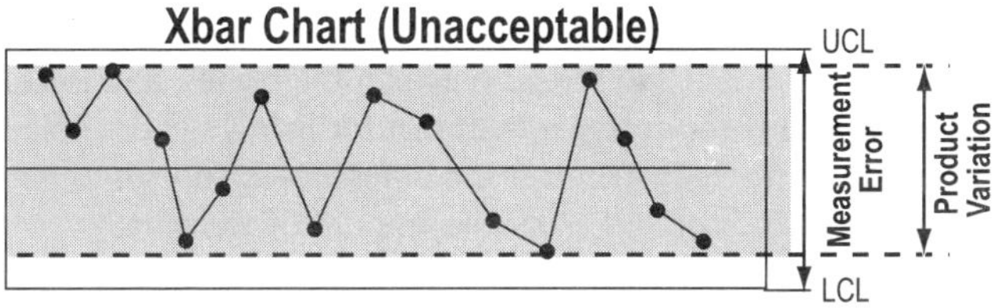

- Also compare patterns between operators. If they are *not* similar, there may be significant operator/part or operator/equipment interactions (meaning different operators are using the equipment differently or measuring parts differently).
- Note: if the samples do not represent the total variability of the process, the gage (repeatability) variance may be larger than the part variance and invalidate the results here.

By Part chart

The **By Part graph** shows the data for the parts for all operators plotted together. It displays the raw data and highlights the average of those measurements. This chart shows the measurements (taken by three different operators) for each of 10 parts.

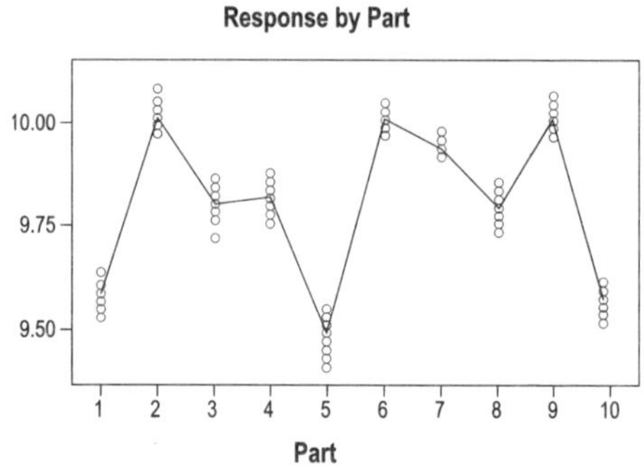

Want the range of readings for each part to be consistent with the range for other parts. That is NOT the case here (Ex: compare range for Part 7 with range for Part 3).

What you're looking for:

- The chart should show a consistent range of variation (smallest to the largest dimensions) for the same parts.
- If the spread between the biggest and smallest values varies a lot between different sets of points, that may mean that the parts chosen for the calibration were not truly representative of the variation within the process
- In this example, the spread between the highest and lowest value for Part 3 is much bigger than that for Part 7 (where points are closely clustered). Whether the difference is enough to be significant depends on the allowable amount of variation.
- Note: If a part shows a large spread, it may be a poor candidate for the test because the feature may not be clear or it may be difficult to measure that characteristic every time the same way.

By Operator chart

The **By Operator graph** groups data by who was collecting the data ("running the process") rather than by part, so it will help you identify operator issues (such as inconsistent use of operational definitions or of measuring devices). In this example, each of three operators measured the same 10 parts. The 10 data points for each operator are stacked.

What you're looking for:

- The line connecting the averages (of all parts measured by an operator) should be flat or almost flat.

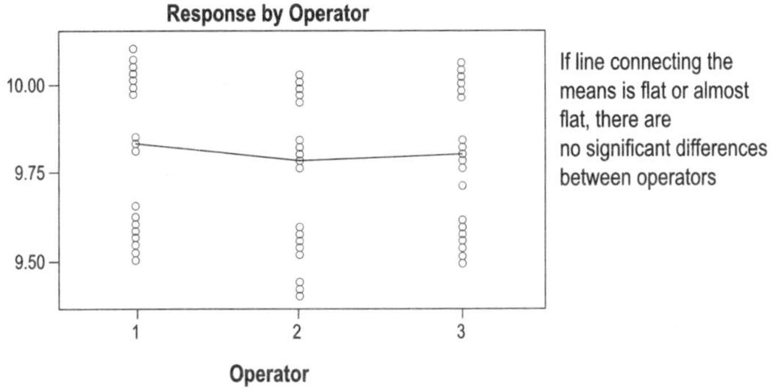

- Any significant slope indicates that at least one operator has a bias to measure larger or smaller than the other operators.
- In the example, Operator 2 tends to measure slightly smaller than Operators 1 and 3. Whether that is significant will depend on the allowable level of variation.

Operator*Part chart

This graph shows the data for each operator involved in the study. It is the best chart for exposing operator-and-part interaction (meaning differences in how different people measure different parts).

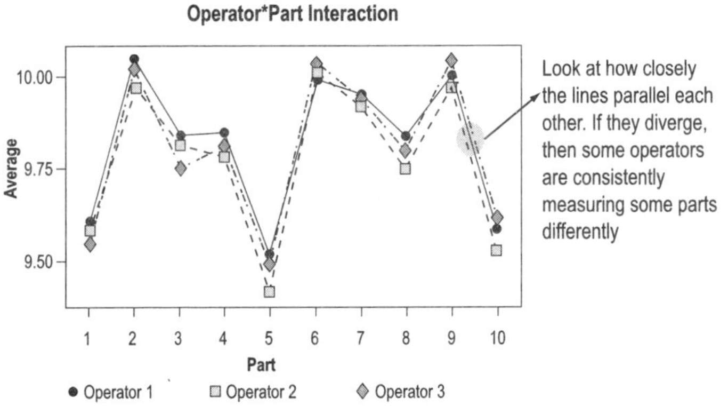

What you're looking for

- If the lines connecting the plotted averages diverge significantly, then there is a relationship between the operator making the measurements and the part being measured. This is not good and needs to be investigated.

MSA: Evaluating bias

Accuracy vs. bias

Accuracy is the extent to which the averages of the measurements deviate from the true value. In simple terms, it deals with the question, "On average, do I get the 'right' answer?" If the answer is yes, then the measurement system is accurate. If the answer is no, the measurement system is inaccurate.

Bias is the term given to the distance between the observed average measurement and the true value, or "right" answer.

In statistical terms, bias is identified when the averages of measurements differ by a fixed amount from the "true" value. Bias effects include:

Operator bias – Different operators get detectable different averages for the same value. Can be evaluated using the Gage R&R graphs covered on previous pages.

Instrument bias – Different instruments get detectably different averages for the same measurement on the same part. If instrument bias is suspected, set up a specific test where one operator uses multiple devices to measure the same parts under otherwise identical conditions. Create a "by instrument" chart similar to the "by part" and "by operator" charts discussed on pp. 94 to 95.

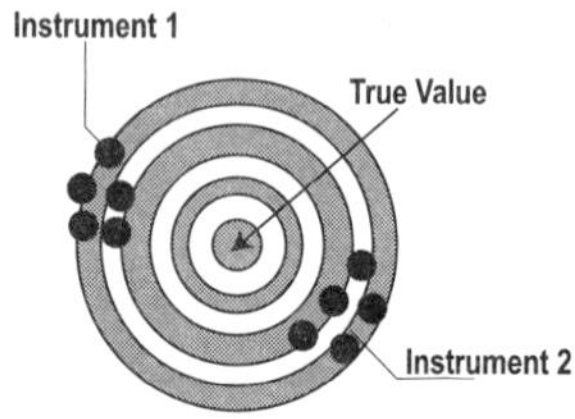

Other forms of bias – Day-to-day (environment), customer and supplier (sites). Talk to data experts (such as a Master Black Belt) to determine how to detect these forms of bias and counteract or eliminate them.

Testing overall measurement bias

1. Assemble a set of parts to be used for the test. Determine "master values" (the agreed-on measurement) for the characteristic for each part.
2. Calculate the difference between the measured values and the master value.
3. Test the hypothesis (*see* p. 156) that the average bias is equal to 0.
4. Interpret the position of 0 relative to the 95% confidence interval of the individual differences. You want the 95% confidence interval for the average to overlap the "true" value. In the boxplot below; the confidence interval overlaps the H_0 value, so we cannot reject the null hypothesis that the sample is the same as the master value.

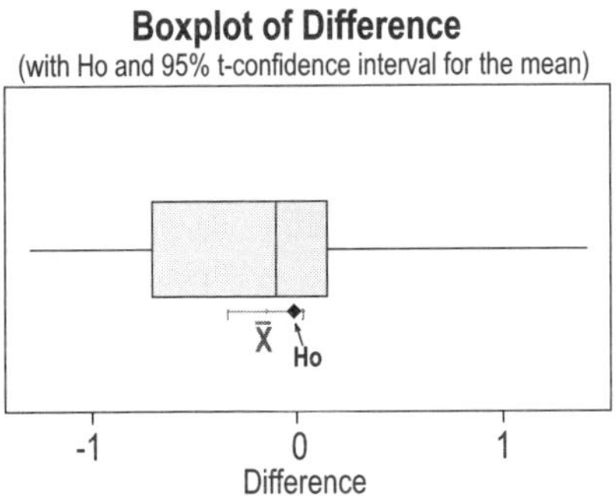

If the confidence interval for Xbar overlaps "0," then the measurements are not statistically different from the "master values"

MSA: Evaluating stability

If measurements do not change or drift over time, the instrument is considered to be stable. Loss of stability can be due to:

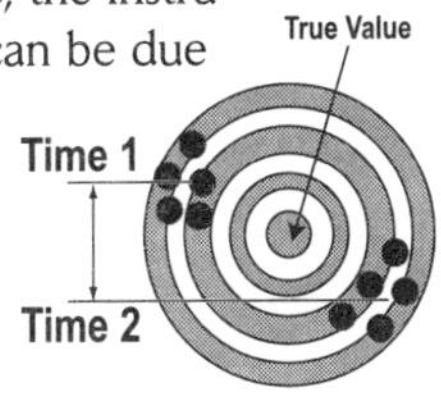

- deterioration of measurement devices
- increase in variability of operator actions (such as people forgetting to refer to operational definitions)

A common and recurring source of instability is the lack of enforced Standard Operating Procedures. Ask:

- Do standard operating procedures exist?
- Are they understood?
- Are they being followed?
- Are they current?
- Is operator certification performed?
- How and how often do you perform audits to test stability?

Measurement System stability can be tested by maintaining a control chart on the measurement system (*see* charts below).

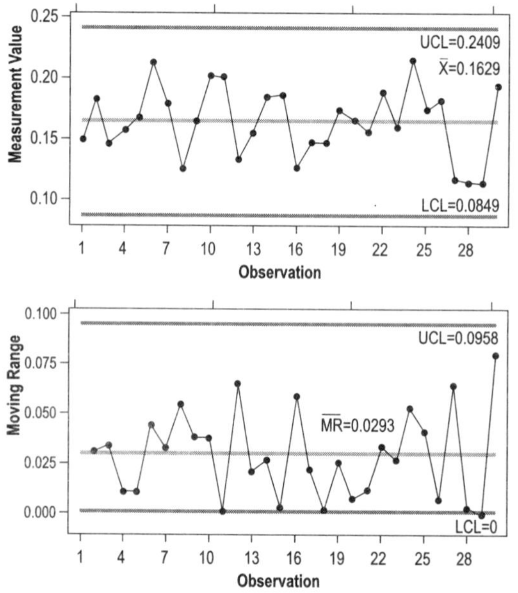

Measurement stability is monitored the same as process stability—with a control chart. This is an "Individuals, moving range" (ImR) chart on measurements. You want both charts to be in control. (See p. 124 for more on interpreting ImR control charts.)

MSA: Evaluating discrimination

Discrimination is the measurement system's ability to detect changes in the characteristic. A measurement system is unacceptable if it cannot detect the variation of the process, and/or cannot differentiate between special and common cause levels of variation. (Ex: A timing device with a discrimination of 1/100th of a second is needed to evaluate differences in most track events.)

In concept, the measurement system should be able to divide the smaller of the tolerance or six standard deviations into at least five data categories. A good way to evaluate discrimination graphically is to study a range chart. (The distance between the UCL and LCL is approximately 6 standard deviations.)

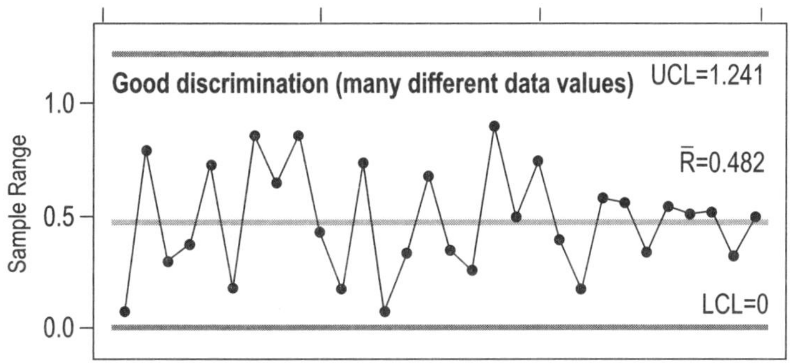

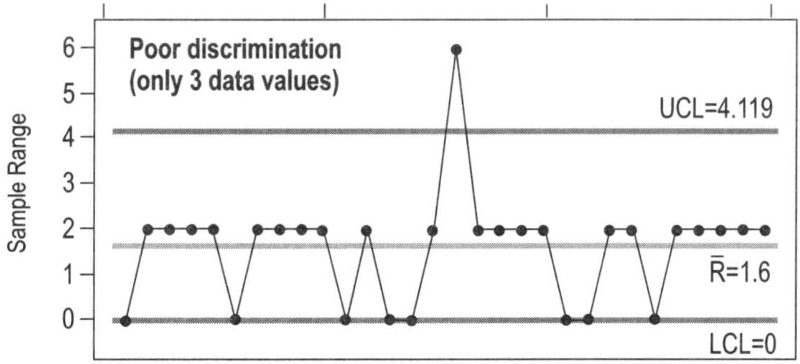

MSA for attribute/ discrete data

Attribute and ordinal measurements often rely on subjective classifications or ratings.

Ex: Rating features as good or bad, rating wine bouquet, taste, and aftertaste; rating employee performance from 1 to 5; scoring gymnastics

The Measurement System Analysis procedures described previously in this book are useful only for continuous data. When there is no alternative—when you cannot change an attribute metric to a continuous data type—a calculation called **Kappa** is used. Kappa is suitable for non-quantitative (attribute) systems such as:

Good or bad

Go/No Go

Differentiating noises (hiss, clank, thump)

Pass/fail

Notes on Kappa for Attribute Data

a) Treats all non-acceptable categories equally

Ex: It doesn't matter whether the numeric values from two different raters are close together (a 5 vs. a 4, for instance) or far apart (5 vs. 1). All differences are treated the same.

Ex: A "clank" is neither worse nor better than a "thump"

b) Does not assume that the ratings are equally distributed across the possible range

Ex: If you had a "done-ness" rating system with 6 categories (raw, rare, medium rare, medium, medium well, well done), it doesn't matter whether each category is "20% more done" than the prior category or if the done-ness varies between categories (which is a good thing because usually it's impossible to assign numbers in situations like this)

c) Requires that the units be independent

- The measurement or classification of one unit is not influenced by any other unit
- All judges or raters make classifications independently (so they don't bias one another)

d) Requires that the assessment categories be mutually exclusive (no overlap—something that falls into one category cannot also fall into a second category)

How to determine Kappa

1. **Select sample items for the study.**
   - If you have only **two categories**, good and bad, you should have a minimum of 20 good and 20 bad items (= 40 items total) and a maximum of 50 good and 50 bad (= 100 items total)
     - Try to keep approximately 50% good and 50% bad
     - Choose items of varying degrees of good and bad
   - If you have **more than two categories**, one of which is good and the other categories reflecting different defect modes, make 50% of the items good and have a minimum of 10% of the items in each defect mode.
     - You might combine some defect modes as "other"
     - The categories should be mutually exclusive (there is no overlap) or, if not, combine any categories that overlap

2. **Have each rater evaluate the same unit at least twice.**

3. **Calculate a Kappa for each rater** by creating separate Kappa tables, one per rater. (*See* instructions on next page.)

4. **Calculate a between-rater Kappa** by creating a Kappa table from the first judgment of each rater.
   - Between-rater Kappa will be made as Pairwise comparisons (A to B, B to C, A to C, etc.)

5. **Interpret the results**
   - If Kappa is lower than 0.7, the measurement system is not adequate
   - If Kappa is 0.9 or above, the measurement system is considered excellent
   - If P observed = P chance, then K=0
     - A Kappa of 0 indicates that the agreement is the same as that expected by random chance
   - Warning: One bad apple can spoil this bunch! A small Kappa means a rater must be changing how he/she takes the measurement each time (low repeatability). One rater with low repeatability skews the comparison with other raters.

Doing the Kappa calculation

$$K = \frac{P_{observed} - P_{chance}}{1 - P_{chance}}$$

$P_{observed}$: Proportion of units on which both Raters agree

= proportion both raters agree are good + the proportion both Raters agree are bad

Pchance: Proportion of agreements expected by chance

= (proportion that Rater A grades as good * proportion that Rater B grades as good) + (proportion that Rater A grades as bad * proportion that Rater B grades as bad)

Note: This equation applies to a two-category (binary) analysis, where every item can fall into only one of two categories.

Example: Kappa for repeatability by a single Rater

		Rater A First Measure		
		Good	Bad	
Rater A Second Measure	Good	0.5	0.1	0.6
	Bad	0.05	0.35	0.4
		0.55	0.45	

$P_{observed}$ is the sum of the probabilities on the diagonal:

$$P_{observed} = (0.500 + 0.350) = 0.850$$

P_{chance} is the probabilities for each classification multiplied and then summed:

$$P_{chance} = (0.600*0.55) + (0.400*0.45) = 0.51$$

Then $K_{rater\ A} = (0.85 - 0.51)/(1 - 0.51) = 0.693$

This Kappa value is below the generally accepted benchmark of 0.85 for good reliability.

Example: Kappa reproducibility for comparing two different raters

Rater A to Rater B comparison		**Rater A First Measure**		
		Good	Bad	
Rater B First Measure	Good	9	3	12
	Bad	2	6	8
		11	9	

9 = Number of times both raters agreed the unit was good (using their first measurements)

3 = Number of times Rater A judged a unit bad and Rater B judged a unit good (using their first measurements)

2 = Number of times Rater A judged a unit good and Rater B judged a unit bad (using their first measurements)

6 = Number of times both raters agreed the unit was bad (using their first measurements)

This figures are converted to percentages:

Rater A to Rater B comparison		**Rater A First Measure**		
		Good	Bad	
Rater B First Measure	Good	0.45	0.15	0.6
	Bad	0.1	0.3	0.4
		0.55	0.45	

$P_{observed}$ is the sum of the probabilities on the diagonal:

$$P_{observed} = (0.450 + 0.300) = 0.750$$

P_{chance} is the probabilities for each classification multiplied and then summed:

$$P_{chance} = (0.600*0.55) + (0.400*0.45) = 0.51$$

Then $K_{rater\ A/B} = (0.75 - 0.51)/(1 - 0.51) = 0.489$

This Kappa value is well below the acceptable threshold of 0.7. It means that these two raters grade the items differently too often.

CHAPTER 6

Descriptive Statistics and Data Displays

Purpose of these tools

To provide basic information about the distribution and properties of a set of data

Deciding which tool to use

- **Statistical term conventions**, p. 105, covers standards used for symbols and terminology in statistical equations. Review as needed.
- **Measures of Central Tendency,** p. 106, covers how to calculate **mean**, **median**, and **mode**. Calculate these values manually for any set of continuous data if not provided by software.
- **Measures of Spread,** p. 108, reviews how to calculate **range**, **standard deviation**, and **variance**. You will need these calculations for many types of statistical tools (control charts, hypothesis tests, etc.).
- **Box plots**, p. 110, describes one type of chart that summarizes the distribution of continuous data. You will rarely generate one by hand, but will see them often if you use statistical software programs. Review as needed.
- **Frequency plot/histogram,** p. 111, reviews the types of frequency plots and interpretation of patterns they reveal. Essential for evaluating the normality; recommended for any set of continuous data.
- **Normal Distribution,** p. 114, describes the properties of the "normal" or "bell-shaped" distribution. Review as needed.
- **Non-Normal Distributions/Central Limit Theorem,** p. 114, reviews other types of distributions commonly encountered with continuous data, and how you can make statistically valid inferences even if they are not normally distributed. Review as needed.

Quick Take

Statistical term conventions

The field of statistics is typically divided into two areas of study:

1) **Descriptive statistics** represent a characteristic of a large group of observations (a population or a sample representing a population).

   Ex: Mean and standard deviation are descriptive statistics about a set of data

2) **Inferential Statistics** draw conclusions about a population based upon analysis of sample data. A small set of numbers (a sample) is used to make inferences about a much larger set of numbers (the population).

   Ex: You'll use inferential statistics when hypothesis testing (*see* Chapter 9)

Parameters are terms used to describe the key characteristics of a **population**.

- Population parameters are denoted by a small Greek letter, such as sigma (σ) for standard deviation or mu (μ) for mean
- The capital letter **N** is used for the number of values in a population when the population size is not infinite

In most cases, the data used in process improvement is a **sample** (a subset) taken from a population..

- **Statistics** (also called "sample statistics") are terms used to describe the key characteristics of a sample
- Statistics are usually denoted by Latin letters, such as **s**, $\bar{\mathbf{X}}$ (often spelled out as Xbar in text), and $\tilde{\mathbf{X}}$ (spelled out as X-tilde)
- The lowercase letter **n** is used for the number of values in a sample (the sample size)

In general mathematics as well as in statistics, capital Greek letters are also used. These big letters serve as "operators" in equations, telling us what mathematical calculation to perform. In this book, you'll see a "capital sigma" in many equations:

Σ (capital sigma) indicates that the values should be added together (summing)

Quick Take

Measures of central tendency (mean, median, mode)

Highlights

- Central tendency tells you how tightly data cluster around a central point.
- The three most common measures of central tendency are **mean** (or average), **median**, and **mode.**
- These are measures of central tendency, not a measure of variation. However, a mean is required to calculate some of the statistical measures of variation.

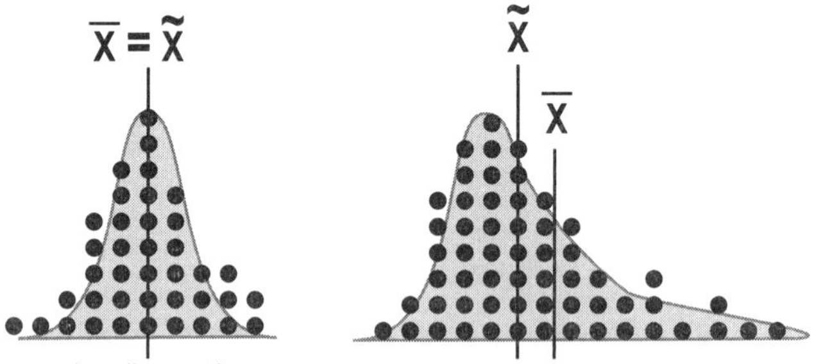

Mean and median are the same with a normal distribution

Mean and median are different when distributions are not normal

Mean/average

The **mean** is the arithmetic average of a set of data.

- To calculate the mean, add together all data values then divide by the number of values.
- Using the statistical conventions described on p. 105, there are two forms of the expression—one for a population mean and the other for a sample of data:

POPULATION MEAN

$$\mu = \frac{\sum_{i=1}^{N} X_i}{N}$$

SAMPLE MEAN

$$\bar{X} = \frac{\sum_{i=1}^{n} X_i}{n}$$

Median

The **median** is the midpoint of a ranked order set of data.

To determine the median, arrange the data in ascending or descending order. The median is the value at the center (if there is an odd number of data points), or the average of the two middle values (if there is an even number of data points). The symbol for the median is X with a tilde (~) over it.

$$\text{Median} = \tilde{X}$$

Mode

The **mode** of a set of data is the most frequently observed value(s).

Example

Scores from 10 students arranged in ascending order:

32, 33, 34, 34, 35, 37, 37, 39, 41, 44

Mean: Xbar = (32 + 33 + 34 + 34 + 35 + 37 + 37 + 39 + 41 + 44) / 10 = **36.6**

Median: X-tilde = (35 + 37) / 2 = 36

Mode: There are two modes (34 & 37)

Tips

- While the mean is most frequently used, the median is occasionally helpful because it is not affected as much by outliers.
  - Ex: In the student scores data above, changing the "44" to a "99" would make the mean = 42.1 (up nearly 6 points) but the median would stay at 36. In that instance, the median would be far more representative of the data set as a whole.

Quick Take

Measures of spread (range, variance, standard deviation)

Highlights

- Spread tells us how the data are distributed around the center point. A lot of spread = high variation.
- Common measures of spread include range, variance, and standard deviation.
- Variation is often depicted graphically with a frequency plot or histogram (*see* p. 111).

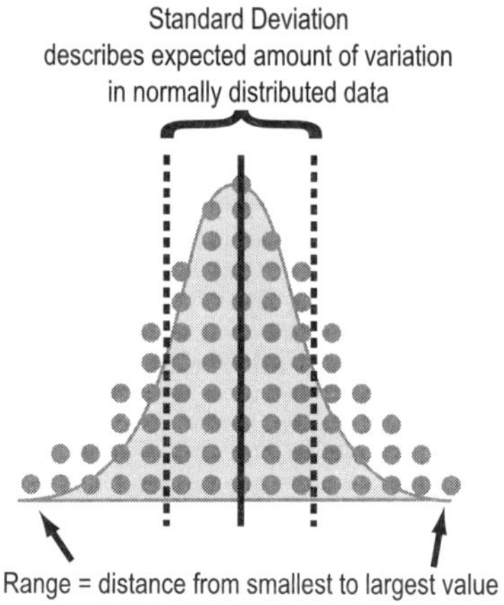

Range

Range is the difference between the largest and smallest values in a data set.

The **Min** is the *smallest* value in a data set

The **Max** is the *largest* value in a data set

The **Range** is the *difference* between the Max and the Min

Ex: Here are ten ages in ascending order: 32, 33, 34, 34, 35, 37, 37, 39, 41, 44

Min = **32**, Max = **44**

Range = Max – Min = **44** - **32** = **12**

Variance

Variance tells you how far off the data values are from the mean overall.

1) Calculate the mean of all the data points, Xbar
2) Calculate the difference between each data point and the average (X_i – Xbar)

3) Square those figures for all data points
   - This ensures that you'll always be dealing with a positive number–otherwise, all of the values would cancel each other out and sum to zero
4) Add the squared values together (a value called the **sum of squares** in statistics)
5) Divide that total by n-1 (the number of data values minus 1)

$$s^2 = \frac{\text{sum of squares}}{n-1} = \frac{\sum_{i=1}^{n}(X_i - \bar{X})^2}{n-1}$$

Note that the equation above follows statistical conventions (p. 105) for describing sample statistics. Variance for a population uses a sigma as shown here.

$$\sigma^2 = \frac{\sum_{i=1}^{N}(X_i - \mu)^2}{N}$$

Though more people are familiar with standard deviation (*see* below), variance has one big advantage: it is **additive** while standard deviations are not. That means, for example, that the total variance for a process can be determined by adding together the variances for all the process steps.

- So to calculate a standard deviation for an entire process, first calculate the variances for each process step, add those variances together, *then* take the square root. Do not add together the standard deviations of each step.

A drawback to using variance is that it is not in the same units of measure as the data points. Ex: for cycle times, the variance would be in units of "minutes squared," which doesn't make logical sense.

Standard deviation

Think of standard deviation as the "average distance from each data point to the mean." Calculate the standard deviation for a sample or population by doing the same steps as for the variance, then simply taking the square root. Here's how the equation would look for the 10 ages listed on the previous page:

$$s = \sqrt{\frac{\sum_{i=1}^{n}(X_i - \bar{X})^2}{n-1}}$$

$$s = \sqrt{\frac{(32-36.6)^2 + (33-36.6)^2 + (34-36.6)^2 + (34-36.6)^2 \ldots}{(10-1)}}$$

Just as with variance, the standard deviation of a population is denoted with sigma instead of "s," as shown here:

$$\sigma = \sqrt{\frac{\sum_{i=1}^{N}(X_i - \mu)^2}{N}}$$

The standard deviation is a handy measure of variability because it is stated in the same units as the data points. But as noted above, you CANNOT add standard deviations together to get a combined standard deviation for multiple process steps. If you want an indication of spread for a process overall, add together the variances for each step then take the square root.

Quick Take

Boxplots

Highlights

- Boxplots, or box-and-whisker diagrams, give a quick look at the distribution of a set of data
- They provide an instant picture of variation and some insight into strategies for finding what caused the variation
- They allows easy comparison of multiple data sets

Boxplot Structure

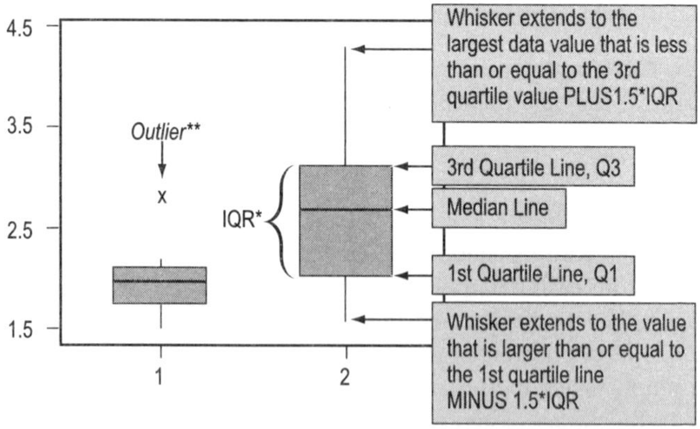

* IQR = InterQuartile Range (the distance encompassed by the 2nd and 3rd quartiles)

** A value is considered an outlier if

- it is above the upper whisker (= 3rd quartile + (1.5*IQR))
- below the lower whisker (= 1rd quartile – (1.5*IQR))

To use boxplots…

- Boxplots are typically provided as output from statistical packages such as Minitab (you will rarely construct one by hand)
- The "box" shows the range of data values comprising 50% of the data set (the 2nd and 3rd quartiles)
  - The line that divides the box shows the **median** (*see* definition on p. 107)
  - The width of the box defines the InterQuartile Range (IQR)
- Single-line "whiskers" extend below and above the box (or the left and right, if the box is horizontal) showing the data value (1) at or below the 3rd quartile PLUS 1.5 times the IQR and (2) at or above the 1st quartile MINUS 1.5 times the IQR
- Data values that fall far above the upper whisker or below the lower whisker are plotted separately and labeled as **outliers**
  - Often, outliers reflect errors in recording data
  - If the data value is real, you should investigate what was going on in the process at the time

Frequency plot (histogram)

Purpose

To evaluate the distribution of a set of data (to learn about its basic properties and to evaluate whether you can apply certain statistical tests)

When to use frequency plots

- Any time you have a set of continuous data. You will be evaluating the distribution for normality (*see* p. 114), which affects what statistical tests you can use.

  Ex: When dealing with data collected at different times, first plot them on a time series plot (p. 119), then create a histogram of the series data. If the data are not normally distributed, you cannot calculate control limits or use the "tests for special causes."

Types of frequency plots

Though they all basically do the same thing, there are several different types of frequency plots you may encounter:

1) Dot plot

Dot plots display a dot (or other mark) for each observation along a number line. If there are multiple occurrences of an observation, or if observations are too close together, then dots will be stacked vertically.

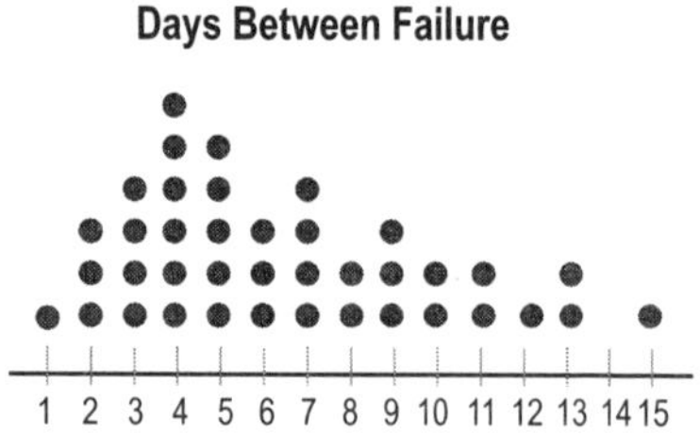

- Dot plots are very easy to construct by hand, so they can be used "in the field" for relatively small sets of data.
- Dot plots are typically used for data sets with fewer than 30 to 50 points. Larger data sets use histograms (*see* below) and box plots (*see* p. 110).
- Unlike histograms, dot plots show you how often specific data values occur.

2) Histogram

Histograms display bars representing the *count* within different ranges of data rather than plotting individual data points. The groups represent **non-overlapping** segments in the range of data.

Ex: All the values between 0.5 and 1.49 might be grouped in an interval labeled "1," all the values between 1.5 and 2.49 might be grouped in an interval labeled "2," etc.

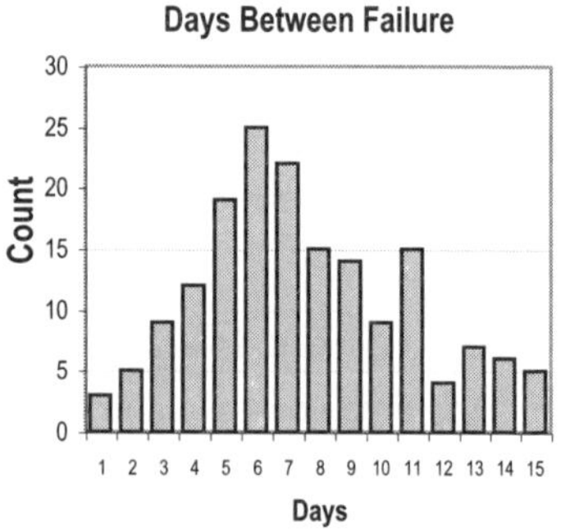

How to create a histogram

1. Take the difference between the min and max values in your observations to get the range of observed values
2. Divide the range into evenly spaced intervals
   - This is often trickier than it seems. Having too many intervals will exaggerate the variation; too few intervals will obscure the amount of variation.
3. Count the number of observations in each interval
4. Create bars whose heights represent the count in each interval

Interpreting histogram patterns

Histograms and dot plots tell you about the underlying distribution of the data, which in turn tells you what kind of statistical tests you can perform and also point out potential improvement opportunities.

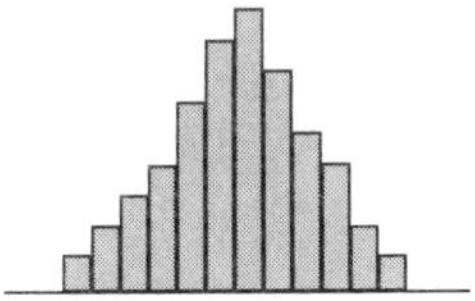

1) This first pattern is what a normal distribution would look like, with data more-or-less symmetric about a central mean.

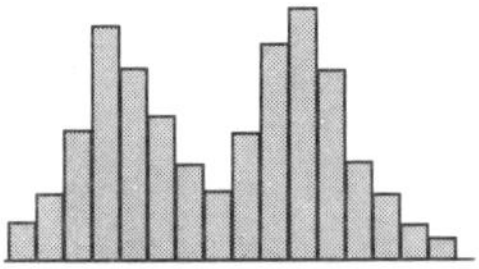

2) A histogram with two peaks is called **bimodal.** This usually indicates that there are two distinct pathways through the process. You need to define customer requirements for this process, investigate what accounts for the systematic differences, and improve the pathways to shift both paths towards the requirements.

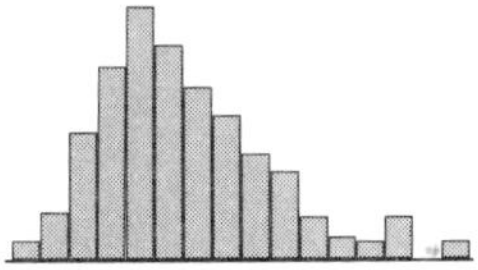

3) You may see a number of distributions that are **skewed**–meaning data values pile up towards one end and tail off towards the other end. The pattern is common with data such as time measurements (where a relatively small number of jobs can take much longer than the majority). This type of patterns occurs when the data have an underlying distribution that is not normal or when measurement devices or methods are inadequate. If a non-normal distribution is at work, you cannot use hypothesis tests or calculate control limits for this kind of data unless you take subgroup averages (*see* Central Limit Theorem, p. 114).

Quick Take

Normal distribution

In many situations, data follow a normal distribution (bell-shaped curve). One of the key properties of the normal distribution is the relationship between the shape of the curve and the standard deviation (σ for population; s for sample).

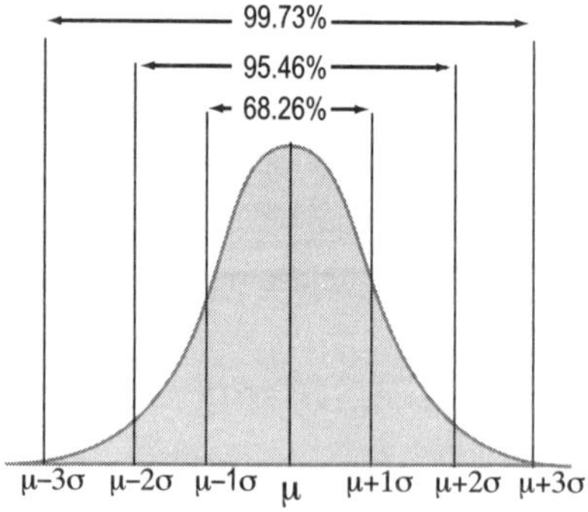

- 99.73% of the area under the curve of the normal distribution is contained between –3 standard deviations and +3 standard deviations from the mean.
- Another way of expressing this is that 0.27% of the data is more than 3 standard deviations from the mean; 0.135% will fall below –3 standard deviations and 0.135% will be above +3 standard deviations.

To use these probabilities, your data must be random, independent, and normally distributed.

Quick Take

Non-normal distributions and the Central Limit Theorem

Highlights

- Many statistical tests or inferences (such as the percentages associated with standard deviations) apply only if data are normally distributed
- However, many data sets will NOT be normally distributed

  Ex: Data on time often tail off towards one end (a skewed distribution)

- You will still want to use a dot plot or histogram to display the raw data
- However, because normality is a requirement for many statistical tests, you may want to convert non-normal data into something that does have a normal distribution
  - The distribution of the **averages (Xbars)** approaches normality if you take big enough samples
  - This property is called the **Central Limit Theorem**
  - Calculating averages on subsets of data is therefore a common practice when you have an underlying distribution that is non-normal

Central Limit Theorem

Regardless of the shape of the parent population, the distribution of the means calculated from samples quickly *approaches the normal distribution* as shown below:

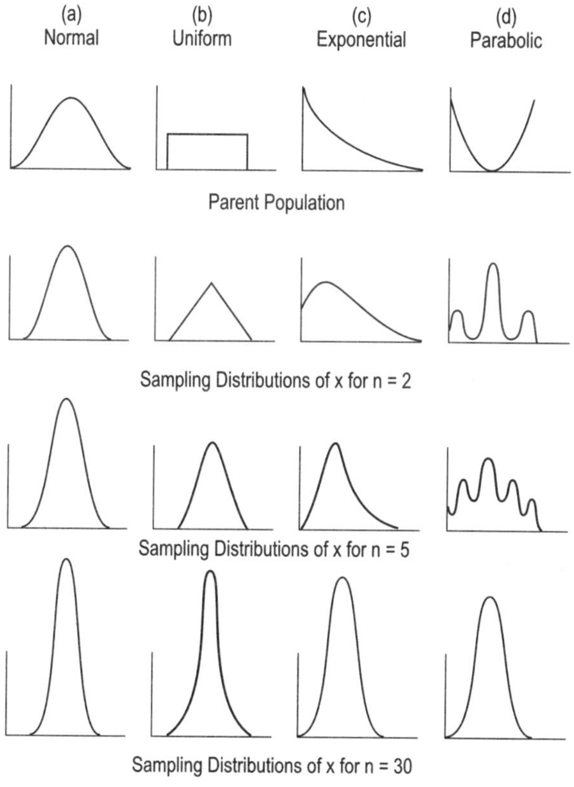

Practical Rules of Thumb

- If the population is normal, Xbar will always be normal for any sample size
- If the population is at least symmetric, sample sizes of 5 to 20 should be OK
- Worst-case scenario: Sample sizes of 30 should be sufficient to make Xbar approximately normal no matter how far the population is from being normal (*see* diagrams on previous page)
- Use a standard subgroup size to calculate Xbars (Ex: all subgroups contain 5 observations, or all contain 30 observations)
- The sets of data used to calculate Xbar must be **rational subgroups** (*see* p. 125)

CHAPTER 7

Variation Analysis

Purpose of these tools

- To separate special cause from common cause variation
- To detect trends and patterns in data that provide clues about the sources of variation (with the ultimate goal of reducing or eliminating those sources)

Deciding which tool to use

This section features two types of tools used to understand variation:

1) **Time series charts,** on which you plot data in the order of their occurrence
2) **Capability calculations,** which compare the range of actual process output against the range (specifications or tolerance) that meet customer requirements

When collecting process data, plot the data on one of the following charts before continuing with other analyses:

a) **Time series plots** (also called **run charts**): Simple charts of process data that require calculation only of a median (*see* p. 119). Easy to do "in the field" for up to 50 data points with just a pencil and paper.
   - Use the **run chart table** (p. 121) to identify patterns associated with special cause variation

b) **Control charts:** Time series plots that have the added features of a **centerline** (the mean) and **control limits**, calculated from the data, which show the expected range of variation in the process (usually ± 3 standard deviations from the mean). These are a bit more complicated than time series plots because additional calculations are required. However, they are better at detecting several kinds of special cause variation.
   - Different kinds of data require different formulas for calculating the centerline and control limits. *See* p. 123 for instructions on how to select the right set of calculations.
   - Use the **tests for special cause variation** (p. 133) for identifying patterns that indicate the presence of special cause variation.

Quick Take

Review of variation concepts

Variation is the term applied to any differences that occur in products, services, and processes. There are two types of variation:

1) **Common cause**–the variation due to random shifts in factors that are always present in the process.
   - A process with **only common cause variation** is said to be "**in control"** (or "in statistical control").
   - Though random, the variation will be stable and predictable with a determined range
   - An "in control" process may still be unacceptable because it has too much variation–meaning the output can be unacceptable to the customer and/or can incur too many internal costs.
   - The only way to reduce common cause variation is by fundamentally **changing the system**–redesigning the process so a different mix of factors affects the output.

2) **Special cause** (also called "assignable" cause variation)–variation above and beyond common cause variation, arising from factors that are not always present in the process.
   - Every process has common cause variation. One that ALSO has **special cause variation** is said to be **out of control.**
   - Variation from special causes is not random (that is, it generates identifiable patterns)–but you can't predict when it will appear or what its impact will be (so is unstable and unpredictable).
   - Reduce special cause variation by **tracking down and eliminating the specific, assignable root cause(s)**, looking for "what's different" in the process when the special cause variation appears.

Note that there are different strategies for dealing with the two types of variation: To reduce common cause variation, you have to develop new methods for doing the work everyday. To eliminate special cause variation, you have to look for something that was temporary or that has changed in the process, and find ways to prevent that cause from affecting the process again.

Time series plots (Run charts)

Purpose

- To show data points in the order in which they occurred
- To show if the process is changing over time

When to use time series plots

- Easy to construct, even by hand, and require fewer data points than control charts, so often used in the field to get an immediate sense of process performance (though you can also go immediately to control charts if you have easy access to statistical software for data analysis)
- Easy to interpret using some basic guidelines, so used to detect trends and significant changes in the underlying process generating the data

How to create and use time series plots

1. Collect data and be sure to track the order in which the data were generated by the process.
2. Mark off the data units on the vertical (y) axis and mark the sequence (1, 2, 3...) or time unit (11 Mar, 12 Mar, 13 Mar...) on the horizontal (X) axis.
3. Plot the data points on the chart and draw a line connecting them in sequence.

OPTIONAL: If you have done a histogram or have reason to believe the data are from a normal distribution (see p. 114), you can use the Run Chart Table (p. 121) to look for patterns of special causes. If this is the case...

4. Determine the median (*see* p. 107) and draw a line at that value on the chart.

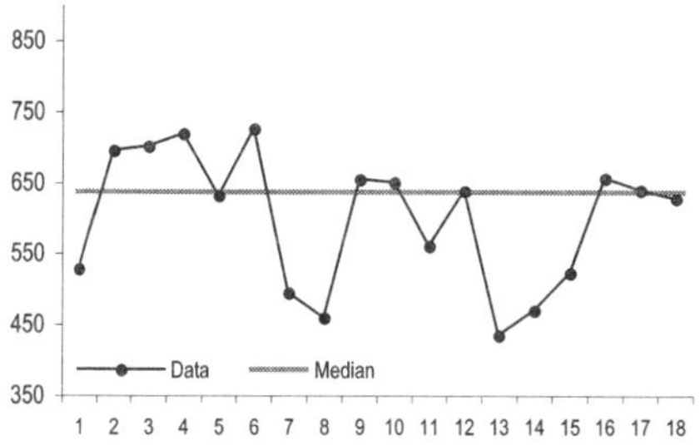

5. Count the number of points *not on the median.*
6. Circle then count the number of **runs**.
   - A "run" is defined as series of consecutive points that do not cross the median
   - Points on the median are not counted toward total points
   - Points on the median do not interrupt the run if the median

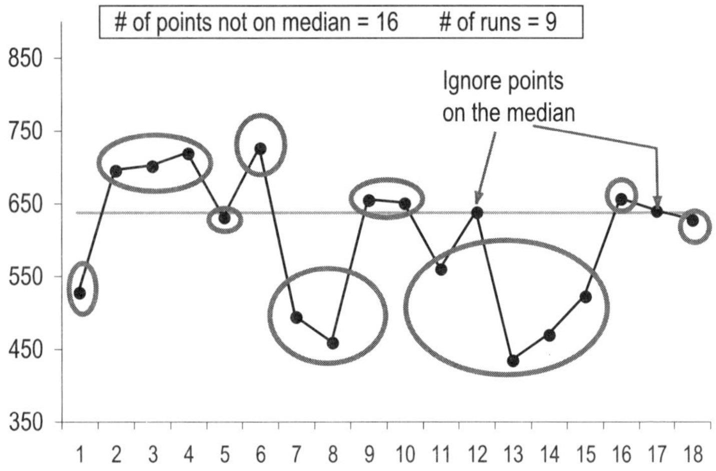

is not crossed (see points 11 to 15 in the example below)

7. Use the Run Chart Table (next page) to interpret the results.
   - The table gives you a range of runs you can expect to see if the data are random (common cause variation only) and from a normal distribution.
   - If the number of counted runs is bigger or smaller than expected, you may have special cause variation in the process or the data are not normal.
     - Plot the points on a histogram to look at the distribution
     - Look to see what was different or what changed in the process during the time those data points were collected to discover the source of special cause variation

Run chart table

# pts not on median	Lower limit of runs	Upper limit of runs	# pts not on median	Lower limit of runs	Upper limit of runs
10	3	8	34	12	23
11	3	9	35	19	23
12	3	10	36	13	23
13	4	10	37	13	25
14	4	11	38	14	25
15	4	12	39	14	26
16	6	12	40	15	26
17	5	13	41	16	26
18	6	13	42	16	27
19	6	14	43	17	27
20	6	14	44	17	28
21	7	15	45	17	29
22	7	16	46	17	30
23	8	16	47	18	30
24	8	17	48	18	31
25	9	17	49	19	31
26	9	18	50	19	32
27	9	19	60	24	37
28	10	19	70	28	43
29	10	20	80	33	48
30	11	20	90	37	54
31	11	21	100	42	59
32	11	22	110	46	65
33	11	22	120	48	70

Quick Take

Control chart basics

Highlights

- **Control charts** are similar to run charts in that they display measurement data in time order
- Additional lines help you identify special cause variation
  - The **average** (mean) is used for the centerline (instead of the median, used on a run chart).

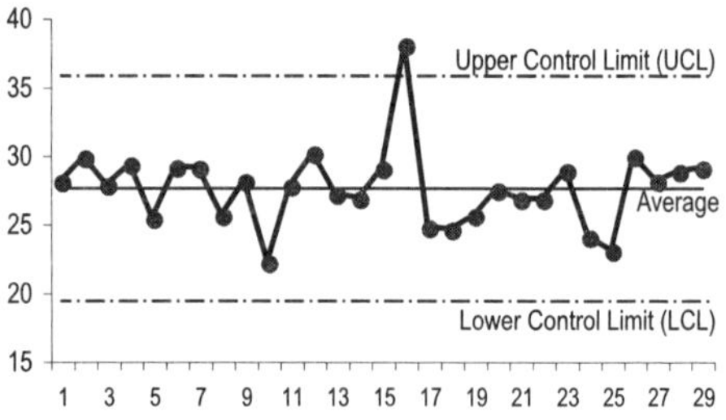

  - **Control limits** are added, representing the range of expected variation.
  - The control limits are approximately ± 3 standard deviations off of the average (99.7% of the points in a set of normally distributed data will fall between the limits).
  - **Control limits are not specification limits.** Control limits are based on data and tell you how a process is actually performing. Spec limits are based on customer requirements and tell you how you *want* a process to perform.

Uses for control charts

- Establishing a measurement baseline
- Detecting special cause variation
- Ensuring process stability and enabling predictability
- Monitoring process over time
- Confirming the impact of process improvement activities

Data requirements

- Minimum of 25 consecutive subgroups, or
- Minimum of 100 consecutive observations
- Must be in time series order

Quick Take

Selecting a control chart

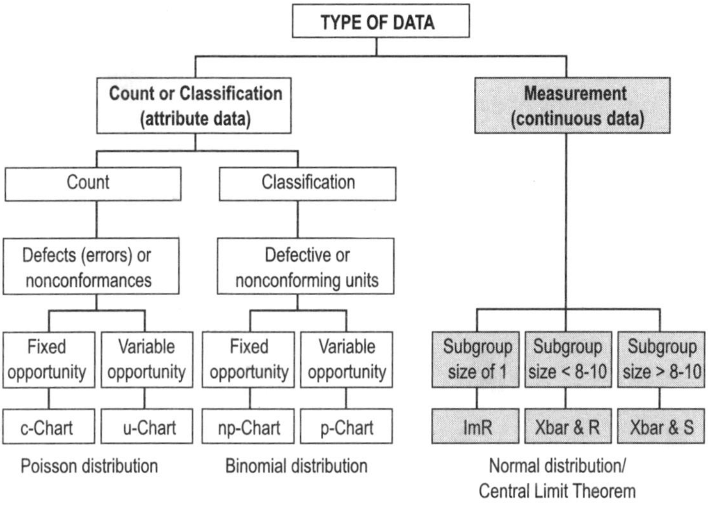

Fixed opportunity: the sample size or "unit" being sampled is constant
Variable opportunity: the sample size or "unit" being sampled changes

If you aren't sure what kind of data you have, *see* p. 70.

See below for more details on selecting charts for continuous data and *see* p. 130 for selecting charts for attribute data.

Control charts for continuous data

In most cases, you will be creating **two charts** for each set of continuous data. The first chart shows the actual data points or averages, the second chart shows the ranges or standard deviations. Why use both?

The **data (I or Xbar) chart** ...

- Shows changes in the average value of the process
- Is a visualization of the **longer-term variation**

- For an Xbar chart the key question: "Is the variation **between** the averages of the subgroups more than that predicted by the variation **within** the subgroups?"

The **range (mR or R) chart...**

- Reflects **short-term variation**
- The **R**-charts used with Xbar charts depict the ranges within **subgroups** of data; the key question: "Is the variation **within** subgroups consistent?"
- Range charts must be "in control" before we can build or use the I or Xbar charts

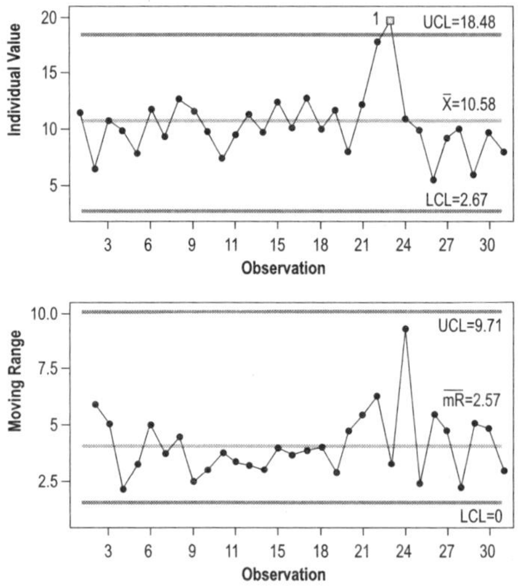

Selecting a control chart for continuous data

ImR chart (Individuals, moving Range)

Plots **individuals data (I)** on one chart and moving ranges (**mR**—the differences between each two adjacent points) on a second chart. Use when the best subgroup size is one, which will happen when...

- There are very few units produced (= low output rate) relative to how often process variables (sources of variation) may change
- There is little choice due to data scarcity
- A process drifts over time and needs to be monitored
- Sampling is very expensive or involves destructive testing

ImR is a good chart to start with when evaluating continuous data. You can often do a quick chart by hand then use it to build a different or more elaborate chart later.

$\bar{X}$,R chart (Xbar&R, Average + Range)

Plots averages of subgroups (Xbar) on one chart and the ranges (R) within the subgroups on the other chart. The Xbar&R Chart is used with a sampling plan to monitor repetitive processes.

- Subgroup sizes typically range from 3 to 9 items. Frequently, practitioners will choose subgroups of 5
- All of the Tests for Special Causes (p. 133) can be applied with these charts
- The Xbar chart will highlight changes to the average ("between subgroups" or process accuracy)
- The R-chart will detect changes to "within subgroup" dispersion (process precision)

The Xbar&R chart is the most commonly used control chart because it uses the Central Limit Theorem (p. 114) to normalize data—meaning it doesn't matter as much what the underlying distribution of the data is. It is also more sensitive than the ImR to process shifts.

$\bar{X}$,S chart (Xbar&S, Average + Standard Deviation)

Plots subgroup averages (Xbar) plus standard deviations of the subgroups (S). Similar in use to Xbar&R charts except these can be used only when you have sample sizes of at least 10 units (statisticians believe that the standard deviation is reliable only when sample sizes are 9 or larger). It's far more common to use smaller sample sizes (≤9) so in most cases an Xbar&R chart will be a better choice.

See below for instructions on rational subgrouping for Xbar&R and Xbar&S charts.

Quick Take

Subgrouping for continuous data

For both Xbar&R and Xbar&S charts, you'll need to collect data in sets of points called subgroups, then calculate and plot the averages for those subgroups. **Rational subgrouping** is the process of selecting a subgroup based upon "logical" grouping criteria or statistical considerations.

Often, you can use **natural breakpoints** to determine subgroups:

Ex: If you have 3 shifts operating per day, collect 1 data point per shift and calculate the average for those 3 data points (you'll plot one "average" reading per day)

Or if you want to look for differences between shifts, collect, say, 5 data points per shift (you'll plot 3 average readings every day, 1 per shift)

If the data are not normally distributed, use the guidelines on the **Central Limit Theorem**, p. 114, and rational subgrouping guidelines to determine the proper subgroup size.

Subgroup size selection can also be used to address the following data problems:

1) **Trends and patterns** – Use subgrouping to "average out" special cause patterns caused by logical grouping or time cycles. Examples:
   - A predictable difference in size from different injection mold diameters grouped together into one shot
   - A predictable difference in the output of 3 shifts grouped into 1 day
   - A predictable difference in incoming calls per day (M–F) grouped into 1 week

2) **Too much data** – Sometimes it is necessary to use subgrouping to reduce the number of data points plotted on a chart, which can make it easier to spot trends and other types of special cause variation.

Tips

- Always try to convert attribute (discrete) data to continuous data and use Xbar&R or ImR charts. Convert attribute data to length, area, volume, etc.
- For data that occur infrequently (such as safety accidents), use the **time between incidents** (a **continuous** measure) rather than binary attribute data (yes/no did an incident occur). Add a measure for leading indicators (such as days between near misses).

Quick Take

Control limit formulas for continuous data

The constants in these formulas will change as the subgroup size changes (*see* second table on next page).

Individuals + Moving Range Charts (ImR chart)		
Centerline	$\overline{X}$ Average of data points	$\overline{mR}$ Average of the moving ranges
UCL	$\overline{X} + 2.66\overline{mR}$	$D_4\overline{R}$
LCL	$\overline{X} - 2.66\overline{mR}$	$D_3\overline{R}$
Subgroup Averages + Range ($\overline{X}$&R chart)		
Centerline	$\overline{\overline{X}}$ Average of subgroup averages	$\overline{R}$ Average of subgroup ranges
UCL	$\overline{\overline{X}} + A_2\overline{R}$	$D_4\overline{R}$
LCL	$\overline{\overline{X}}_2 - A_2\overline{R}$	$D_3\overline{R}$
Subgroup Averages + Std Dev ($\overline{X}$&S chart)		
Centerline	$\overline{\overline{X}}$ Average of subgroup averages	$\overline{S}$ Average of subgroup std. dev.
UCL	$\overline{\overline{X}} + A_3\overline{R}$	$B_4\overline{S}$
LCL	$\overline{\overline{X}} - A_3\overline{R}$	$B_3\overline{S}$

Note: The X, R, and S symbols should technically be in lower-case letters, but (except for statistics books) are more often seen with capitals, so that is the convention used here. The A, D, and B factors are on the next page.

Quick Take

Factors for Control Chart Formulas

n	A_2	A_3	B_3	B_4	d_2	D_3	D_4
2	1.88	2.66	.00	3.27	1.13	.00	3.27
3	1.02	1.95	.00	2.57	1.69	.00	2.57
4	.73	1.63	.00	2.27	2.06	.00	2.28
5	.58	1.43	.00	2.09	2.33	.00	2.11
6	.48	1.29	.03	1.97	2.53	.00	2.00
7	.42	1.18	.12	1.88	2.70	.08	1.92
8	.37	1.10	.19	1.82	2.85	.14	1.86
9	.34	1.03	.24	1.76	2.97	.18	1.82
10	.31	.98	.28	1.72	3.08	.22	1.78
11	.29	.93	.32	1.68	3.17	.26	1.74
12	.27	.89	.35	1.65	3.26	.28	1.72
13	.25	.85	.38	1.62	3.34	.31	1.69
14	.24	.82	.41	1.59	3.41	.33	1.67
15	.22	.79	.43	1.57	3.47	.35	1.65
16	.21	.76	.45	1.55	3.53	.36	1.64
17	.20	.74	.47	1.53	3.59	.38	1.62
18	.19	.72	.48	1.52	3.64	.39	1.61
19	.19	.70	.50	1.50	3.69	.40	1.60
20	.18	.68	.51	1.49	3.74	.42	1.59

Quick Take

Creating an ImR Chart

1. Determine sampling plan
2. Take a sample at each specified time or production interval
3. Calculate the moving ranges for the sample
    - To calculate each moving range, subtract each measurement from the previous one

  - Ex: subtract Observation 2 from Observation 1; or Observation 15 from Observation 14)
  - Treat all ranges as positive even if the difference is negative. (Ex: 10 – 15 = -5 but is recorded as a range of +5)
- There will be no moving range for the first observation on the chart (because no data value preceded it)

4. Plot the data (the original data values on one chart and the and moving ranges on another)
5. After 20 or more sets of measurements, calculate control limits for moving Range chart
6. If the Range chart is not in control, take appropriate action
7. If the Range chart is in control, calculate control limits for the Individuals chart
8. If the Individuals chart is not in control, take appropriate action

Quick Take

Creating $\overline{X}$,R charts or $\overline{X}$,S charts

1. Determine an appropriate subgroup size and sampling plan
2. Collect the samples at specified intervals of time or production
3. Calculate the mean and range (or standard deviation) for each subgroup
4. Plot the data. The subgroup means go on one chart and the subgroup ranges or standard deviations on another
5. After 20 or more sets of measurements, calculate control limits for the Range chart
6. If the Range chart is not in control, take appropriate action
7. If the Range chart is in control, calculate control limits for the Xbar chart
8. If the Xbar chart is not in control, take appropriate action

Control charts for attribute data

- Review the definition of data types on p. 70
- Attribute control charts are similar to variables control charts except they plot **proportion** or **count** data rather than variable measurements
- Attribute control charts have only **one chart** which tracks proportions or counts over time (there is no range chart or standard deviation chart like there is with continuous data)

Binomial data

When data points can have only one of two values—such as when comparing a product or service to a standard and classifying it as being acceptable or not (pass/fail)—it is called binomial data. Use one of the following control charts for binomial data:

p-chart: Charts the **proportion** of defectives in each subgroup

np-chart: Charts the **number** of defectives in each subgroup (must have same sample size each time)

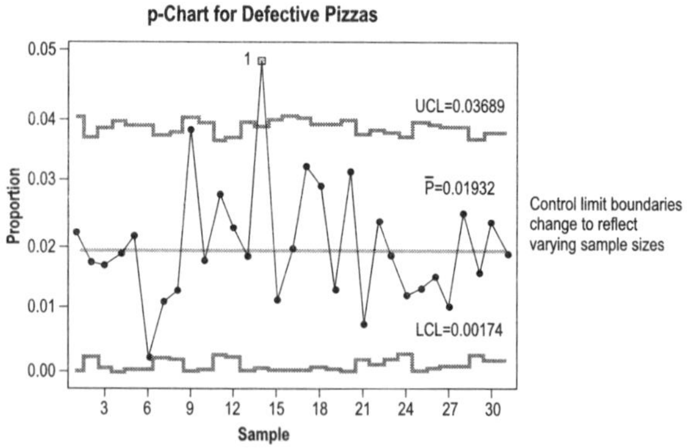

Note how Control Limits change as subgroup size changes (the p-chart has variable subgroup sizes)

P-charts are often used in transactional situations: billing errors, defective loan applications, proportion of invoices with errors, defective room service orders, sales order data, etc.

Poisson data

A Poisson (pronounced pwa-sahn) distribution describes count data where you can easily count the number of occurrence (Ex: errors on a form, dents on a car), but not the number of non-occurrences (there is no such thing as a "non-dent"). These data are best charted on either:

c-chart: Charts the **defect count per sample** (must have the same sample size each time)

u-chart: Charts the **number of defects per unit sampled** in each subgroup (uses a proportion, so it's OK if sample size varies)

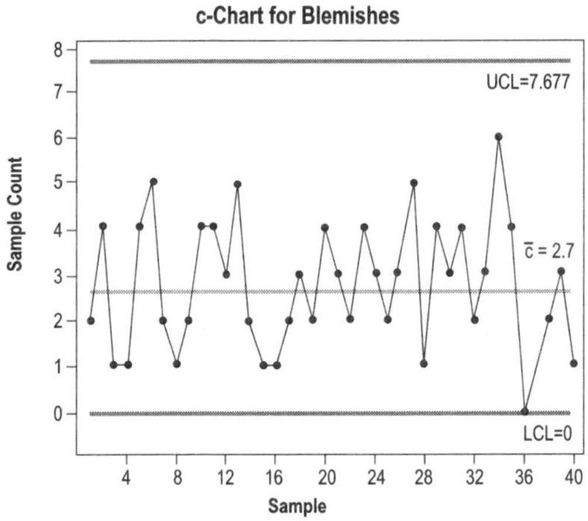

"Counts of blemishes" is one example of Poisson data—you can count blemishes but not non-blemishes. Also, the number of blemishes is relatively rare given the area of opportunity (having two small dents in a car is a relatively rare event compared to the proportion of the car that is NOT dented). Poisson data is plotted on either c-charts or u-charts depending on whether sample size varies.

If the sample size is always the same (10% variation in sample size is OK) use c–charts. If the sample size varies use the u-chart.

Tips for converting attribute data to continuous data

In general, much more information is contained in continuous data than in attribute data, so control charts for continuous data are preferred. Possible alternatives to attribute charting for different situations:

Situation	**Possible Solution**
Infrequent failures	*Plot time between failures on an ImR chart*
Similar subgroup size	*Plot the failure rate on an ImR chart*

Creating p-, np-, c-, and u-charts

When charting continuous data, you normally create two charts, one for the data and one for ranges (ImR, Xbar&R, etc.). In contrast, charts for attribute data use only the chart of the count or percentage.

1. Determine an appropriate sampling plan
2. Collect the sample data: Take a set of readings at each specified interval of time
3. Calculate the relevant metric (n, np, c, or u)
4. Calculate the appropriate centerline
5. Plot the data
6. After 20 or more measurements, calculate control limits
7. If the chart is not in control, take appropriate action

Control limit formulas for attribute data

Chart Type	Centerline	Upper Control Limit	Lower Control Limit
p	$\bar{p}$	$UCL = \bar{p} + 3\sqrt{\frac{\bar{p}(1-\bar{p})}{n}}$	$LCL = \bar{p} - 3\sqrt{\frac{\bar{p}(1-\bar{p})}{n}}$
np	$\overline{np}$	$UCL = \overline{np} + 3\sqrt{n\bar{p}(1-\bar{p})}$	$LCL = n\bar{p} - 3\sqrt{n\bar{p}(1-\bar{p})}$
c	$\bar{c}$	$UCL = \bar{c} + 3\sqrt{\bar{c}}$	$LCL = \bar{c} - 3\sqrt{\bar{c}}$
u	$\bar{u}$ $\bar{u} = c/n$	$UCL = \bar{u} + 3\sqrt{\bar{u}/n}$	$LCL = \bar{u} - 3\sqrt{\bar{u}/n}$

Quick Take

Assumptions for interpreting control charts

The "test for special causes" described on the following pages assume that you have **normally distributed data** (*see* p. 114)**:**

- Control limits are ± 3 standard deviations from the mean—and calculation of std. dev. assumes normal distribution
- If the distribution of the plotted points is **not normal**, the control limits cannot be used to detect out-of-control conditions such as outliers
  - To fix this problem, use the Central Limit Theorem (p. 114) to determine what subgroup sample sizes will allow you to plot data averages that are normally distributed

All tests for special causes also assume you have **independent observations:**

- Independence means the value of any given data point is not influenced by the value of any other data point
- If data are **not independent**, the data values will **not be random**
- This means the rules for determining special cause variation cannot be applied (because they are based on rules of statistical probability)

Interpreting control charts (Tests for Special Cause Variation)

Many of these tests relate to "zones," which mark off the standard deviations from the mean. Zone C is ± 1 std dev.; Zone B is between 1 and 2 std. dev.; and Zone A is between 2 and 3 std dev.

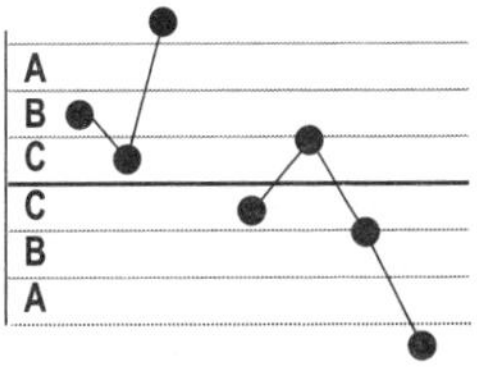

1 point beyond Zone A: Detects a shift in the mean, an increase in the standard deviation, or a single aberration in the process. Check your R-chart to rule out increases in variation.

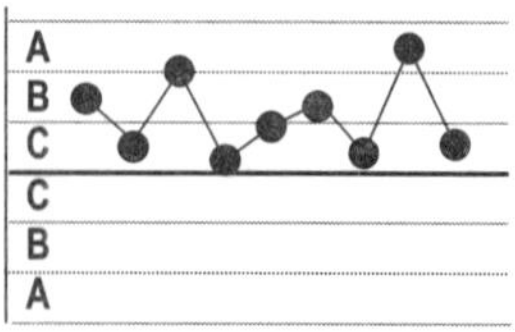

9 points in a row on one side of the average in Zone C or beyond: Detects a shift in the process mean.

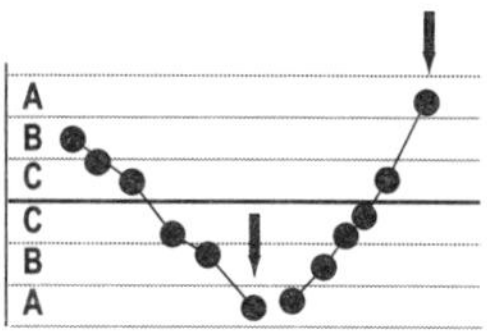

6 points in a row steadily increasing or decreasing: Detects a trend or drift in the process mean. Small trends will be signaled by this test before the first test.

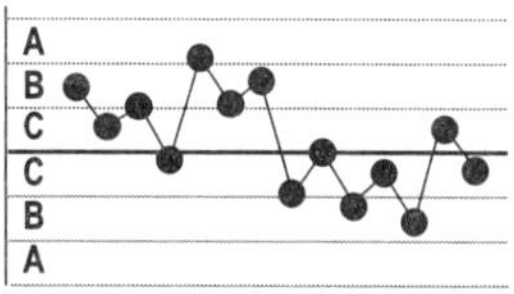

14 points in a row alternating up and down: Detects systematic effects, such as two alternately used machines, vendors, or operators.

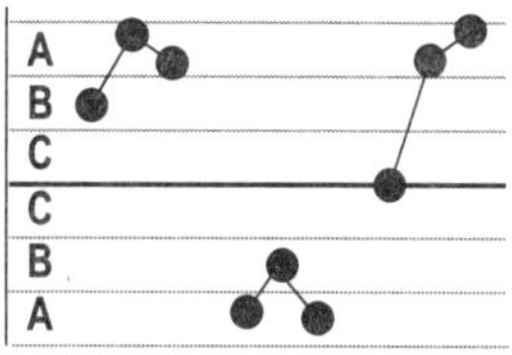

2 out of 3 points in a row in Zone A or beyond: Detects a shift in the process average or increase in the standard deviation. Any two out of three points provide a positive test.

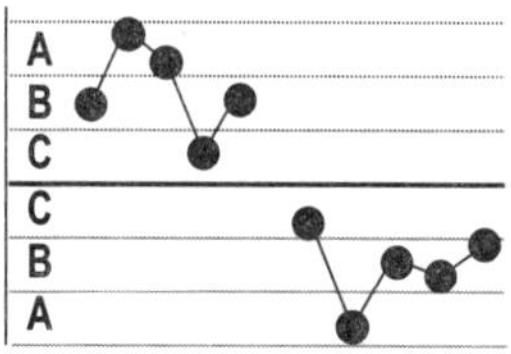

4 out of 5 points in Zone B or beyond: Detects a shift in the process mean. Any four out of five points provide a positive test.

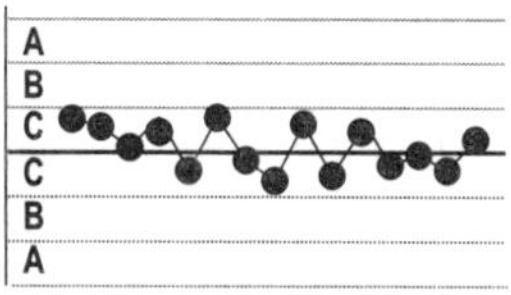

15 points in a row in Zone C, above and below the centerline: Detects stratification of subgroups—appears when observations in a subgroup come from sources with different means.

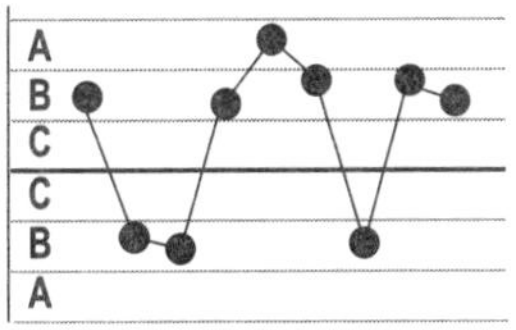

8 points in a row on both sides of the centerline with none in Zone C: Detects stratification of subgroups when the observations in one subgroup come from a single source, but subgroups come from different sources with different means.

Background on process capability calculations

Purpose

To compare the actual variation in a process (Voice of the Process) to its allowed variation limits (Voice of the Customer):

- The Voice of the Process is reflected in the control limits
- The Voice of the Customer is reflected in process specifications

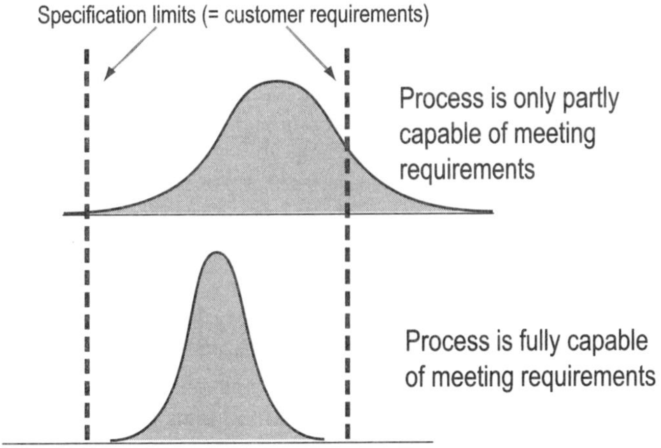

The proportion of current values that fall inside specification limits tells us whether the process is capable of meeting customer expectations.

When to use process capability calculations

Can be done on any process that has a specification established, whether manufacturing or transactional, and that has a capable measuring system. More specifically, in manufacturing and engineering...

- Performed on new equipment as part of the qualification and approval process
- Performed on existing processes to establish a baseline of current operations
- Performed on a pilot process prior to widespread rollout to prove actual performance capability meets or exceeds required performance
- Done periodically to monitor wear and tear on equipment, and deterioration of a process for whatever reason (material, personnel, environment, etc.)

In services...

- Performed on a pilot process prior to widespread rollout to prove actual performance capability meets or exceeds required performance
- Performed periodically to assure that performance standards are maintained or to highlight the need to reinforce existing standards
- Performed whenever outside or inside factors change, to prove the process is still capable of delivering high-quality, timely service

Tip

- Because capability indices are "unitless" (*not* associated with a unit like inches, minutes, etc.), you can use capability statistics to compare the capability of one process to another

Prework for Capability Analysis

When beginning to measure/monitor a parameter always:

- Calibrate measuring system (unless done recently)
- Perform Measuring System Analysis (MSA)
  - *See* p. 87 for Gage R&R for continuous data
  - *See* p. 100 for MSA for discrete/attribute data
- Ensure the process is in statistical control
- Confirm customer requirements to establish specification limits
- Requirements are the same as for control charts:
  - Minimum of 25 consecutive subgroups (representing a minimum of 100 observations) or individual data points
  - Must be in time series

Quick Take

Confusion in short-term vs. long-term process capability calculations

Any process experiences *more variation in the long term than in the short term,* so "capability" will vary depending on whether you're collecting data for a short period of time (a day, week) or for much longer (several months or years).

- For practical purposes, "long term" means data have been collected over a long enough period that you believe it likely that you've seen 80% of the process variation

The equations and basic concepts are identical for calculating short-term and long-term capability except for how the standard deviation is calculated:

- In the **C metrics**, the standard deviation is calculated from the subgroups and therefore represents **short-term variation** (which means C metrics represent **short-term capability**)
- In the **P metrics**, the standard deviation is calculated from all the data, and therefore represents **long-term variation**, and P metrics represent long-term capability

Be alert: Many companies calculate process capability statistics using long-term variation, but use the "C" labels; others are careful to distinguish between long- and short-term variation. Check with data experts in your company to see what standards they follow.

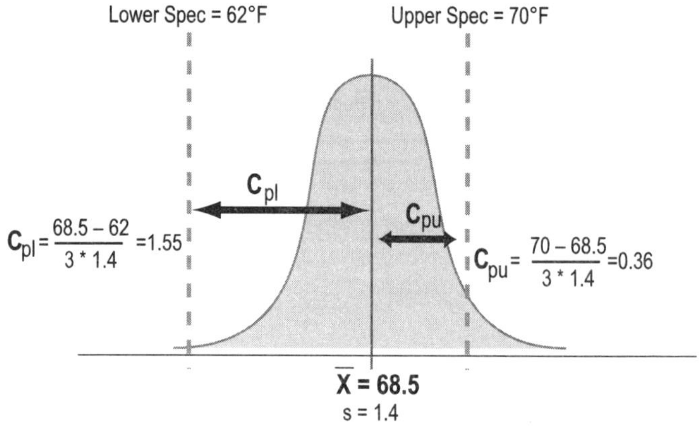

Calculating process capability

NOTE: The calculations here are for continuous, normal data. Refer to any good statistics textbook for capability analysis on attribute data.

The choice: C_p vs. C_{pk} (or "P" versions)

- $\mathbf{C_p}$ and $\mathbf{P_p}$ calculations represent an overall comparison of process output vs. desired limits. These calculations are based on the full range of variation compared to specification (they don't compare performance to a mean), so are best used when:
  - The mean can easily be adjusted (such as transactional processes where resources can easily be added with no or minor impact on quality) AND
  - The mean is monitored (so process owner will know when adjustment is necessary—doing control charting is one way of monitoring)
- $\mathbf{C_{pk}}$ and $\mathbf{P_{pk}}$ calculations build on comparisons of variation against the upper and lower specification limits separately. The

calculations include the mean, so are best used when the mean is not easily adjusted.

- For process improvement efforts, you will most likely use P_{pk} because it is most representative of what the customer experiences over time
- C_{pl} and C_{pu} (and P versions) are intermediate steps for determining C_{pk}

Calculating and interpreting C_p or P_p

$$C_p \text{ or } P_p = \frac{\text{Allowed variation (specifications or requirements)}}{\text{Normal variation of the process}}$$

$$\text{Normal variation (short term for C metrics)} = \frac{\overline{R}}{d_2}$$

(d_2 comes from table on p.128)

$$\text{Normal variation (long term for P metrics)} = s = \sqrt{\frac{\sum_{i=1}^{n}(X_i - \overline{X})^2}{n-1}}$$

C_p and P_p are ratios of total variation allowed by the specification to the total variation actually measured from the process.

- Formulas are the same for P_p except "normal variation" is calculated from long-term process variation
- If $C_p < 1$ then the variability of the process is greater than the size of the specification range
- Typical goals for C_p are greater than 1.33 (or 1.67 for mission critical/safety items)

Calculating and interpreting C_{pk} or P_{pk}

$$C_{pk} = \text{Min}\left[\frac{USL - \overline{X}}{3\sigma} \text{ or } \frac{\overline{X} - LSL}{3\sigma}\right]$$

C_{pk} is the smaller of C_{pu} or C_{pl} (same for the P versions) when a process has both an upper and lower specification limit.

- **C_{pl}** or **P_{pl}** = Indicates capability when only a **lower** specification limit exists (Ex: amt. of chicken in frozen pot pie cannot be less than 1 oz)

- $\mathbf{C_{pu}}$ or $\mathbf{P_{pu}}$ = Indicates capability when only an **upper** specification limit exists (Ex: delivery time cannot exceed 24 hours)
- Calculate both values and report the smaller number
- Typical goals for capability indices are greater than 1.33 (or 1.67 if safety related)
- Give highest priority to parameters with capability indices of less than 1.0 (you want to center the process around the specification, reduce the variation, or both)
  - If product/process is mature, and there have been no customer problems, see if defined tolerances can be changed–what is the need for a formal spec if another "de facto" spec has been used historically?
  - May need to perform 100% inspection, measuring, and sorting until the process is improved

Tips

- Check short-term capability first. If unacceptable, implement fixes. If acceptable, then run a long-term capability analysis. (Repeat customers, after all, experience the long-term capability of the process.)
  - Research the sources of variability and identify as best you can how often each is likely to appear
  - Calculate the process capability performance once you have determined that it's likely at least 80% of the variability has been seen
- Check what really happens in the workplace to see if there are unwritten specifications that people use in addition to or instead of the documented specifications. Evaluating results against written specifications when people are using unwritten specifications can lead to false conclusions.

CHAPTER 8

Identifying and Verifying Causes

Purpose of these tools

To increase the chances that you can identify the true root causes of problems, which can then be targeted for improvement.

The tools in this chapter fall into two very different categories:

a) Tools for **identifying potential causes** (starts below) are techniques for sparking creative thinking about the causes of observed problems. The emphasis is on thinking broadly about what's going on in your process.

b) Tools for **verifying potential causes** (starts on p. 149) are at the opposite end of the spectrum. Here the emphasis is on rigorous data analysis or specific statistical tests used to verify whether a cause-and-effect relationship exists and how strong it is.

Part A: Identifying potential causes

Purpose of these tools

To help you consider a wide range of potential causes when trying to find explanations for patterns in your data.

They will help you…

- **Propose Critical Xs** – Suggest ideas (hypotheses) about factors (Xs) that are contributing to problems in a targeted process, product, or service
- **Prioritize Critical Xs** – Identify the most likely causes that should be investigated further

Be sure to check the tools in part B to validate the suspected Xs.

Deciding which tool to use

This guide covers two types of tools used to identify potential causes:

- **Data displays:** Many basic tools covered elsewhere in this guide (time series plots, control charts, histograms, etc.) may spark your thinking about potential causes. Your team should simply review any of those charts created as part of your investigative efforts. One addition tool covered here is…
  - **Pareto charts** (below): specialized bar charts that help you focus on the "vital few" sources of trouble. You can then focus your cause-identification efforts on the areas where your work will have the biggest impact.
- **Cause-focused brainstorming tools:** All three of these tools are variations on brainstorming.
  - **5 Whys** (p. 145): A basic technique used to push your thinking about a potential cause down to the root level. Very quick and focused.
  - **Fishbone diagram** (cause-and-effect diagrams or Ishikawa diagrams, p. 146): A format that helps you arrange and organize many potential causes. Encourages broad thinking.
  - **C&E Matrix** (p. 148): A table that forces you to think about how specific process inputs may affect outputs (and how the outputs relate to customer requirements). Similar in function to a fishbone diagram, but more targeted in showing the input-output linkages.

Quick Take

Pareto charts

Highlights

- Pareto charts are a type of bar chart in which the horizontal axis represents categories rather than a continuous scale
  - The categories are often defects, errors or sources (causes) of defects/errors
- The height of the bars can represent a *count* or *percent* of errors/defects or their *impact* in terms of delays, rework, cost, etc.
- By arranging the bars from largest to smallest, a Pareto chart can help you determine which categories will yield the biggest gains if addressed, and which are only minor contributors to the problem

To create a Pareto chart...

1. Collect data on different types or categories of problems.
2. Tabulate the scores. Determine the *total* number of problems observed and/or the *total* impact. Also determine the counts or impact for *each category*.
   - If there are a lot of small or infrequent problems, consider adding them together into an "other" category
3. Sort the problems by frequency or by level of impact.
4. Draw a vertical axis and divide into increments equal to the total number you observed.
   - In the example here, the total number of problems was 42, so the vertical axis on the left goes to 42
   - People often mistakenly make the vertical axis only as tall as the tallest bar, which can overemphasize the importance of the tall bars and lead to false conclusions
5. Draw bars for each category, starting with the largest and working down.
   - The "other" category always goes last even if it is not the shortest bar
6. OPTIONAL: Add in the cumulative percentage line. (Convert the raw counts to percentages of the total, then draw a vertical axis on the right that represents percentage. Plot a point above the first bar at the percentage represented by that bar, then another above the second bar representing the combined percentage, and so on. Connect the points.)
7. Interpret the results (*see* next page).

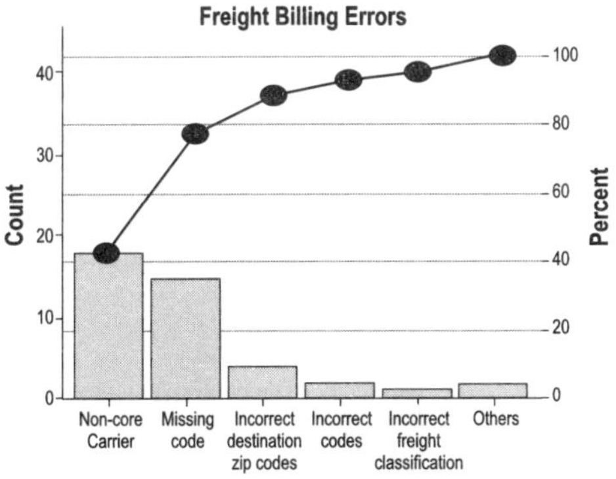

Count	18	15	4	2	1	2
Percent	42.9	35.7	9.5	4.8	2.4	4.8
Cum %	42.9	78.6	88.1	92.9	95.2	100.0

Interpreting a Pareto chart

1) Clear Pareto effect

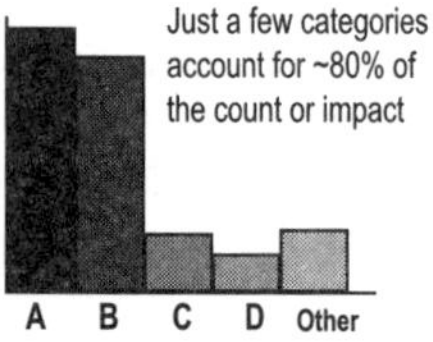

- This pattern shows that just a few categories of the problem account for the most occurrences or impact
- Focus your improvement efforts on those categories

2) No Pareto effect

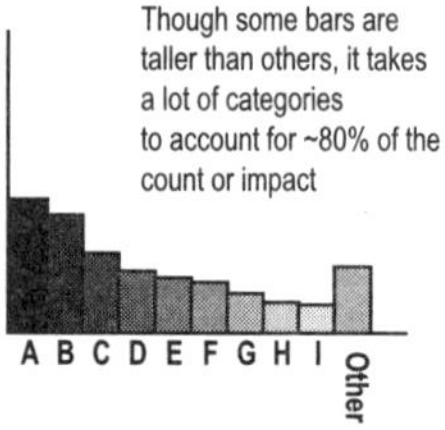

- This pattern shows that no cause you've identified is more important than any other
  - If working with counts or percentages, convert to an "impact" Pareto by calculating impacts such as "cost to fix" or "time to fix"
  - A pattern often shows up in impact that is not apparent by count or percentage alone
- Revisit your fishbone diagram or list of potential causes, then…
  - Ask which factors could be contributing to *all* of the potential causes you've identified
  - Think about other stratification factors you may not have considered; collect additional data if necessary and create another Pareto based on the new stratification factor

Tips

- The most frequent problems may not have the biggest impact in terms of quality, time, or costs. When possible, construct two Pareto charts on a set of data, one that uses count or frequency data and another that looks at impact (time required to fix the problem, dollar impact, etc.) You may end up targeting both the most frequent problems and the ones with the biggest impact.

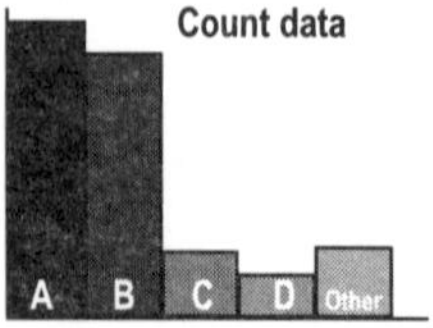

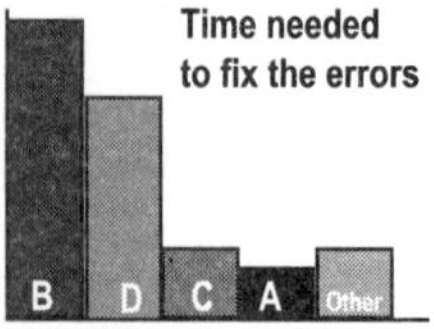

Category A errors happen a lot but don't take long to fix
Category D errors are rare, but very expensive in terms of time

Quick Take

5 Whys

Highlights

- Method for pushing people to think about root causes
- Prevents a team from being satisfied with superficial solutions that won't fix the problem in the long run

To use 5 Whys...

1. Select any cause (from a cause-and-effect diagram, or a tall bar on a Pareto chart). Make sure everyone has a common understanding of what that cause means. ("Why 1")
2. Ask "why does this outcome occur"? (Why 2)
3. Select one of the reasons for Why 2 and ask "why does that occur"? (Why 3)
4. Continue in this way until you feel you've reached a potential root cause.

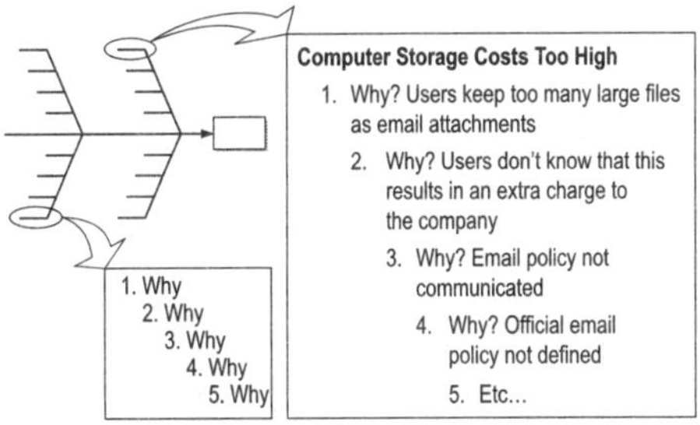

Tips

- There's nothing sacred about the number 5. Sometimes you may reach a root cause after two or three whys, sometimes you may have to go more than five layers down.
- Stop whenever you've reached a potential cause that the team can act on.

  Ex: "**Why** are we late in delivery?"... Because the copier jams..."**Why** does the copier jam?"... Because of high humidity in the copier room ..."**Why** does high humidity cause jams?" ... Because the paper absorbs moisture and sticks together.
  (If you can't do anything about paper that absorbs moisture, go back to solving the problem of high humidity in the copier room– "What can we do to control or reduce humidity in the copier room?")

Cause-and-effect diagrams (fishbone or Ishikawa diagrams)

Purpose

- To help teams push beyond symptoms to uncover potential root causes
- To provide structure to cause identification effort
- To ensure that a balanced list of ideas have been generated during brainstorming or that major possible causes are not overlooked

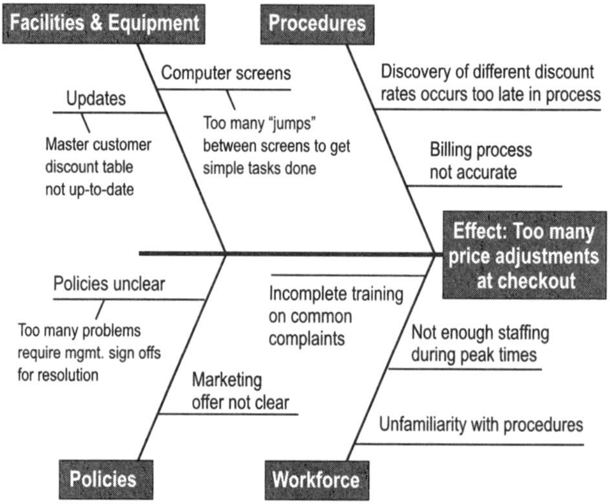

When to use cause-and-effect diagrams

- Best used for cause identification once you have a focused definition of the problem (which may not happen until Analyze or Improve)
- Can also be used as a cause-*prevention* tool by brainstorming ways to maintain or prevent future problems (include in planning efforts in Improve or Control)

How to create and use a cause-and-effect diagram

1. Name the problem or effect of interest. Be as specific as possible.
   - Write the problem at the head of a fishbone "skeleton"
2. Decide the major categories for causes and create the basic diagram on a flip chart or whiteboard.
   - Typical categories include the 6 Ms: manpower (personnel), machines, materials, methods, measurements, and Mother Nature (or environment)
3. Brainstorm for more detailed causes and create the diagram.
   - Option 1: Work through each category, brainstorming potential causes and asking "why" each major cause happens. (*See* 5 Whys, p. 145).
   - Option 2: Do silent or open brainstorming (people come up with ideas in any order).
   - Write suggestions onto self-stick notes and arrange in the fishbone format, placing each idea under the appropriate categories.
4. Review the diagram for completeness.
   - Eliminate causes that do not apply
   - Brainstorm for more ideas in categories that contain fewer items (this will help you avoid the "groupthink" effect that can sometimes limit creativity)
5. Discuss the final diagram. Identify causes you think are most critical for follow-up investigation.
   - OK to rely on people's instincts or experience (you still need to collect data before taking action).
   - Mark the causes you plan to investigate. (This will help you keep track of team decisions and explain them to your sponsor or other advisors.)
6. Develop plans for confirming that the potential causes are actual causes. DO NOT GENERATE ACTION PLANS until you've verified the cause.

C&E Matrix

Purpose

To identify the few key process input variables that must be addressed to improve the key process output variable(s).

When to use a C&E matrix

- Similar in purpose to a fishbone diagram, but allows you to see what effect various inputs and outputs have on ranked customer priorities
- Use in Measure to prioritize inputs being considered for data collection
- Use in Improve to pinpoint the focus of improvement efforts

		Temp of Coffee	Taste	Strength		Process Outputs
	Importance	*8*	*10*	*6*		
Process Steps	**Process Inputs**	**Correlation of Input to Output**				**Total**
						0
Clean Carafe		[blank]	3	1		36
Fill Carafe with Water			9	9		144
Pour Water into Maker			1	1		16
Place Filter in Maker			3	1		36

How to create a C&E matrix

1. Identify **key** customer requirements (outputs) from the process map or Voice of the Customer (VOC) studies. (This should be a relatively small number, say 5 or fewer outputs.) List the outputs across the top of a matrix.
2. Assign a priority score to each output according to importance to the customer.
   - Usually on a 1 to 10 scale, with 10 being most important
   - If available, review existing customer surveys or other customer data to make sure your scores reflect customer needs and priorities
3. Identify all process steps and key inputs from the process map. List down the side of the matrix.
4. Rate each input against each output based on the strength of their relationship:

Blank = no correlation 1 = remote correlation

3 = moderate correlation 9 = strong correlation

Tip: At least 50% to 60% of the cells should be blank. If you have too many filled-in cells, you are likely forcing relationships that don't exist.

5. Cross-multiply correlation scores with priority scores and add across for each input.

   Ex: Clean Carafe = (3*10) + (1 * 6) = 30 + 6 = 36

6. Create a Pareto chart and focus on the variables relationships with the highest total scores. Especially focus on those where there are acknowledged performance gaps (shortfalls).

Part B: Confirming causal effects and results

Purpose of these tools

To confirm whether a potential cause contributes to the problem. The tools in this section will help you confirm a cause-and-effect relationship and quantify the magnitude of the effect.

Deciding between these tools

Often in the early stages of improvement, the problems are so obvious or dramatic that you don't need sophisticated tools to verify the impact. In such cases, try confirming the effect by **creating stratified data plots** (p. 150) or **scatter plots** (p. 154) of cause variables vs. the outcome of interest, or by **testing quick fixes/obvious solutions** (seeing what happens if you remove or change the potential cause, p. 152).

However, there are times when more rigor, precision, or sophistication is needed. The options are:

- **Basic hypothesis testing principles and techniques** (p. 156). The basic statistical calculations for determining whether two values are statistically different within a certain range of probability.

- **Specific cause-and-effect (hypothesis) testing techniques.** The choice depends in part on what kinds of data you have (*see* table below).

		Dependent Variable (Y)	
		Continuous	Attribute
Independent Variable (X)	Continuous	**Regression** (p. 167)	**Logistic Regression** (not covered in this book)
	Attribute	**ANOVA** (p. 173)	**Chi-Square (χ^2) Test** (p. 182)

- **Design of Experiments** (pp. 184 to 194), a discipline of planned experimentation that allows investigation of multiple potential causes. It is an excellent choice whenever there are a number of factors that may be affecting the outcome of interest, or when you suspect there are interactions between different causal factors.

Quick Take

Stratified data charts

Highlights

- Simple technique for visually displaying the source of data points
- Allows you to discover patterns that can narrow your improvement focus and/or point towards potential causes

To use stratified data charts...

1. Before collecting data, identify factors that you think may affect the impact or frequency of problems
    - Typical factors include: work shift, supplier, time of day, type of customer, type of order. *See* stratification factors, p. 75, for details.
2. Collect the stratification information at the same time as you collect the basic data

3. During analysis, visually distinguish the "strata" or categories on the chart (*see* examples)

Option 1: Create different charts for each strata

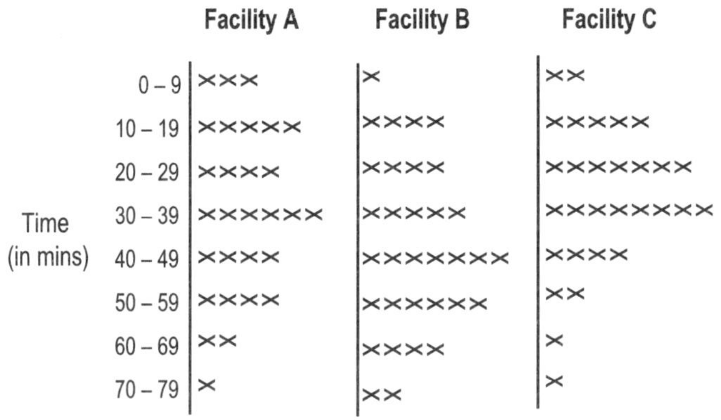

These stratified dot plots show the differences in delivery times in three locations. You'd need to use hypothesis testing to find out if the differences are statistically significant.

Option 2: Color code or use symbols for different strata

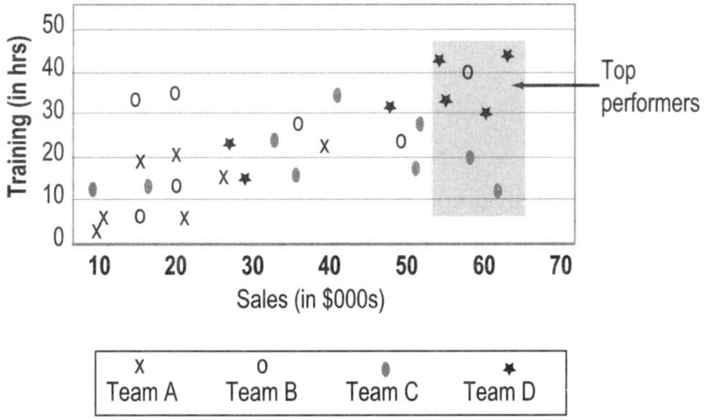

This chart uses symbols to show performance differences between people from different work teams. Training seems to have paid off for Team D (all its top performers are in the upper right corner); Team C has high performers who received little training (they are in the lower right corner).

Testing quick fixes or obvious solutions

Purpose

- To confirm cause-and-effect relationships and prevent unanticipated problems from obvious "quick fixes"

Why test quick fixes

- Your team may stumble on what you think are quick fixes or obvious solutions. On the one hand, you don't want to exhaustively test every idea that comes along (doing so can delay the gains from good ideas). But you also don't want to plunge into making changes without any planning (that's why so many "solutions" do nothing to reduce or eliminate problems). Testing the quick fix/obvious solution provides some structure to help you take advantage of good ideas while minimizing the risks.

When to test quick fixes

- Done only when experimental changes can be done safely:
  - No or minimal disruption to the workplace and customers
  - No chance that defective output can reach customers
  - Relatively quick feedback loop (so you can quickly judge the impact of changes)
- Done in limited circumstances where it may be difficult or impossible to verify suspected causes without making changes

  Ex: Changing a job application form to see if a new design reduces the number of errors (it would be difficult to verify that "form design" was a causal factor unless you tested several alternative forms)

  Ex: Changing labeling on materials to see if that reduces cross-contamination or mixing errors (difficult to verify "poor labeling" as a cause by other means)

How to test quick fixes

1. Confirm the potential cause you want to experiment with, and document the expected impact on the process output.

2. Develop a plan for the experiment.
   - What change you will make
   - What data you will be measuring to evaluate the effect on the outcome
   - Who will collect data
   - How long the experiment will be run
   - Who will be involved (which team members, process staff, work areas, types of work items, etc.)
   - How you can make sure that the disruption to the workplace is minimal and that customers will not feel any effects from the experiment
3. Present your plan to the process owner and get approval for conducting the experiment.
4. Train data collectors. Alert process staff of the impending experiment; get their involvement if possible.
5. Conduct the experiment and gather data.
6. Analyze results and develop a plan for the next steps.
   - Did you conduct the experiment as planned?
   - Did making the process change have the desired impact on the outcome? Were problems reduced or eliminated?
   - If the problem was reduced, make plans for trying the changes on a larger scale (*see* pilot testing, p. 273)

Tips

- **Note:** Testing quick fixes is similar to doing a pilot test EXCEPT the purpose is to confirm a cause-and-effect relationship. You are not proposing a solution per se—you're doing a quick test to see if you've found a contributing cause. If the test shows an effect, continue with your regular procedures for planning and testing full-scale implementation.
- **Caution:** Do not confuse this testing with the kind of unplanned changes that often occur in the workplace. You need to approach quick fixes with an experimental mindset: predicting what changes you expect to see, planning specifically what changes to make, knowing what data you will collect to measure the effect, and so on.
- Before the experiment, imagine that you have the results in hand and determine what type of analysis will be needed (confirm that you will get the type of data you need for the analysis).

Quick Take

Scatter plots

Highlights

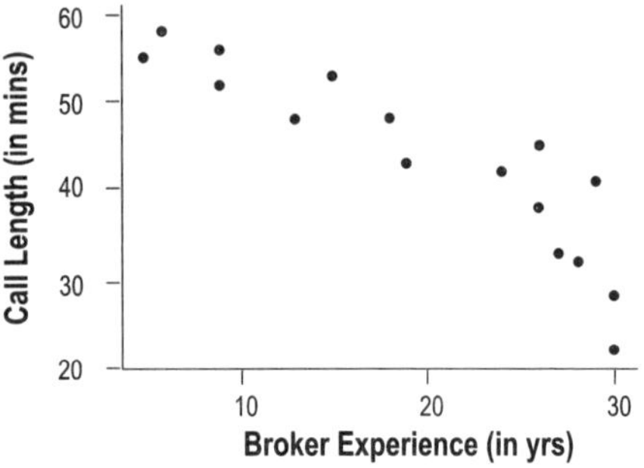

- A graph showing a relationship (or correlation) between two factors or variables
- Lets you see patterns in data
- Helps support or refute theories about the data
- Helps create or refine hypotheses
- Predicts effects under other circumstances
- The width or tightness of scatter reflects the strength of the relationship
- Caution: seeing a relationship in the pattern does not guarantee that there is a cause-and-effect relationship between the variables (*see* p. 165)

To use scatter plots...

1. Collect **paired data**

   To create a scatter plot, you must have two measurements for each observation point or item

   – Ex: in the chart above, the team needed to know both the call length and the broker's experience to determine where each point should go on the plot

2. Determine appropriate measures and increments for the axes on the plot

   – Mark units for the suspected cause (input) on the horizontal X-axis

   – Mark the units for the output (Y) on the vertical Y-axis

3. Plot the points on the chart

Interpreting scatter plot patterns

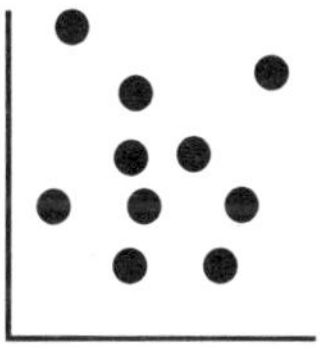

No pattern. Data points are scattered randomly in the chart.

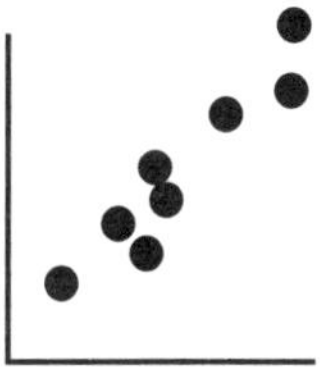

Positive correlation (line slopes from bottom left to top right). Larger values of one variable are associated with larger values of the other variable.

Negative correlation (line slopes from upper left down to lower right). Larger values of one variable are associated with smaller values of the other variable.

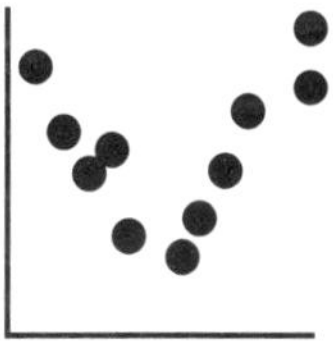

Complex patterns. These often occur when there is some other factor at work that interacts with one of the factors. Multiple regression or design of experiments can help you discover the source of these patterns.

Tips

- Use your SIPOC diagram (p. 38) to identify Xs and Ys.
- By convention, scatter plots are used to compare an independent (X) variable (placed on the horizontal axis) and a dependent (Y) variable (on the vertical axis). But sometimes you may want to compare two input variables (Xs) or two output variables (Ys) to each other. In these cases, it doesn't matter which variable goes on the horizontal and which on the vertical axis.

Quick Take

Hypothesis testing overview

Highlights

- Hypothesis testing is a branch of statistics that specifically determines whether a particular value of interest is contained within a calculated range (the confidence interval)
- Whether the value falls within or beyond the confidence interval determines whether you conclude that two things are the same or different
- A common application of hypothesis testing is to see if two means are equal
  - Because of variation, no two data sets will ever be exactly the same even if they come from the same population
  - Hypothesis testing will tell you if differences you observe are likely due to *true* differences in the underlying populations or to random variation

Hypothesis testing terms and concepts

- The ***null hypothesis*** (H_0) is a statement being testing to determine whether or not it is true. It is usually expressed as an equation, such as this one:

$$H_0\colon \mu_1 = \mu_2 \qquad \text{or} \qquad H_0\colon \mu_1 - \mu_2 = 0$$

  - This notation means the null hypothesis is that the means from two sets of data are the same. (If that's true, then subtracting one mean from the other gives you 0.)
  - We assume the null hypothesis is true, unless we have enough evidence to prove otherwise
  - If we can prove otherwise, then we reject the null hypothesis

- The ***alternative hypothesis*** (H_a) is a statement that represents reality if there is enough evidence to reject H_O. Ex:

$$H_a\colon \mu_1 \neq \mu_2 \qquad \text{or} \qquad H_a\colon \mu_1 - \mu_2 \neq 0$$

  This notation means the alternative hypothesis is that the means from these two populations are not the same.

  - If we reject the null hypothesis then practically speaking we accept the alternative hypothesis

- NOTE: From a statistician's viewpoint, we can never accept or prove a null hypothesis–we can only fail to reject the null based on certain probability. Similarly, we never accept or prove that the alternative is right–we reject the null. To the layperson, this kind of language can be confusing. So this book uses the language of rejecting/accepting hypotheses.

Uses for hypothesis testing

- Allows us to determine statistically whether or not a value is cause for alarm
- Tells us whether or not two sets of data are truly different (with a certain level of confidence)
- Tells us whether or not a statistical parameter (mean, standard deviation, etc.) is different from a value of interest
- Allows us to assess the "strength" of our conclusion (our probability of being correct or wrong)

Assumptions of hypothesis tests

- Independence between and within samples
- Random samples
- Normally distributed data
- Unknown Variance

Quick Take

Confidence intervals

- Rarely will any value (such as a mean or standard deviation) that we calculate from a sample of data be exactly the same as the true value of the population (or of another sample)
- A confidence interval is a range of values, calculated from a data set, that gives us an assigned probability that the true value lies within that range
- Usually, confidence intervals have an additive uncertainty: *Estimate ± margin of error*

  Ex: Saying that a 95% confidence interval for the mean is 35 ±

2, means that we are 95% certain that the true mean of the population lies somewhere at or between 33 to 37

Calculating confidence intervals

The formulas for calculating confidence intervals are not included in this book because most people get them automatically from statistical software. What you may want to know is that the Z (normal) distribution is used when the standard deviation is known. Since that is rarely the case, more often the intervals are calculated from what's called a *t*-distribution. The *t*-distribution "relaxes" or "expands" the confidence intervals to allow for the uncertainty associated with having to use an estimate of the mean. (So a 95% confidence interval calculated with an unknown standard deviation will be wider than one where the standard deviation is known.)

Quick Take

Type I and Type II errors, Confidence, Power, and

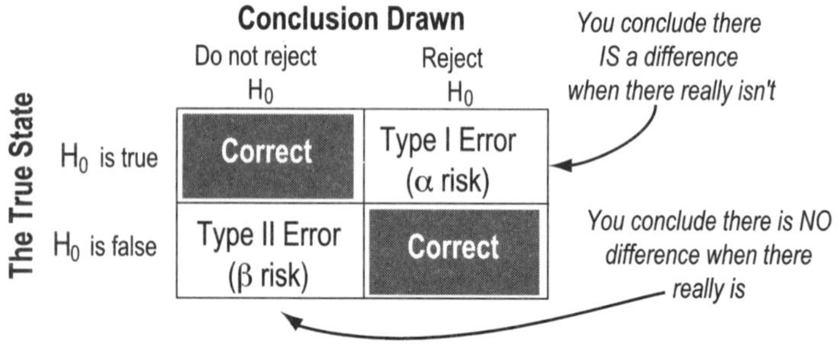

p-values

Type I Error: Alpha (α) Risk or Producer risk

- Rejecting the null when you should not
- **You've "discovered" something that isn't really there**
  Ex: If the null hypothesis is that two samples are the same, you would *wrongly* conclude they are different ("rejecting the null") even though they are the same
- Impact of Alpha errors: You will reach wrong conclusions and likely implement wrong solutions

Type II Error: Beta (β) Risk or Consumer Risk

- Description: Do not reject the null when you should
- **You've missed a significant effect**
  Ex: If the null hypothesis is that two samples are the same, you would *wrongly* conclude that they are the same ("NOT rejecting the null") when, in fact, they are different
- Impact of Beta errors: You will treat solution options as identical even though they aren't
- Type II error is determined from the circumstances of the situation

Balancing Alpha and Beta risks

- You select upfront how much Type I error you are willing to accept (that's the alpha value you choose).
- **Confidence level = 1 − α**
  - Often an alpha level of 0.05 is chosen, which leads to a 95% confidence level. Selecting an alpha of 0.10 (increasing the chances of rejecting the null when you should accept it) would lead to a 90% confidence level.
- If alpha is made very small, then beta increases (all else being equal).
- If you require overwhelming evidence to reject the null, that will increase the chances of a Type II error (not rejecting it even when you should)
- **Power = 1 − β** (Power is the probability of rejecting the null hypothesis when it is false); power can also be described as the ability of the test to detect an effect of a given magnitude.
- If two populations truly have different means, but only by a very small amount, then you are more likely to conclude they are the same. This means that the beta risk is greater.
- Beta comes into play only if the null hypothesis truly is false. The "more" false it is, the greater your chances of detecting it, and the lower your beta risk.

p-values

- If we reject the null hypothesis, the p-value is the probability of being wrong
  - The p-value is the probability of making a Type I error
  - It is the critical alpha value at which the null hypothesis is rejected
- If we don't want alpha to be more than 0.05, then we simply reject the null hypothesis when the p-value is 0.05 or less

Quick Take

Confidence intervals and sample size

There is a direct correlation between sample size and confidence level

- Larger samples increase our confidence level
- If you can live with less confidence, smaller sample sizes are OK

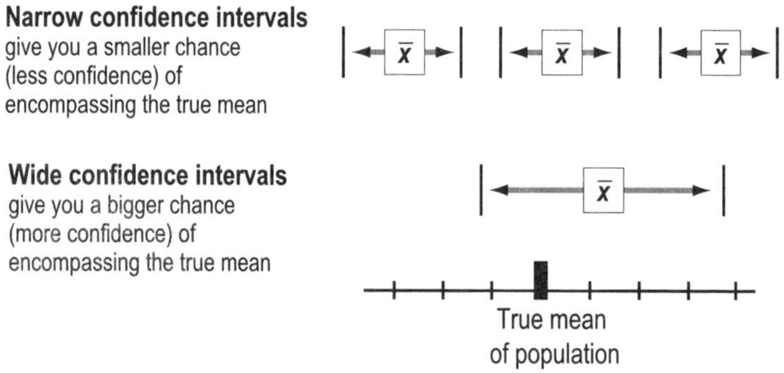

- To minimize beta risk at a given alpha level, increase sample size
- All of these translate into a specific confidence interval for a given parameter, set of data, confidence level and sample size
- They also translate into what types of conclusions result from hypothesis tests
- Testing for larger differences (delta, Δ) between the samples reduces the required sample size

Quick Take

t–test Overview

Highlights

- A statistical test that allows us to make judgments about the average of a process or population
- The judgment is whether the null hypothesis is likely to be true (*see* p. 156 for more on basic hypothesis testing)
- We calculate a *t*-statistic and determine probabilities comparing the statistic to a *t*-distribution (*see* below)
  - In cases where you know the standard deviation of a population you should use a Z-statistic not a *t*-statistic. Z-distributions are not covered in this book since they are rarely used in practice.
- The data should be normally distributed. However, because of the Central Limit Theorem (p. 114) concerning the distribution of averages, this assumption is not as critical here as it is with other tests
- Used in two situations:

  a) Comparing a sample to a point of interest (a 1-sample *t*-test) or

  b) Comparing a sample to another sample (a 2-sample *t*-test)

t-Distribution

- The *t*-distribution is actually a ***family*** of distributions
- They are similar in shape to the normal distribution (symmetric and bell-shaped), although wider and flatter in the tails.
  - *How* wide and flat depends on the sample size. The smaller the sample size, the wider and flatter the distribution tails (that means intervals between confidence levels get broader and broader)
  - As sample size increases, the *t*-distribution approaches the exact shape of the normal distribution
- Most statistical packages (such as Minitab) will automatically report the *t*-statistic and probability values to you. On the following pages, we show how these calculations are done. Refer to any good statistics textbook for *t*-distribution tables.

Quick Take

1-Sample *t*-test

- Tells us whether or not a statistical parameter (average, standard deviation, etc.) is different from a value of interest
- Allows us to assess the "strength" of our conclusion (our probability of being correct)
- The hypotheses take the basic form:

H_0: μ = a target or known value

The null hypothesis is that the sample mean is equal to a target value.

H_a: μ is > or < or ≠ the target or known value

(choose one symbol for the alternative hypothesis indicating whether you think the mean is bigger than, less than, or simply not equal to the target value)

- Here is the equation for calculating the *t*-test statistic:

$$t = \frac{(\overline{X}_1 - \overline{X}_2) - \Delta_0}{s_{\overline{X}_1 - \overline{X}_2}}$$

  - Δ_0 (delta) is the hypothesized difference between the two population means.
  - The methods for determining the factor in the denominator varies depending on whether you can assume that the new data has the same variation as the known standard (this affects what options you check in Minitab).
  - Details on calculating s are beyond the scope of this book (and besides, is usually done automatically if you use a statistics program). Refer to any good statistics text if you need to do these calculations by hand.

Example

An automobile manufacturer has a target length for camshafts of 599.5 mm., with an allowable range of ± 2.5 mm (= 597.0 mm to 602.0 mm). Here are data on the lengths of camshafts from Supplier 2:

mean = 600.23 std. dev. = 1.87

95% CI for mean is 599.86 to 600.60

The null hypothesis in plain English: the camshafts from Supplier 2 are the same as the target value. Printouts from Minitab showing the results of this hypothesis test are shown on the next page.

One-Sample T: Supp2

Test of mu = 599.5 vs. not 599.5

Variable	N	Mean	StDev	SE Mean	95% CI	T	P
Supp2	100	600.230	1.874	0.187	(599.858, 600.602)	3.90	0.000

Confidence Intervals, Hypothesis Tests and Power

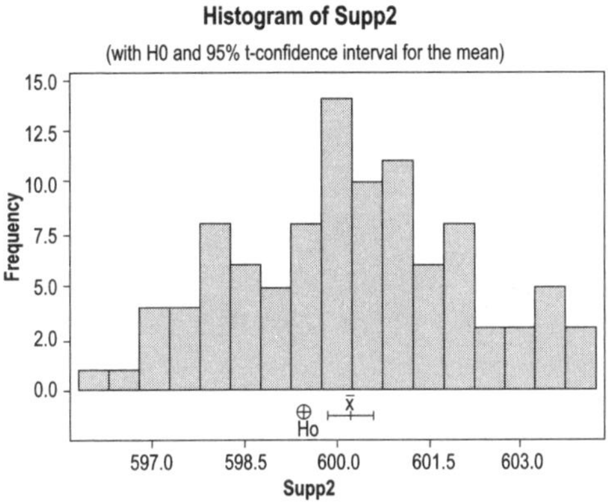

Results

Clues that we should reject the null hypothesis (which, for practical purposes, means the same as concluding that camshafts from Supplier 2 are not on target):

1) On the histogram, the circle marking the target mean value is *outside* the confidence interval for the mean from the data
2) The p-value is 0.00 (which is less than the alpha of 0.05)

Quick Take

2-Sample *t*-test

Highlights

- The ***2-Sample t*** is used to test whether or not the means of two samples are the same

Using a 2-sample *t*-test

- The null hypothesis for a 2-sample *t* is

$$H_0: \mu_1 = \mu_2 \qquad \text{or} \qquad H_0: \mu_1 - \mu_2 = 0$$

(the mean of population 1 is the same as the mean of population 2)

- The ***alternative hypothesis*** is a statement that represents reality if there is enough evidence to reject H_0
- Here is the alternative hypothesis for this situation:

$$H_a: \mu_1 \neq \mu_2 \quad \text{or} \quad H_a: \mu_1 - \mu_2 \neq 0$$

- If we reject the null hypothesis then we accept ("do not reject") the alternative hypothesis

2-Sample *t*-test example

The same automobile manufacturer has data on another supplier and wants to compare the two:

Supplier 1: mean = 599.55, std. dev =.62 (95% CI for mean is 599.43 to 599.67)

Supplier 2: mean = 600.23, std. dev. = 1.87 (95% CI for mean is 599.86 to 600.60)

The null hypothesis in plain English: the mean length of camshafts from Supplier 1 is the same as the mean length of camshafts from Supplier 2. Here is the printout from Minitab along with a boxplot:

Two-Sample T-Test and CI: Supp1, Supp2

Two-sample T for Supp1 vs Supp2

	N	Mean	StDev	SE Mean
Supp1	100	599.548	0.619	0.062
Supp2	100	600.23	1.87	0.19

Difference = mu (Supp1) – mu (Supp2)

Estimate for difference: -0.682000

95% CI for difference: (-1.072751, -0.291249)

T-Test of difference = 0 (vs not =) : T-Value = -3.46 P-Value = 0.001 DF = 120

Confidence Intervals, Hypothesis Tests and Power

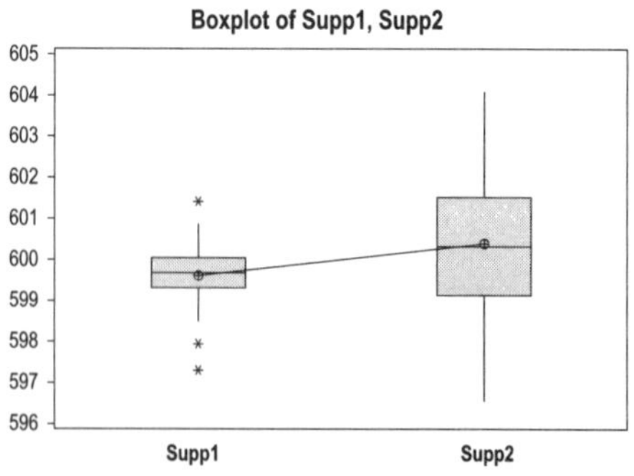

Results

There are two indicators in these results that we have to reject the null hypothesis (which, in practice, means concluding that the two suppliers are statistically different):

- The 95% CI for the difference does NOT encompass "0" (both values are negative)
- The p-value 0.001 (we usually reject a null if p ≤.05)

(Given the spread of values displayed on this boxplot, you may also want to test for equal variances.)

Quick

Take

Overview of correlation

Highlights

- Correlation is a term used to indicate whether there is a relationship between the values of different measurements
  - A **positive correlation** means that higher values of one measurement are associated with higher values of the other measurement (both rise together)
  - A **negative correlation** means that higher values of one measurement are associated with *lower* values of another (as one goes up, the other goes down)
- Correlation itself **does not** imply a cause-and-effect relationship!
  - Sometimes an apparent correlation can be coincidence
  - Other times, the two cause-and-effect variables are both related to an underlying cause—called a **lurking variable**—that is not included in your analysis
  - In the example shown here, the lurking variable is the weight of the car

The price of automobiles shows a negative correlation to gas mileage (meaning as price goes up, mileage goes down). But higher prices do not CAUSE lower mileage, nor does lower mileage cause higher car prices.

Quick Take

Correlation statistics (coefficients)

Regression analysis and other types of hypothesis tests generate **correlation coefficients** that indicate the strength of the relationship between the two variables you are studying. These coefficients are used to determine whether the relationship is statistically significant (the likelihood that certain values of one variable are associated with certain values of the other variable). For example:

- The **Pearson correlation coefficient** (designated as **r**) reflects the strength and the direction of the relationship
- $\mathbf{r^2}$ [r-squared], the square of the Pearson correlation coefficient, tells us the percentage of variation in Y that is attributable to the independent variable X ("r" can be positive or negative; r^2 is always positive)

As you've probably heard before, "correlation does not mean causation." That means you can't conclude that high values of one variable cause high or low values of the other variable based solely on the correlation coefficients.

Interpreting correlation coefficients

- r falls on or between -1 and 1
- Use to calculate r^2
- r^2 is on or between 0 and 1

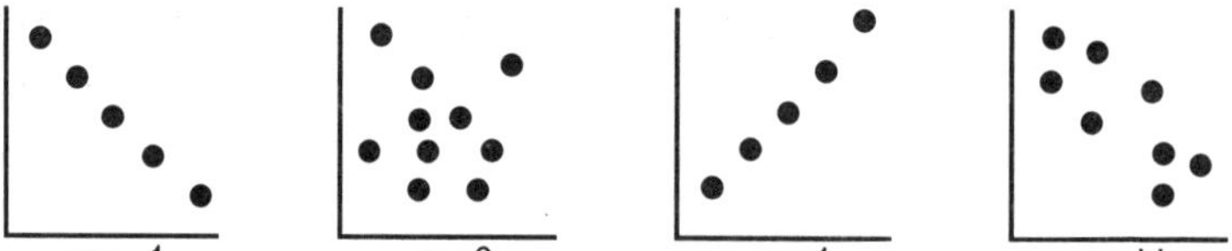

r = –1 perfect negative correlation	r = 0 no correlation	r = 1 perfect positive correlation	consider r > + .65 or < -.65 as evidence of a strong relationship

Quick Take

Regression overview

Highlights

Regression Analysis is used in conjunction with correlation calculations and scatter plots to predict future performance based on past results.

- Regression defines the relationship more precisely than correlation coefficients alone
- Regression analysis is a tool that uses data on relevant variables to develop a prediction equation, or model [Y = f(x)]

Overview of regression analysis

1. **Plan data collection**
   - What inputs or potential causes will you study?
     - Also called predictor variables or independent variables
     - Best if the variables are continuous, but they can be count or categorical
   - What output variable(s) are key?
     - Also called response or dependent variables
     - Best if the variables are continuous, but they can be count or categorical
   - How can you get data? How much data do you need?

2. **Perform analysis and eliminate unimportant variables**
   - Collect the data and generate a regression equation:
     - Which factors (predictor or independent variables) have the biggest effect on the response variable?
     - What factor or combination of factors is the best predictors of output?
   - Remember to perform residuals analysis (p. 195) to check if you can properly interpret the results

3. **Select and refine model**
   - Delete unimportant factors from the model.
   - Should end up with to 2 or 3 factors still in the model

4. **Validate model**
   Collect new data to see how well the model is able to predict actual performance

Quick Take

Simple linear regression

Highlights

- In Simple Linear Regression, a single input variable (X) is used to define/predict a single output (Y)
- The output you'll get from the analysis will include an equation in the form of:

$$Y = B_0 + (B_1 * X) + E$$

B_0 is the **intercept** point on the y-axis (think of this as the average minimum value of the output)

B_1 is the **constant** that tells you how and how much the X variable affects the output

- A "+" sign for the factor means the more of X there is, the more of Y there will be
- A "–" sign means that the more of X there is, the less of Y there will be

E is the amount of error or "noise"

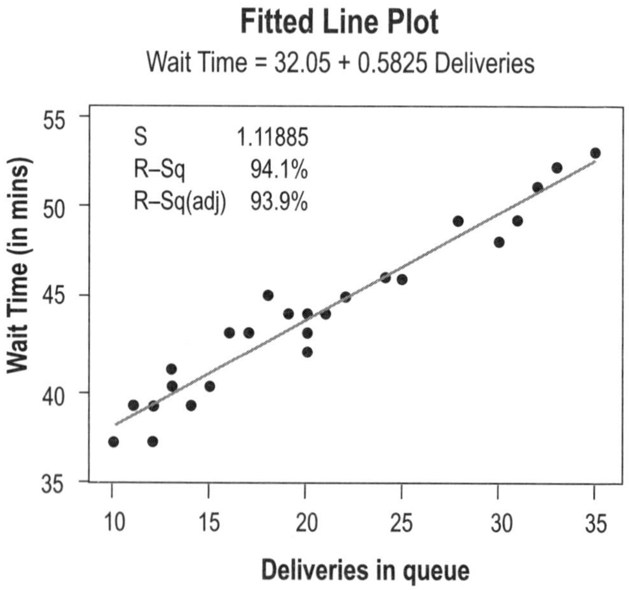

Interpreting simple regression numbers

CAUTION: Be sure to perform residuals analysis (p. 195) as part of your work to verify the validity of the regression. If the residuals show unusual patterns, you cannot trust the results.

The graph shown on the previous page was generated to depict how the number of pizza deliveries affected how long customers had to wait. The form of the simple regression equation is:

$$\text{Wait Time} = B_0 + (B_1 \text{*Deliveries}) + E \text{ (error)}$$

The actual data showed

$$\text{Wait Time} = 32.05 + 0.5825 \text{ Deliveries}$$

This means that, on average, customers have to wait about 32 minutes even when there are no deliveries in queue, and that (within the range of the study) each new delivery in queue adds just over half a minute (0.58 min) to the waiting time. The company can use this equation to predict wait time for customers. For example, if there are 30 deliveries in queue, the predicted wait time would be:

$$\text{Wait time} = 32 \text{ mins} + (.58 * 30) = 49.4 \text{ mins}$$

- Percent of variation in the data that is explained by the model = R-Sq = .970 *.970 = 94.1%

Quick Take

Multiple regression

Highlights

- Same principles as simple regression except you're studying the impact of multiple Xs (predictor variables) on one output (Y)
- Using more predictors often helps to improve the accuracy of the predictor equation ("the model")
- The equation form is...

$$\mathbf{Y = B_0 + B_1X_1 + B_2X_2 + B_3X_3}$$

  - **Y** is what we are looking to predict
  - **Xs** are our input variables
  - The **Bs** are the constants that we are trying to find–they tell us how much, and in what way, the inputs affect the output

Interpreting multiple regression results

Below is the Minitab session output. The predictor equation proceeds the same as for simple regression (p. 168).

The regression equation is

Delivery Time = 30.5 + 0.343 Total Pizzas + 0.113 Defects - 0.010 Incorrect Order

Predictor	Coef	SE Coef	T	P
Constant	30.4663	0.7932	38.41	0.000
Total Pizzas	0.34256	0.0340	10.06	0.000
Defects	0.11307	0.0412	2.75	0.012
Incorrect Order	-0.0097	0.2133	-0.05	0.964

S = 1.102 R-Sq = 94.8% R-Sq(adj) = 94.1%

The factors here mean:

- Delivery time is 30.5 mins, plus...
- Each pizza adds 0.343 mins to delivery
- Each error in creating the pizzas adds 0.113 min
- Each incorrect order subtracts 0.01 mins–which means that incorrect orders do not have much of an effect on delivery time or that including "incorrect orders" in the equation is just adding random variation to the model (*see* p-value, below)

R-squared is the percent of variation that is explained by the model. This model explains 94.8% of the variability in Pizza Delivery Time.

R-squared(adj) is the percent of variation that is explained by the model *adjusted for* the number of terms in the model and the size of the sample (more factors and smaller sample sizes increase uncertainty). In Multiple regression, you will use R-Sq(adj) as the amount of variation explained by the model.

S is the estimate of the standard deviation about the regression model. We want S to be as small as possible.

The P-values tell us that this must have been a hypothesis test.

H_0: No correlation H_a: Correlation

If $p < 0.05$, then the term is significant (there is a correlation).

If a p-value is greater than 0.10, the term is removed from the model. A practitioner might leave the term in the model if the p-value is within the gray region between these two probability levels.

Output charts: Matrix plot and correlation matrix

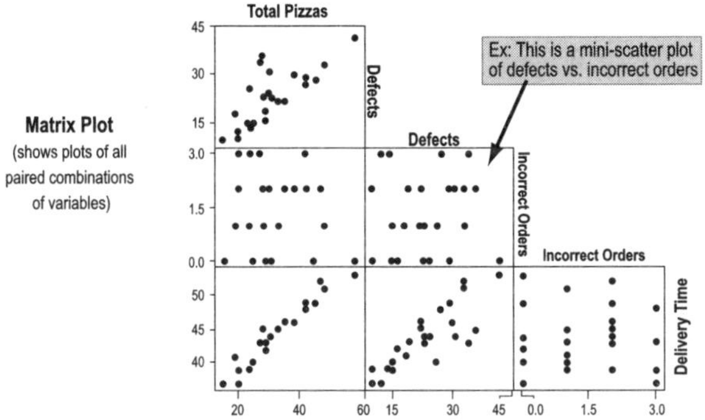

- Delivery Time appears to increase when there's an increasing number of Total Pizzas and Defects
- Incorrect Order appears to have no effect
- Total Pizzas and Defects appear to be related, as well

These observations are confirmed by the **correlation matrix** (below). In the following example, the table shows the relationship between different pairs of factors (correlations tested among Total Pizzas, Defects, Incorrect Order, Delivery Time on a pairwise basis).

	Total Pizzas	Defects	Incorrect Order
Defects	0.769 0.000		
Incorrect Order	0.082 0.695	0.051 0.807	
Delivery	0.964 0.000	0.829 0.000	-0.057 0.787

In each pair of numbers:

- The **top number** is the Pearson Coefficient of Correlation, r

  As a rule of thumb, look for r > 0.65 or r < –0.65 to indicate correlation

- The **bottom number** is the p-value

  Look for p-values ≤0.05 to indicate correlation at the 95% confidence level

Cautions

1) Relative importance of predictors cannot be determined from the size of their coefficients:

- The coefficients are scale-dependent–they depend on the units and increments in the original data
  Ex: If Factor A has a coefficient of 5.0 and Factor B has a coefficient of 50, that does *not* mean that Factor B has ten times the impact of Factor A
- The coefficients are influenced by correlation among the input variables

2) At times, some of the Xs will be correlated with each other. This condition is known as **multicollinearity,** which causes:

- Estimates of the coefficients to be unstable with inflated P-values
- Difficulty isolating the effects of each X
- Coefficients to vary widely depending on which Xs are included in the model

Use a metric called **Variance Inflation Factor** (VIF) to check for multicollinearity:

$$VIF = \frac{1}{1 - r_i^2}$$

r_i^2 is the r^2 value from regressing X_i against the other Xs

A large r_i^2 suggests that a variable is redundant

Rule of Thumb:

$r_i^2 > 0.9$ is a cause for concern (VIF > 10; high degree of collinearity)

$0.8 < r_i^2 < 0.9$ will occur when VIF > 5; indicates a moderate degree of collinearity

If two predictor variables show multicollinearity, you need to remove one of them from the model.

Tips

- Use scatterplots (p. 154) to visualize the data and validate your interpretation of the statistical analysis.
- Use a measurement selection matrix (p. 74) to help identify the multiple factors you want to study.
- Gather enough observations to adequately measure error and check the model assumptions.

- Make sure that the sample of data is representative of the population. (Need a valid sampling strategy.)
- Excessive measurement error of the inputs (Xs) creates uncertainty in the estimated coefficients, predictions, etc. (Need an acceptable MSA.)
- Be sure to collect data on all potentially important variables.
- When you're deciding which inputs to include in the model, consider the time and effort of gathering the data on those additional variables.
- Statistical software packages such as Minitab will usually help you find the best combination of variables (**best subsets** analysis). Rather than relying on the p-values alone, the computer looks at all possible combinations of variables and prints the resulting model characteristics.
- When you have found the best subset, **recalculate** the regression equation with only those factors.
- Validate the equation by collecting additional data.

ANOVA (ANalysis Of VAriance)

Purpose

To compare three or more samples to each other to see if any of the sample means is statistically different from the others.

- An ANOVA is used to analyze the relationships between several categorical inputs (KPIVs) and one continuous output (KPOV)

When to use ANOVA

- Use in Analyze to confirm the impact of variables
- Use in Improve to help select the best option from several alternatives

Overview of ANOVA

In the statistical world, inputs are sometimes referred to as **factors**. The samples may be drawn from several different sources or under several different circumstances. These are referred to as **levels**.

- Ex: We might want to compare on-time delivery performance at three different facilities (A, B, and C). "Facility" is considered to be a factor in the ANOVA, and A, B, and C are the "levels."

To tell whether the three or more options are statistically different, ANOVA looks at three sources of variability…

Total – Total variability among all observations

Between – Variation between subgroup means (factor)

Within – Random (chance) variation within each subgroup (noise, or statistical error)

In One-Way ANOVA (below), we look at how different levels of a single factor affect a response variable.

In Two-Way ANOVA (p. 180), we examine how different levels of two factors and the interaction between those two factors affect a response variable.

One-way ANOVA

A one-way ANOVA (involving just one factor) tests whether the mean (average) result of any alternative is different from the others. It does not tell us *which* one(s) is different. You'll need to supplement ANOVA with multiple comparison procedures to determine which means differ. A common approach for accomplishing this is to use Tukey's Pairwise comparison tests. (*See* p. 178) Form of the hypotheses:

H_0: $\mu_1 = \mu_2 = \mu_3 = \mu_4 \ldots = \mu_k$

H_a: At least one μ_k is different from one other μ_k (or "at least one pair of means is different")

The comparisons are done through "sum of squares" calculations (shown here and depicted in the graph on the next page):

$$\sum_{j=1}^{g}\sum_{i=1}^{n_j}(y_{ij}-\bar{\bar{y}})^2 = \sum_{j=1}^{g} n_j(\bar{y}_j-\bar{\bar{y}})^2 + \sum_{j=1}^{g}\sum_{i=1}^{n_j}(y_{ij}-\bar{y}_j)^2$$

SS(Total) = SS(Factor) + SS(Error)

SS (Total) = Total Sum of Squares of the Experiment (individual values – grand mean)

SS (Factor) = Sum of Squares of the Factor (Group mean – Grand mean)

SS (Error) = Sum of Squares within the Group (Individual values – Group mean)

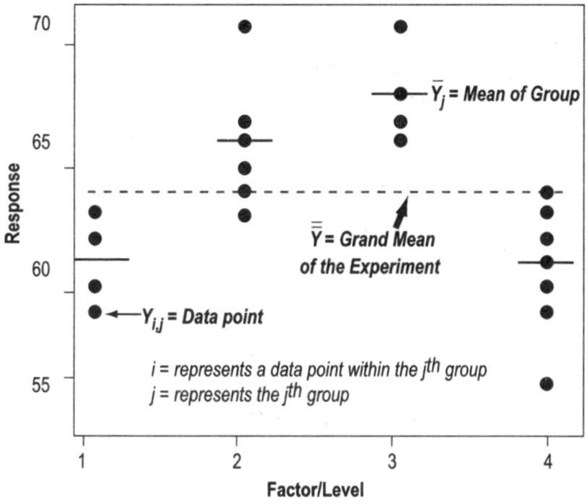

One-way ANOVA Steps

1. Select a sample size and factor levels.
2. Randomly conduct your trials and collect the data.
3. Conduct the ANOVA analysis (typically done through statistical software; see below for interpretation of results).
4. Follow up with pairwise comparisons, if needed. If the ANOVA shows that at least one of the means is different, pairwise comparisons are done to show which ones are different.
5. Examine the residuals, variance and normality assumptions.
6. Generate main effects plots, interval plots, etc.
7. Draw conclusions.

One-way ANOVA reports

By comparing the Sums of Squares, we can tell if the observed difference is due to a true difference or random chance.

- If the factor we are interested in has little or no effect on the average response then these two estimates ("Between" and "Within") should be almost equal and we will conclude all subgroups could have come from one larger population
- If the "Between" variation becomes larger than the "Within" variation, that can indicate a significant difference in the means of the subgroups

Interpreting the F-ratio

- The **F-ratio** compares the denominator to the numerator
  - The denominator is calculated to establish the amount of variation we would normally expect. It becomes a sort of standard of variability that other values are checked against.
  - The numerator is the "others" that are being checked.
- When the F-ratio value is small (close to 1), the value of the numerator is close to the value of the denominator, and you cannot reject the null hypothesis that the two are the same
- A larger F-ratio indicates that the value of the numerator is substantially different than that of the denominator (MS Error), and we reject the null hypothesis

Checking for outliers

- Outliers in the data set can affect both the variability of a subgroup and its mean—and that affects the results of the F-ratio (perhaps causing faulty conclusions)
- The smaller the sample size, the greater the impact an outlier will have
- When performing ANOVA, examine the raw data to see if any values are far away from the main cluster of values

Tip

- Be sure to perform a residuals analysis as well (*see* p. 195)

Example: Invoice processing cycle time by Facility (One-way ANOVA)

```
One-way ANOVA: Order Processing Cycle Time versus Location

Analysis of Variance for Order Pr
Source        DF      SS       MS      F      P
Location       2    13.404   6.702   6.89   0.004
Error         27    26.261   0.973
Total         29    39.665
                           Individual 95% CIs For Mean
                           Based on Pooled StDev
Level    N    Mean    StDev  -----+---------+---------+---------+-
CA      10  4.2914   0.6703  (------*------)
NY      10  5.2304   0.8715           (------*------)
TX      10  5.9225   1.3074                      (------*------)
                             -----+---------+---------+---------+-
Pooled StDev =  0.9862          4.00      4.80      5.60      6.40
```

Conclusion: Because the p-value is 0.004, we can conclude that ***at least one pair of means is different,*** or one of the facilities is statistically significantly different from ***at least one*** other facility.

Further analysis is needed to see there are more than one significant differences. For example, one facility could differ from all the others, or several facilities could differ significantly from each other.

To tell which pair(s) of facilities is/are significant, perform a **Tukey Pairwise Comparisons**, which provides confidence intervals for the difference between the tabulated pairs (Facility A vs. Facility B; Facility A vs. Facility C; Facility B vs. Facility C, etc.). Alpha is determined by the individual error rate–and will be less for the individual test than the alpha for the family. (*See* chart on next page.)

Tukey's pairwise comparisons
Family error rate = 0.0500
Individual error rate = 0.0196
Critical value = 3.51
Intervals for (column level mean) – (row level mean)

	CA	NY
NY	-2.0337 0.1556	
TX	-2.7258 -0.5364	-1.7867 0.4026

- The two numbers describe the end points of the confidence interval for the difference between each pair of factors. (Top number in each set is the lower limit; bottom number is the upper limit). If the range encompasses 0, we have to accept ("not reject") the hypothesis that the two means are the same.
- In this example, we can conclude that NY is *not* statistically different from CA or from TX because the CI ranges for those pairs both encompass 0. But it appears that CA *is* statistically different from TX–both numbers in the CI range are negative.

Quick Take

Degrees of Freedom

The number of independent data points in the samples determines the available **degrees of freedom** (df) for the analysis.

- We *earn* a degree of freedom for every data point we collect.
- We *spend* a degree of freedom for each parameter we estimate

In other words, the total number of degrees of freedom is equal to the number in independent data points minus one. The degrees of freedom for the factors calculation, interactions calculation, and the error term calculation are shown below:

$$df_{total} = N - 1 = \#\text{ of observations} - 1$$

$$df_{factor} = L - 1 = \#\text{ of levels} - 1$$

$$df_{interaction} = df_{factorA} * df_{factorB}$$

$$df_{error} = df_{total} - df_{everything\ else}$$

Quick Take

ANOVA assumptions

1) Model errors are assumed to be normally distributed with a mean of zero, and are to be randomly distributed
2) The samples are assumed to come from normally distributed populations. Test this with residuals plots (*see* p. 195).
3) Variance is assumed approximately constant for all factor levels
   - Minitab and other statistical software packages will perform both the Bartlett's (if data is normal) or Levene tests (if cannot assume normality) under options labeled *Test for Equal Variances*

Test for Equal Variances for Order Processing Time

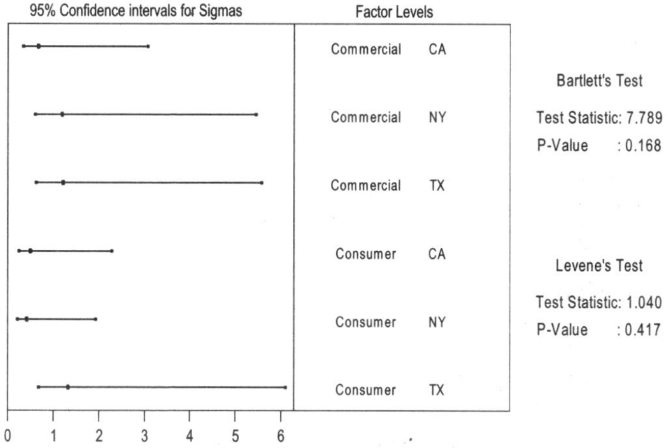

In this example, the p-values are very high, so we cannot reject the hypothesis that variance is the same for all the factors

Practical Note: Balanced designs (consistent sample size for all the different factor levels) are, in the language of statisticians, said to be "very robust to the constant variance assumption." That means the results will be valid even if variance is not perfectly constant. Still, make a habit of checking for constant variances. It is an opportunity to learn if factor levels have different amounts of variability, which is useful information.

Two-way ANOVA

Same principles as one-way ANOVA, and similar Minitab output (see below):

- The factors can take on many levels; you are not limited to two levels for each
- Total variability is represented as:

$$SS_T = SS_A + SS_B + SS_{AB} + SS_e$$

SS_T is the total sum of squares,

SS_A is the sum of squares for factor A,

SS_B is the sum of squares for factor B,

SS_{AB} is the sum of squares due to the interaction between factor A and factor B

SS_e is the sum of squares from error

Two-Way ANOVA Reports

A) Session window output

Analysis of Variance for Order Processing time

Source	DF	SS	MS	F	P
Order Ty	1	3.968	3.968	4.34	0.048
Location	2	13.404	6.702	7.34	0.003
Interaction	2	0.364	0.182	0.20	0.821
Error	24	21.929	0.914		
Total	29	39.665			

As with other hypothesis tests, look at the p-values to make a judgment based on your chosen alpha level (typically .05 or .10) as to whether the levels of the factors make a significant difference.

B) Main effects plots

- These plots show the average or **mean** values for the individual factors being compared (you'll have one plot for every factor)
- Differences between the factor levels will show up in "non-flat" lines: slopes going up or down or zig-zagging up and down

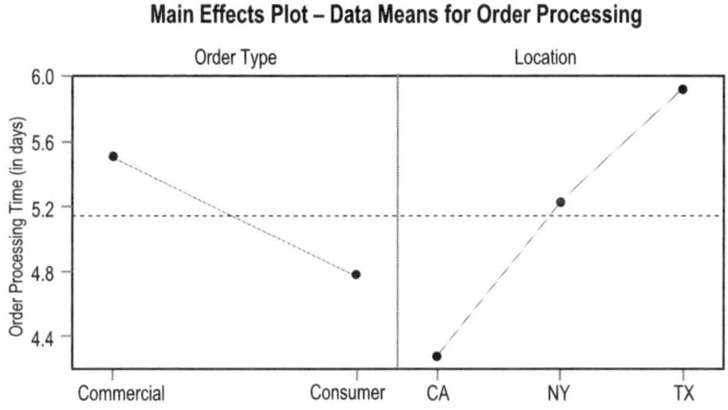

- For example, the left side of the chart above shows that consumer orders process faster than commercial orders. The right side shows a difference in times between the three locations (California, New York, and Texas).
- Look at p-values (in the Minitab session output, previous page) to determine if these differences are significant.

C) Interaction plots

- Show the mean for different **combinations** of factors
- The example below, taken from a standard Minitab data set, shows a different pattern for each region (meaning the factors "act differently" at different locations:
  - In Region 1, color and plain packaging drive higher sales than point-of-sale displays
  - In Region 2, color and point-of-sale promotions have higher sales than color
  - Region 3 has lower overall sales; unlike in Region 1 and Region 2, color alone does not improve sales

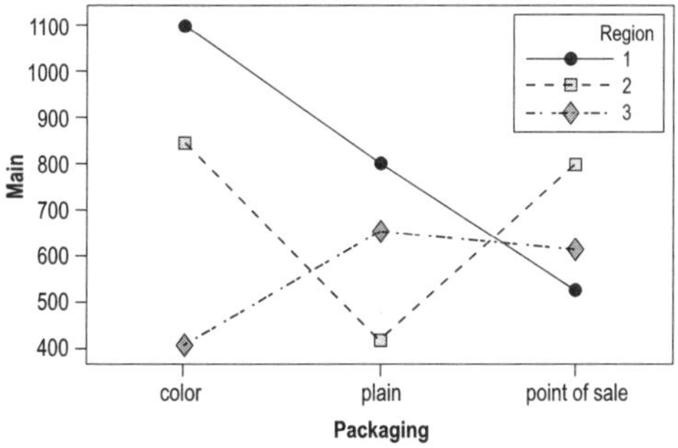

Quick Take

Chi-square test

Highlights

- A hypothesis testing method when both the contributing factor (X) and result (Y) are categorical/attribute data

  Ex: Does customer location affect products/services ordered?

  Ex: Does supplier affect whether end product passes performance tests

- The Greek letter χ or chi (pronounced "kye"—rhymes with "eye") is used to represent the statistic (the final figure is "squared" before interpretation, hence the "chi-square" label)
- Chi-square is the *sum* of the "squared differences" between the expected and observed number of observations in each category

Form of the hypothesis

With the chi-square test for independence, statisticians assume most variables in life are independent, therefore:

H_0: data is independent (not related)
H_a: data is dependent (related)

If the p-value is $<.05$, then reject H_o

How to calculate chi-square

1. Identify different levels of both the X and Y variables

Ex: Supplier A vs. Supplier B, Pass or Fail

2. Collect the data

3. Summarize results in an observations table

- Include totals for each column and row
- The table here shows data on whether age (X) affected if a candidate was hired (Y)

	Hired	Not Hired	**Total**
Old	**30**	**150**	**180**
Young	**45**	**230**	**275**
Totals	**75**	**380**	**455**

4. Develop an expected frequency table

- For each cell in the table, multiply the column total by the Row total, then divide by the total number of observations
  Ex: in the table above, the "Old, Hired" cell has an expected frequency of: (75 * 180) / 455 = 29.6%
- For each cell, subtract the Actual number of observations from the expected frequency
  Ex: in the table above, the "Old, Hired" cell would be: 30 – 29.6 = 0.4

5. Compute the relative squared differences

- Square each figure in the table (negative numbers will become positive)
  Ex: 0.4 * 0.4 = 0.16
- Divide by the expected number of observances for that cell
  Ex: 0.16 / 29.6 =.005

6. Add together all the relative squared differences to get chi-square

Ex: in the table on the previous page:

Chi-square = $\chi^2 = 0.004 + 0.001 + 0.002 + 0.000 = 0.007$

7. Determine and interpret the p-value

For this example: df = 1, p-value = 0.932

NOTE: Minitab or other statistical software will generate the table and compute the chi-square and p-values once you enter the data. All you need to do is interpret the p-value.

Tips

- Your data should have been gathered to ensure randomness. Beware of other hidden factors (Xs).

Quick Take

Design of Experiments (DOE) notation and terms

Response Variable – An output which is measured or observed.

Factor – A controlled or uncontrolled input variable.

Fractional Factorial DOE – Looks at only a fraction of all the possible combinations contained in a full factorial. If many factors are being investigated, information can be obtained with smaller investment. *See* p. 190 for notation.

Full Factorial DOE – Full factorials examine every possible combination of factors at the levels tested. The full factorial design is an experimental strategy that allows us to answer most questions completely. The general notation for a full factorial design run at 2 levels is: $\mathbf{2^k = \# Runs.}$

Level – A specific value or setting of a factor.

Effect – The change in the response variable that occurs as experimental conditions change.

Interaction – Occurs when the effect of one factor on the response depends on the setting of another factor.

Repetition – Running several samples during one experimental setup run.

Replication – Replicating (duplicating) the entire experiment in a time sequence with different setups between each run.

Randomization – A technique used to spread the effect of nuisance variables across the entire experimental region. Use random numbers to determine the order of the experimental runs or the assignment of experimental units to the different factor-level combinations.

Resolution – how much sensitivity the results have to different levels of interactions.

Run – A single setup in a DOE from which data is gathered. A 3-factor full factorial DOE run at 2 levels has $2^3 = 8$ runs.

Trial – *See Run*

Treatment Combination – *See Run*

Design terminology

In most software programs, each factor in the experiment will automatically be assigned a letter: A, B, C, etc.

- Any results labeled with one letter refer to that variable only

Interaction effects are labeled with the letters of the corresponding factors:

"Two-way" interactions (second-order effects)

AB, AC, AC, BC, etc....

"Three-way" interactions (third-order effects)

ABC, ACD, BCD, BCG, etc.

Tip: It's common to find main effects and second-order effects (the interaction of one factor with another) and not unusual to find third-order effects in certain types of experiments (such as chemical processes). However, it's rare that interactions at a higher order are significant (this is referred to as "Sparsity of Effects"). Minitab and other programs can calculate the higher-order effects, but generally such effects are of little importance and are ignored in the analysis.

Planning a designed experiment

Design of Experiments is one of the most powerful tools for understanding and reducing variation in *any* process. DOE is useful whenever you want to:

- Find **optimal process settings** that produce the best results at lowest cost
- Identify *and quantify* the factors that have the biggest impact on the output
- Identify factors that do *not* have a big impact on quality or time (and therefore can be set at the most convenient and/or least costly levels)
- Quickly screen a large number of factors to determine the most important ones
- Reduce the time and number of experiments needed to test multiple factors

Developing an experimental plan

1. Define the problem in business terms, such as cost, response time, customer satisfaction, service level.
2. Identify a measurable objective that you can quantify as a **response variable**. (*see* p. 187)

   Ex: Improve the yield of a process by 20%

   Ex: Achieve a quarterly target in quality or service level
3. Identify input variables and their levels (*see* p. 187).
4. Determine the experimental strategy to be used:
   - Determine if you will do a few medium to large experiments or several smaller experiments that will allow quick cycles of learning
   - Determine whether you will do a full factorial or fractional factorial design (*see* p. 189)
   - Use a software program such as Minitab or other references to help you identify the combinations of factors to be tested and the order in which they will be tested (the "run order")
5. Plan the execution of **all** phases (including a confirmation experiment):
   - What is the plan for randomization? replication? repetition?
   - What if any restrictions are there on randomization (factors that are difficult/impossible to randomize)?
   - Have we talked to internal customers about this?
   - How long will it take? What resources will it take?
   - How are we going to analyze the data?
   - Have we planned a ***pilot run***?
   - Make sure sufficient resources are allocated for data collection and analysis
6. Perform an experiment and analyze the results. What was learned? What is the next course of action? Carry out more experimentation or apply knowledge gained and stabilize the process at the new level of performance.

Defining response variables

- Is the output qualitative or quantitative? (Quantitative is much preferred)
- Try for outputs tied to customer requirements and preferences, and aligned with or linked to your business strategy (not just factors that are easy to measure)
- What effect would you like to *see* in the response variable (retargeting, centering, variation reduction, or all three?)
- What is the baseline? (Mean and standard deviation?)
- Is the output under statistical control?
- Does the output vary over time?
- How much change in the output do you want to detect?
- How will you measure the output?
- Is the measurement system adequate?
- What is the anticipated range of the output?
- What are the priorities for these?

Identifying input variables

Review your process map or SIPOC diagram and/or use cause identification methods (*see* pp. 145 to 155) to identify factors that likely have an impact on the response variable. Classify each as one of the following:

1) **Controllable factor (X)** – Factors that can be manipulated to see their effect on the outputs.

   Ex: Quantitative (continuous): temperature, pressure, time, speed

   Ex: Qualitative (categorical): supplier, color, type, method, line, machine, catalyst, material grade/type

2) **Constant (C)** or **Standard Operating Procedure (SOP)** – Procedures that describe how the process is run and identify certain factors which will be held constant, monitored, and maintained during the experiment.

3) **Noise factor (N)** – Factors that are uncontrollable, difficult or too costly to control, or preferably not controlled. Decide how to address these in your plans (*see* details below).

   Ex: weather, shift, supplier, user, machine age, etc.

Selecting factors

Consider factors in the context of whether or not they are:

A) Practical

- Does it make sense to change the factor level? Will it require excessive effort or cost? Would it be something you would be willing to implement and live with?
  Ex: Don't test a slower line speed than would be acceptable for actual production operations
  Ex: Be cautious in testing changes in a service factor that you know customers are happy with

B) Feasible

- Is it physically possible to change the factor?
  Ex: Don't test temperature levels in the lab that you know can't be achieved in the factory

C) Measurable

- Can you measure (and repeat) factor level settings?
  Ex: Operator skill level in a manufacturing process
  Ex: Friendliness of a customer service rep

Tips for treating noise factors

A noise (or nuisance) factor is a factor beyond our control that affects the response variable of interest.

- If the noise factor definitely affects the response variable of interest and is crucial to the process, product, or service performance (such as raw materials)…
  - Incorporate it into the experimental design
  - Limit the scope of the experiment to one case (or level) of the noise factor
- If the noise factor is completely random and uncontrollable (weather, operator differences, etc.), then **randomize the runs** to keep it from invalidating the experiment
- When possible, hold the noise factors constant during the course of the experiment

Tips for selecting factors

- Look for low-hanging fruit
  - High potential for significant impact on key measures
  - No or low cost
  - Easy to implement and change

- Additional items to consider:
  - Cost-effectiveness
  - Manageability
  - Resources
  - Potential for interactions
  - Time
  - How many ideas you generate

DOE: Full-factorial vs. Fractional-factorials (and notations)

Full factorial experiments:

- Examine every possible combination of factors and levels
- Enable us to:
  - Determine main effects that the manipulated factors will have on response variables
  - Determine effects that factor interactions will have on response variables
  - Estimate levels to set factors at for best results
- Advantages
  - Provides a mathematical model to predict results
  - Provides information about all main effects
  - Provides information about all interactions
  - Quantifies the Y=f(x) relationship
- Limitations
  - Requires more time and resources than fractional factorials
- Sometimes labeled as **optimizing designs** because they allow you to determine which factor and setting combination will give the best result within the ranges tested. They are conservative, since information about all main effects and variables can be determined.

- Most common are **2-level designs** because they provide a lot of information, but require fewer trials than would studying 3 or more levels.
- The general notation for a 2-level full factorial design is:

$$2^k = \# \text{ Runs}$$

2 is the number of levels for each factor

k is the number of factors to be investigated

This is the minimum number of tests required for a full factorial

Fractional factorial experiments:

- Look at only **selected subsets** of the possible combinations contained in a full factorial
- Advantages:
  - Allows you to **screen** many factors—separate significant from not-significant factors—with smaller investment in research time and costs
  - Resources necessary to complete a fractional factorial are manageable (economy of time, money, and personnel)
- Limitations/drawbacks
  - Not all interactions will be discovered/known
  - These tests are more complicated statistically and require expert input
- General notation to designate a 2-level fractional factorial design is:

$$2_R^{k-p} = \# \text{ Runs}$$

2 is the number of levels for each factor

k is the number of factors to be investigated

$\mathbf{2^{-p}}$ is the size of the fraction (p = 1 is a 1/2 fraction, p = 2 is a 1/4 fraction, etc.)

$\mathbf{2^{k-p}}$ is the number of runs

R is the **resolution,** an indicator of what levels of effects and interactions are confounded, meaning you can't separate them in your analysis

Loss of resolution with fractional factorials

- When using a fractional factorial design, you cannot estimate all of the interactions
- The amount that we are able to estimate is indicated by the resolution of an experiment
- The higher the resolution, the more interactions you can determine

Example:

$$2_{IV}^{4-1}$$

This experiment will test 4 factors at each of 2 levels, in a half-fraction factorial (2^4 would be 16 runs, this experiment is the equivalent of 2^3 = 8 runs).

The resolution of IV means:

- Main effects are confounded with 3-way interactions (1 + 3 = 4). You have to acknowledge that any measured main effects could be influenced by 3-way interactions. Since 3-way interactions are relatively rare, attributing the measured differences to the main effects only is most often a safe assumption.
- 2-way interactions are confounded with each other (2 + 2 = 4). This design would not be a good way to estimate 2-way interactions.

Quick Take

Interpreting DOE results

Most statistical software packages will give you results for main effects, interactions, and standard deviations.

1. Main effects plots for mean

- Interpretation of slopes is all relative. Lines with steeper slopes (up or down) have a bigger impact on the output means than lines with little or no slope (flat or almost flat lines).

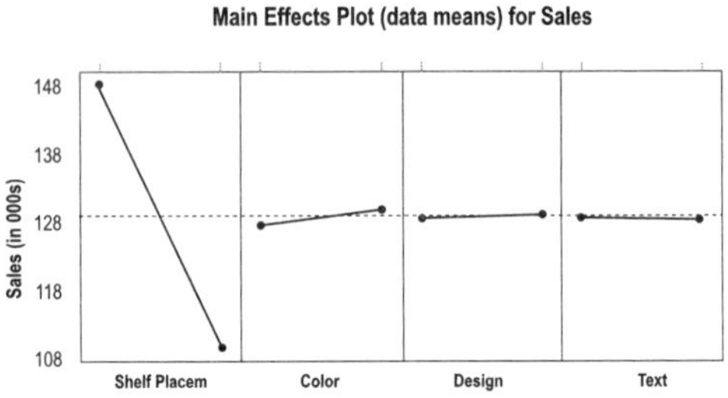

Four factors tested—two factors per level so there are two data points for each level)

- In this example, the line for shelf placement slopes much more steeply than the others–meaning it has a bigger effect on sales than the other factors. The other lines seem flat or almost flat, so the main effects are less likely to be significant.

2. Main effects plots for standard deviation

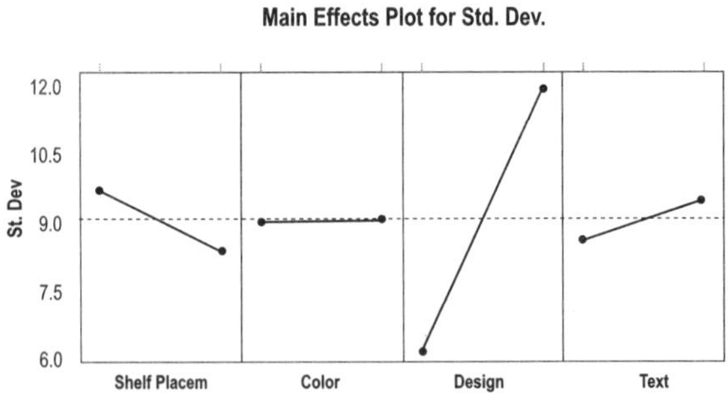

- These plots tell you whether variation changes or is the same between factor levels.
- Again, you want to compare slopes in comparison to each other. Here, Design has much more variation one level than at the factors (so you can expect it to have much more variation at one level than at the other level).

3. Pareto chart of the means for main factor effects and higher-order interactions

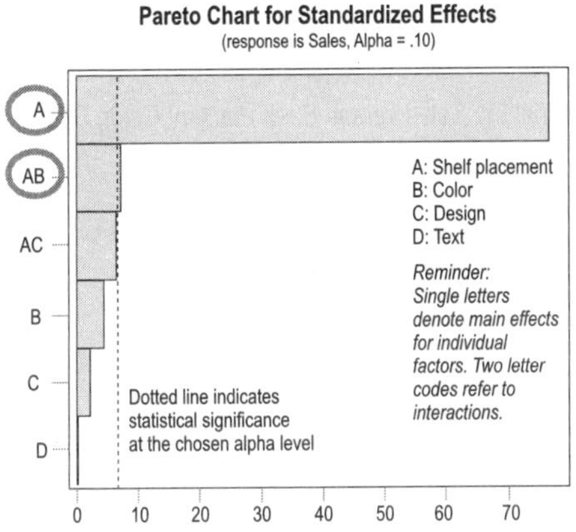

- You're looking for individual factors (labeled with a single letter) and interactions (labeled with multiple letters) that have bars that extend beyond the "significance line"
- Here, main factor A and interaction AB have significant effects, meaning placement, and interaction of placement and color have the biggest impact on sales (compare to the "main effects plot for mean,"previous page).

4. Pareto chart on the standard deviation of factors and interactions

- Same principle as the Pareto chart on means
- Here, only Factor C (Design) shows a significant change in variation between levels

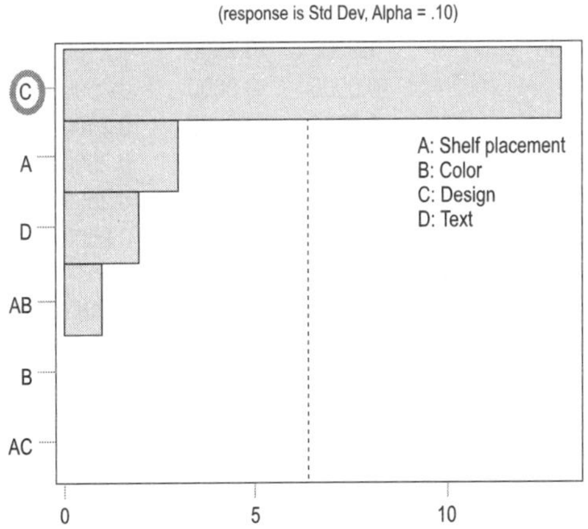

5. Minitab session window reports

- Shelf Placement and the Shelf Placement* Color interactions are the only significant factors at a 90% confidence internal (if alpha were 0.05 instead of 0.10, only placement would be significant)

Fractional Factorial Fit: Sales versus Shelf Placem, Color, Design, Text

Term	Effect	Coef	SE Coef	T	P
Constant	128.50	0.2500	514.00	0.001	
Shelf Pl	**-38.50**	**-19.25**	**0.2500**	**-77.00**	**0.008**
Color	2.00	1.00	0.2500	4.00	0.156
Design	0.50	0.25	0.2500	1.00	0.500
Text	-0.00	-0.00	0.2500	-0.00	1.000
Shelf Pl*Color	**3.50**	**1.75**	**0.2500**	**7.00**	**0.090**
Shelf Pl*Design	-3.00	-1.50	0.2500	-6.00	0.105

Analysis of Variance for Sales (coded units)

Source	DF	Seq SS	Adj SS	Adj MS	F	P
Main Effects	4	2973.00	2973.00	743.250	1E+03	0.019
2-Way Interactions	2	42.50	42.50	21.250	42.50	0.108
Residual Error	1	0.50	0.50	0.500		
Total	7	3016.00				

- Design is the only factor that has a significant effect on variation at the 90% confidence level

Fractional Factorial Fit: Std Dev versus Shelf Placement, Color, ...

Term	Effect	Coef	SE Coef	T	P
Constant	9.0000	0.2500	36.00	0.018	
Shelf Pl	-1.5000	-0.7500	0.2500	-3.00	0.205
Color	-0.0000	-0.0000	0.2500	-0.00	1.000
Design	**6.5000**	**3.2500**	**0.2500**	**13.00**	**0.049**
Text	1.0000	0.5000	0.2500	2.00	0.295
Shelf Pl*Color	0.5000	0.2500	0.2500	1.00	0.500
Shelf Pl*Design	0.0000	0.0000	0.2500	0.00	1.000

Analysis of Variance for Std (coded units)

Source	DF	Seq SS	Adj SS	Adj MS	F	P
Main Effects	4	91.0000	91.0000	22.7500	45.50	0.111
2-Way Interactions	2	0.5000	0.5000	0.2500	0.50	0.707
Residual Error	1	0.5000	0.5000	0.5000		
Total	7	92.0000				

Quick Take

Residual analysis in hypothesis testing

Highlights

- Residual analysis is a standard part of assessing model adequacy any time a mathematical model is generated because residuals are the best estimate of error
- Perform this analysis any time you use ANOVA, regression analysis, or DOE
- See further guidance on the next page

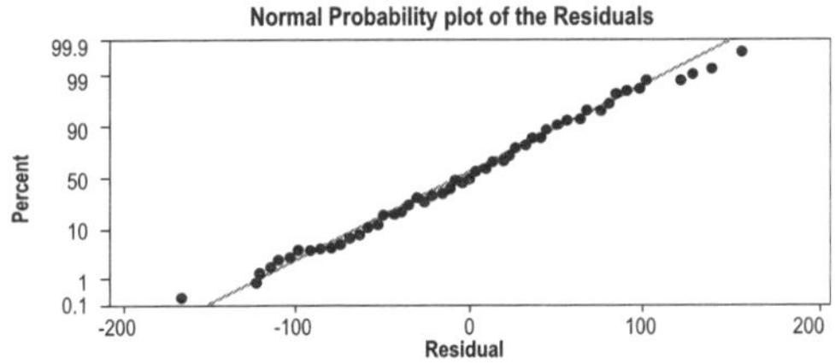

If data points hug the diagonal line, the data are normally distributed

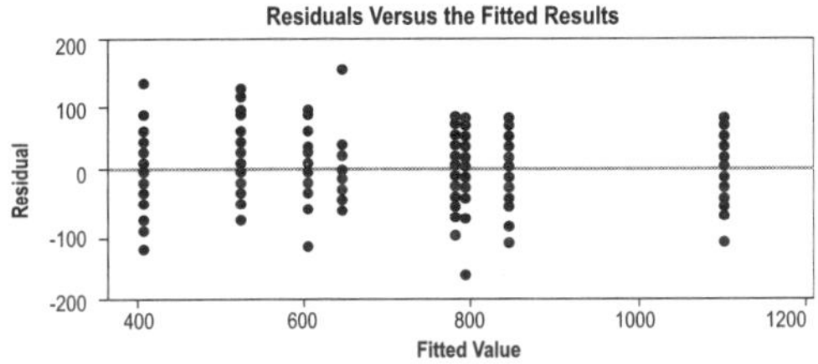

Want to see a similar spread of points across all values (which indicates equal variance)

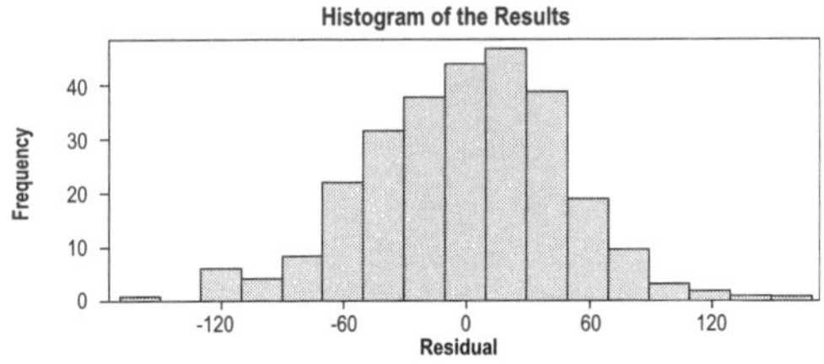

Histograms provide a visual check of normality

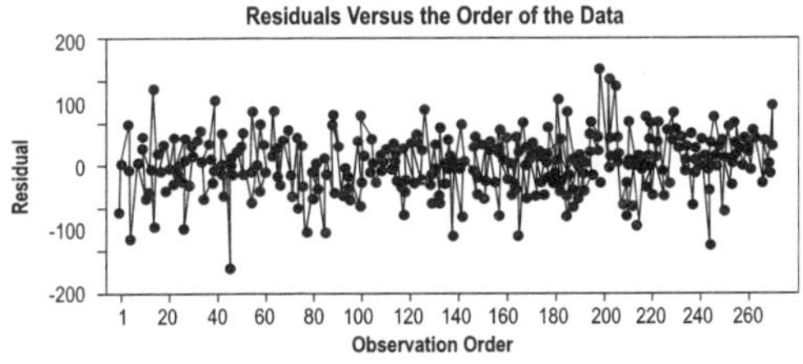

The number of data points here makes this chart difficult to analyze, but the principles are the same as those for time series plots

Interpreting the results

The plots are usually generated in Minitab or other statistical package. The interpretation is based on the following assumptions:

- Errors will all have the same variance (constant variance)
- Residuals should be independent, normally distributed, with a mean equal to 0
- Residual plots should show no pattern relative to any factor
- Residuals should sum to 0

Examine the plots as you would any plot of the varying styles (regression plot, histogram, scatter plot, etc.).

Practical Note: Moderate departures from normality of the residuals are of little concern. We always want to check the residuals, though, because they are an opportunity to learn more about the data.

CHAPTER 9

Reducing Lead Time and Non-Value-Add Cost

Purpose of these tools

- To eliminate constraints in a process
  - ensure that the process can meet customer demand
- To reduce the lead time and cost of a process
  - eliminate non-value-add cost and waste to improve process efficiency and profitability

Deciding which tool to use

Review the **Basic concepts and definitions of Lean** (p. 199). Then:

- Determine where and how time is used in your process:
  - Identify process steps as **value-add or non-value-add** (in the eyes of the customer), *see* Chapter 3, p. 49
  - Calculate the **Process Lead Time** (also known as process cycle time) for the process), p. 199
  - Determine the **desired average completion rate** (customer demand rate, or takt rate), p. 200)
  - Calculate the **Process Cycle Efficiency**, p. 201
  - Locate and quantify the **time traps** and **capacity constraints**, pp. 203 to 206
  - Compute the **Workstation Turnover Times,** p. 202
- Incorporate the data into your **Value Stream Map** (Chapter 3, p. 45)

The choice of tool or method to improve process flow and speed depends on what type of problem(s) you find after completing the value stream map (VSM).

1. **Process produces too much compared to customer demand**
   - Implement a **Replenishment Pull System** to link output directly to customer demand (in conjunction with a Generic Pull System), p. 216

  - Calculate and adjust batch sizes to the minimum safe batch size to meet customer demand, p. 222

2. Process is not producing enough compared to customer demand

- Attack **capacity constraints**. Focus on removing non-value-add work through variation reduction (*see* Chapter 7) and use of the following tools covered in this chapter:
  - Setup reduction, total productive maintenance, mistake proofing, process balancing

3. Process is meeting customer demand but has long process lead times and high overhead cost

- Use **5S** to improve the cleanliness and organization of work-space, p. 206. This is a basic technique that should be used in every workspace.
- Implement a **Generic Pull System** to stabilize, and then reduce, the number of "Things In Process," thus reducing process lead time so that follow-on improvements will have maximum benefit, p. 213.
- **Reduce batch sizes** to the minimum safe batch size for the given process parameters, p. 222.
- Apply Lean and Six Sigma improvement techniques as necessary to time traps in sequence from those injecting the most to the least delay
  - If time trap is a **non-value add step** (p. 49), eliminate it
  - If long setup or changeover times are an issue, implement the **Four Step Rapid Setup method** (p. 223)
  - If downtime is the problem, use **total productive maintenance** (p. 229)
  - If errors are causing rework, *see* **mistake proofing** (Poka-Yoke, etc.)(p. 233)
  - If workload of process steps is uneven, apply **process balancing** principles to move work around (p. 235)
  - If there is variation in demand, compute a **safety stock**, (p. 218)
  - If there is too much variation, review Chapter 7

4. Process steps have uneven workload leading to labor inefficiencies

- Use **process balancing** (p. 234)

5. Process involves much movement of information/material; process flow is inefficient

- Use process flow improvement to reduce distance and time between process steps. *See* **process maps** in Chapter 3 or **work cell optimization** (p. 235)

6. Process flow is efficient, but has too much non-value-add time

- Use **value-add time analysis** (Chapter 3, p. 49) to pinpoint and quantify non-value-added time in process steps, then Lean and Six Sigma methods as needed to implement solutions

Once you've implemented these improvements, use **Visual Process Controls**, p. 237, to maintain the gains.

Quick Take

Basic Lean concepts

Process Lead Time (also called process cycle time, total lead time, or total cycle time): the time from when a work item (product, order, etc.) enters a process until it exits.

Ex: Process Lead Time of a mortgage refinancing process could be measured as the elapsed time from when a homeowner calls to when the mortgage refinancing closes (average = 33 days)

Things-in-Process (TIP) or Work-In-Process (WIP): Any work item that has entered the process and not yet exited. The "work" can be anything: materials, orders, customers, assemblies, emails, etc.

Ex: There were 3300 refinance applications in process at the end of the month

Average Completion Rate (Exit Rate or Throughput): The output of a process over a defined period of time.

Ex: Average completion rate of the mortgage process = 100 mortgage refinance applications closed per day last month.

Capacity: The **maximum** amount of product or service (output) a process can deliver over a continuous period of time.

Ex: The capacity of our process is 120 mortgage applications per day

Takt Rate (customer demand rate): The amount of product or service required by customers over a continuous period of time. **Processes should be timed to produce at the takt rate.** Any lower and you will be disappointing customers; any higher and you will be producing output that cannot be used.

Ex: The takt rate for mortgage applications is 130 applications per day

Time Trap: Any process step (activity) that inserts delay time into a process.

Ex: data entry clerks gather up all mortgage applications for an entire day before entering them into the computer system—this causes delays for the mortgages received during the day, which is a time trap

Capacity Constraint: An activity in the process that is unable to produce at the completion (exit) rate required to meet customer demand (takt rate).

Ex: Property appraisers can evaluate 120 properties per day, but customer demand is currently 130 applications per day—appraisers are a capacity constraint

Value-add (VA) time: any process step or activity that transforms the form, fit, or function of the product or service for which the customer is willing to pay

Ex: The sum of the value-add times in the mortgage refinancing process is 3.2 hours

Non-value-add (NVA) cost: Waste in a process. Customers would be willing to buy a product or service that did *not* have these costs if it meant a lower price.

> Ex: having to print out the refinancing paperwork and walk it over to the appraiser's mailbox is non-value-add—everything should be electronic

See also p. 49 for more on value-add and non-value-add concepts, and the next section for metrics associated with Lean.

Quick Take

Metrics of time efficiency

The purpose of the tools in this chapter is to improve how time and energy are spent in a process. The three metrics described here can help you identify the sources and impact of inefficiency.

1. Process Cycle Efficiency (PCE)

The best measure of overall process health is **Process Cycle Efficiency** (PCE), the percentage of value-add time (work that changes the form, fit, or function as desired by the customer).

$$\text{Process Cycle Efficiency} = \frac{\text{Value-add Time}}{\text{Process Lead Time}}$$

You can either measure process lead time directly by measuring the time it takes "things in process" to transit the process, or use Little's Law (*see* next page) to determine an average.

- PCE indicates how efficiently the process is converting work-in-process into exits/completions.
- Any process with low PCE will have large non-value-add costs and great opportunities for cost reduction. You can find these opportunities with a value stream map (p. 45). PCEs of less than 10% are common pre-improvement.
- The only way you can improve PCE is to get rid of non-value-add work and costs.

2. Little's Law

One component of PCE is Process Lead Time, which can be described by Little's Law:

$$\text{Process Lead Time} = \frac{\text{Number of Things in Process}}{\text{Average Completion Rate}}$$

This shows how lead time is related to the number of things in process (TIP, also known as WIP) and the completion (exit) rate of the process.

To improve Process Lead Time, and in turn PCE, either increase capacity (average completion rate) and/or reduce TIP or WIP.

3. Workstation Turnover Time

Workstation Turnover Time (WTT) for a given process step or workstation is the amount of time needed to set up and complete one cycle of work on all the different "things" (work items, SKUs) at that step. WTT is important in improvement efforts because it helps highlight which process step (time trap) to work on first.

Calculating WTT for a process step

$WTT_k = \Sigma[(\text{Setup Time}_i) + (\text{Process Time}_i * \text{Batch Size}_i)]$

k = the process step (activity) in the process

i = 1 to n (the number of things worked on at that process step)

Quick Take

Time Traps vs. Capacity Constraints

Recap of useful definitions

Capacity: The maximum output a process can deliver over a continuous period of time

Capacity Constraint: An activity in a process that is unable to produce at the exit rate required to meet customer demand

Time Trap: Any process step that inserts delay into a process

Time traps

- Time traps **insert delays** into a process.
  - They are sometimes **erroneously** labeled bottlenecks. The term "bottleneck" is imprecise because it does not distinguish between steps that inject delays (time traps) and those that cannot operate at required levels (capacity constraints)
- Time traps can create long lead times, large *downstream* inventories, and large amounts of WIP—but may not in fact be a capacity constraint
- Time traps are caused by poor management policies (such as launching batch sizes far larger than the minimum required), long setup times, machine or human downtime, or quality problems
- Time traps can change over time (monthly, weekly, even daily) based upon product mixes or special causes (new product introductions, special orders, etc.).

  Focus on identifying time traps if the goal of your project is to improve efficiencies (in inventory, lead time, output rates, etc.). Work on the time trap that is injecting the most amount of delay into your process first.

Capacity constraints

- Capacity constraints **limit the capacity** of the process as measured in units per hour
- Capacity constraints often have less capacity than previous or subsequent steps/operations.
- Capacity constraints can change over time (monthly, weekly, even daily) based on product mixes or special causes (new product introductions, special orders, etc.).

  Focus on identifying capacity constraints if the goal of your project is to increase output to meet real customer demand.

Attacking time traps and capacity constraints

- Fix the capacity constraints first so that you can meet customer demand; then attack time traps
- You can eliminate capacity constraints and time traps only through data and calculation. Relying on intuition will lead you astray.

Identifying Time Traps and Capacity Constraints

Purpose

To quantify how much time delay each step or activity introduces into the process

How to identify traps and capacity constraints: Method 1

The basis of capacity constraint identification is **takt rate** (customer demand rate) **analysis**, which compares the task time of each process (or process step) to:

- Each other, to determine time traps
- Customer demand, to determine if the time traps are capacity constraints

Step 1: Gather needed data

Determine:

- Aggregate customer demand (units/time)
- Net operating time available
  = Gross Operating Time minus breaks, lunch, etc.
- Net resource capacity (units/time) by process step
  = Average output over time

Step 2: Calculate takt rate (customer demand)

Takt rate = (number of units to process)/(net operating time available)

Takt time = inverse of takt rate

(net operating time available)/(number of units to process)

Step 3: Analyze the figures

- The process step with a net resource capacity closest to the takt rate is the Time Trap
- If the time trap does not have enough net resource capacity to meet customer demand, it is also a capacity constraint

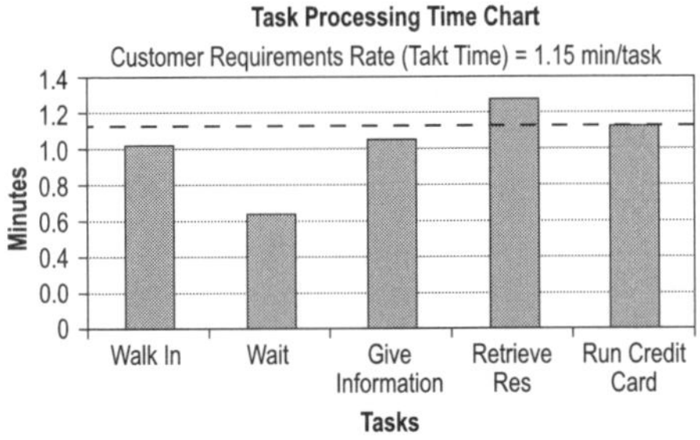

How to identify time traps and capacity constraints, Method 2

To determine which process step is the biggest time trap, simply calculate WTT for each step in the process. Here's the WTT equation from p. 201:

$$WTT_k = \Sigma[(\text{Setup Time}_i) + (\text{Process Time}_i * \text{Batch Size}_i)]$$

The step with the longest WTT is the time trap that is injecting the *most* amount of delay into the process.

Taking action

Examine the data you plugged into the WTT equation for the Time Trap. If the problem lies in setup time, use the Four Step Rapid Setup Method (p. 223); for Process Time, use 5S (*see* below) and other flow-improvement tools. Review Batch Sizing principles on p. 222 if that is the problem. Once improvements have been made, find the new "biggest" time trap and continue until you've reached your improvement goals.

Quick Take

5S Overview

Purpose

To create and maintain an organized, clean, safe, and high-performance workplace.

- 5S enables anyone to distinguish between normal and abnormal conditions at a glance.
- 5S is the foundation for continuous improvement, zero defects, cost reduction, and a safe work area.
- 5S is a systematic way to improve the workplace, processes, and products through production line employee involvement.

Definitions

Sort: Clearly distinguish needed items from unneeded items and eliminate the latter

Set in order (also known as *Simplify*): Keep needed items in the correct place to allow for easy and immediate retrieval

Shine (also known as *Sweep*): Keep the work area swept and clean

Standardize: Standardized cleanup (the first three S's)

Sustain (also known as *Self-Discipline*): Make a habit of maintaining established procedures

When to use 5S

- Whenever a workplace is messy, unorganized
- Whenever people have to spend time tracking down tools, information, etc., required to complete a task
- In any of the DMAIC phases; best implemented…
  - In manufacturing, as one of the *first* Improve actions, because it will make other tools such as setup reduction more efficient
  - In office environments as a *later* Improve step or as part of standardization and cross-training in Control

Implementing 5S

S1: Sort

Goal: Remove all items from the workplace that are not needed for current production or tasks.

- It does **not mean** that you remove only the items that you know you will never need
- It does **not mean** that you simply arrange things in a neater fashion
- When you sort, you leave only the bare essentials–"When in doubt, move it out"

1. **Identify, "red tag," the move potentially unneeded items:** Question the need for each item in that quantity in the workplace. Typical items marked for removal include:
   - Unneeded files, paperwork, reference manuals
   - Defective, excess, or unneeded items that accumulate
   - Outdated or broken tools, supplies, or inspection equipment
   - Old rags and other cleaning supplies
   - Non-working electrical tools/equipment
   - Outdated posters, signs, notices and memos

Put a red tag on any item that is not essential to doing the work and move it to a holding area. (An example tag is shown below.)

RED TAG			
Red Tag No.			
Date Tagged			
Department			
Category	1	Inventory	
	2	Machines and Other Equipment	
	3	Dies, jigs, and fixtures	
	4	Tools and supplies	
	5	Other (Explain)	
Item			
Description			
Qty.			
Total Value $			
Deposition/ Evaluation			Date
	a	Moved to Red Tag Location	
	b	Disposed of	
	c	Moved to More Suitable Location	
	d	Left Exactly Where It Was	

2. Evaluating and dealing with red-tagged (unneeded) items

After one week in a holding area, tagged items should be:

- Disposed of, if determined unnecessary–sold, relocated, thrown away
- Kept, if determined necessary

S2: Set in order (Simplify)

Set in order means to arrange needed items in the area and to identify or label them so that anyone can find them or put them away.

GOAL: To arrange all needed work items in line with the physical workflow, and make them easy to locate and use

1. Draw a current-state map

Show the location of all materials, supplies, forms, etc., needed in this workspace.

2. Draw a future-state map

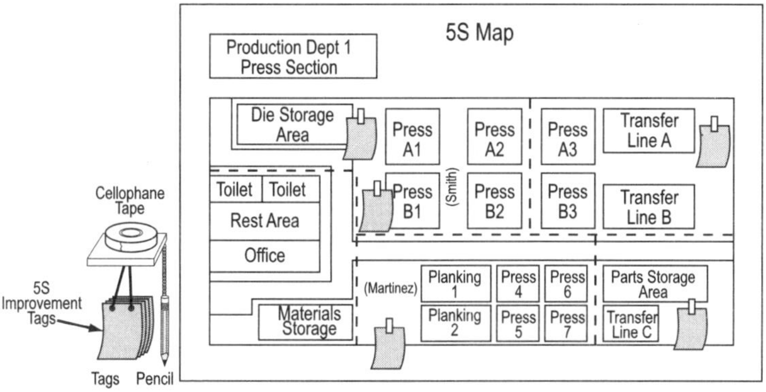

Draw a picture of how you think the workspace could be laid out for better efficiency and effectiveness. Make the map large enough so people can post improvement ideas on "5S tags." The new map should…

- Be based on the principles of motion economy (everything is within arm's reach, body motion kept to a minimum, stored in the sequence used, etc.)

3. Visually organize the workplace

- **Draw borders to differentiate work areas:** Draw a line around an item to identify its area/boundaries. Be sure to highlight: traffic lanes, stationary items, paths covered by mobile items, walkways, surface items
- **Provide a "home address" for each bordered area.** This is often a sign on the "shadowboard" at the item's home, describing what belongs inside the border. Label should include the item name, location, and a picture/silhouette (optional)
- **Put a corresponding label on each item (tool, piece of equipment, etc.).** The label should include name of item and item's home address.

S3: Shine

Shine emphasizes removing the dirt, grime, and dust from the work area. This is a program of keeping the work area swept and clean of debris.

1. Determine the shine targets

Think about...

- •. Safety – Report unsafe conditions, clean up spills on floor
- •. Waste – Empty trash can, remove excess supplies from area
- •. Cleanliness – Sweep floor, place tools on shadowboard

2. Set a housekeeping schedule and assign responsibilities

List responsibilities in detail, including which areas to be cleaned, at which times of the day, and what "cleaning" involves. Assign responsibility for completing housekeeping chores.

IT Dept Housekeeping Assignments
Week Ending ___/___ /___

Task	Assigned To	Mon	Tue	Wed	Thu	Fri	Comments
IT Request Inbox							Daily
Computers in Setup							Daily
Supply Table							Weekly
Repairs/Swaps							Weekly
Swap Cabinet							Weekly
Consumables:							Daily
Paper for Printer							Daily
Printer Cartridge							Daily
Blank CDs							Daily
Floppy Diskc							Daily
Office Furniture							Weekly
Priority Board							Daily
Archive (Equip List)							Daily

3. Create procedures for continued daily shine processes

Create a table that shows which housekeeping tasks must be performed, how often, and by whom.

4. Set periodic inspection and targets for machinery, equipment, computers, furnishings, etc.

S4: Standardize

Standardize means creating a consistent way of implementing the tasks performed daily, including Sort, Set in order, and Shine. It means doing "the right things the right way, every time."

Tips for standardize

- Review procedures conducted for Sort, Set in Order, and Shine and incorporate elements into the everyday work activity
- It should be obvious at a glance when an item is not in its designated place
- Use Visual Process Controls and any other appropriate visual clues that help people keep everything where it should be
- Schedule 5S activities frequently enough to maintain a clean, orderly, and safe work environment.
- Create **5S Agreements** to reflect decisions about which employees in the workplace will have what responsibilities

Elements of a 5S agreement

- Defines how a task should be done and the best way to do it
- Documents the procedures and guidelines for Sorting, Simplifying, Sweeping
  - Guidelines on what visual controls to use; workplace arrangement standards
  - Item and quantity requirements
  - Schedules, including housekeeping standards
- Documents process steps and other operating instructions
- Documents all job aids (user guides, reference materials, trouble-shooting guides)

Radar Chart for Tracking 5S Progress

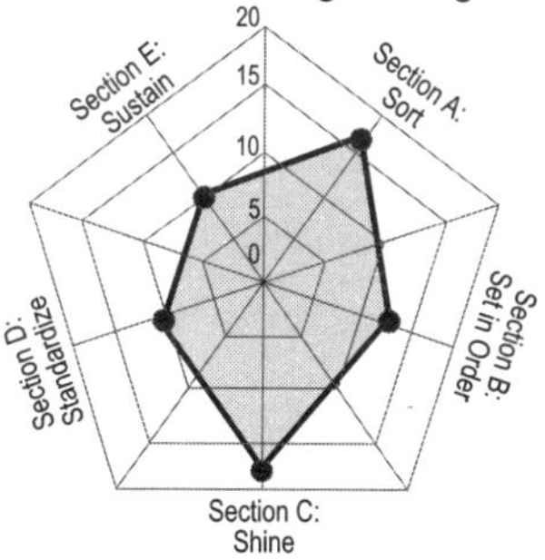

Section	A	B	C	D	E
Score	16	13	19	10	10

Area:
Auditor(s):
Date:

Maximum Score for each section is 20.

Goal is to score highest points possible in each section.

This team is doing well on Sort and Shine, but has work to do in other areas.

S5: Sustain

Sustain means that the 5S program has a discipline that ensures its continued success.

1. Create 5S audit form or radar chart for summarizing results. Establish a company standard for the format.

2. Establish periodic schedule for conducting audits
   - Minimum of weekly for area supervision, monthly for management
   - Participation of management in reviewing and using checklists is critical

Example 5S audit sheet

		0	1	2	3	4	5
A.	**Sort**	**0**	**1**	**2**	**3**	**4**	**5**
1>	Are there unnecessary items (peripherals, supplies) on the setup desk						X
2>	Are there scrap supplies in the supply bins						X
3>	ARE there old computers (off lease) in the swap cabinet						X
4>	Is there more furniture than necessary in the office						X
	Score	0	0	0	0	0	20
B.	**Set in Order**	**0**	**1**	**2**	**3**	**4**	**5**
5>	Is the supply table arranged per drawing/layout						X
6>	Is setup desk arranged per layout (incl. a single computer)						X
7>	Is swap cabinet arranged per layout						X
8>	Can ANYONE determine normal from abnormal						X
	Score	0	0	0	0	0	20
C.	**Shine**	**0**	**1**	**2**	**3**	**4**	**5**
9>	Is the desk clean and maintained or is there clutter (unnecessary supplies, etc.)						X
10>	Is Supply Table/Bins clean and organized						X
11>	Has the shine check sheet been updated (assignments been worked)						X
12>	Is dust filter clean						X
	Score	0	0	0	0	0	20
D.	**Standardize**	**0**	**1**	**2**	**3**	**4**	**5**
13>	Is the IT Dept Process Handbook in plain view						X
14>	Is the IT Dept Process Handbook updated						X
15>	ARE all supply bin, swap cabinet, and software shelf labels intact					X	
16>	Have all setups gone accordingly to instructions this week						X
	Score	0	0	0	0	0	20
E.	**Sustain score**	**0**	**1**	**2**	**3**	**4**	**5**
17>	Was the last audit less than two weeks ago						X
18>	Was the last departmental audit less than one month ago						X
19>	Is the 5S board up to date (pics, metrics, shine, etc.)						X
20>	Has anyone complemented the area on its cleanliness & organization						X
	Score	0	0	0	0	0	20

Area:
Auditor(s):
Date:

Section	A	B	C	D	E
Sub-total Score	20	20	20	20	20

3. Establish checklist for visitors to review
   - With 5S, ANYONE should be able to tell the difference between normal and abnormal conditions

4. Celebrate accomplishments and continue improving
   - Keep everyone aware of 5S and its benefits by giving recognition where it is due
   - Make time each week to brainstorm and implement improvement suggestions

Generic Pull System

Purpose

To place a limit, or **cap**, on the maximum number of things or work in process (TIP or WIP), so that the lead time is known and predictable (*see* Little's Law, p. 201). You can ***then*** apply improvement tools to reduce TIP or WIP by eliminating the effects of variation and batch size.

When to use a Generic Pull System

Whenever lead times are critical to satisfy customers and when non-value-add cost is significant compared to value-add cost.

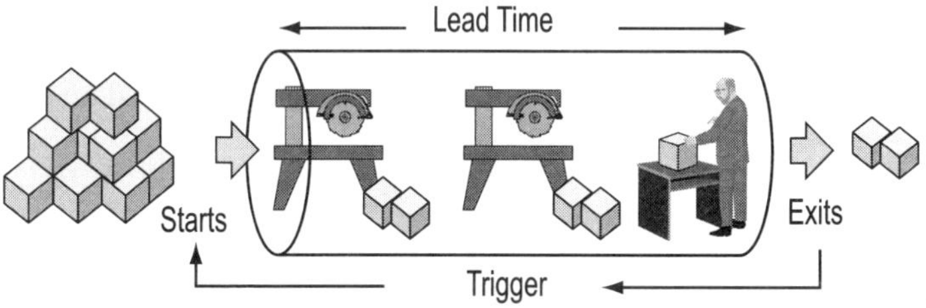

How to create a Generic Pull System

Part 1: Determine the WIP Cap

(maximum amount of work or things that should be in process at any given time)

1. Determine current Process Lead Time (PLT)

- Option 1: Track individual work items through the process to measure lead time
- Option 2: Use Little's Law (p. 202) to get an average lead time

2. Determine current Process Cycle Efficiency (PCE)

(*See* p. 201 for more on PCE)

3. **Identify target PCE.** The target PCE is the level at which the process should be operating based on "world-class" levels. If current PCE is…

Application	Typical (low end)	World-Class (high end)
Machining	1%`	20%
Fabrication	10%	25%
Continuous Manufacturing	5%	30%
Business Processes (Service)	10%	50%
Business Processes (Creative/Cognitive)	5%	25%

   << low end, multiply current PCE by 10 (one order of magnitude improvement) for use as target PCE

   < low end, use low-end figure as target PCE

   = or > low end, use high end as target PCE

   >> high end, move towards one-piece flow

4. **Calculate target lead time for the process.** Target lead time is the "best" or lowest process cycle time achievable based on the process characteristics.

$$\text{Lead Time}_{\text{target}} = \text{LT} = \frac{\text{VA time}_{\text{critical path}}}{\text{Target PCE}}$$

5. **Calculate WIP cap**

   Determine the maximum WIP allowed within the process at any time.

$$\text{WIP Cap} = \text{LT} * \text{Exits}$$

Part 2: Releasing work into the system

Typically the current WIP level will be significantly greater than the WIP Cap level. Therefore, you need a plan to reduce current WIP and to release work into the system to match the exit rate.

1. **Count the WIP in your process**
2. **Determine if you can release work or not:**
   - If the WIP ≥ WIP Cap, do not release any more work
     - If this will harm customers your options are to temporarily increase capacity in order to lower the amount of WIP, or perform a triage of current WIP to see if some work can be set aside to make room for new work (*see* Step 4 for details on triaging)
   - If current WIP < WIP Cap, release enough work to get to the WIP Cap

3. Identify how you will know when more work can be released into the system

CAUTION: as the PCE of a process approaches world-class levels, the effects of variation are magnified. Be careful not to reduce the TIP or WIP too much before addressing issues with variability, or a process step could be "starved" for work, creating a constraint!

4. Create a triage system for determining the order in which future work will be released into the system

Option 1: First-In, First-out (FIFO)–whatever comes in first gets processed first. This is commonly used in manufacturing to prevent obsolescence or degradation of supplies/materials.

Option 2: Triaging–working on highest-potential items first. Not all customer requests or orders, for example, represent the same level of potential for your company. You need to set up criteria for rating or ranking new work requests so you can tell the difference between high- and low-potential requests. This is often used in sales and other service applications.

Alternative to triage if you have the capacity for parallel processing: You can reduce the queue by shifting work from an overloaded step onto another step or adding/shifting resources intelligently. *See* Queue time formula, p. 222.

5. Develop and implement procedures for maintaining the generic pull system

- Identify the person with authority to release work into the process
- Develop signals, alerts, or procedures that will tell that person when WIP has fallen below the Cap (so s/he will know when to release the work)
  Ex: When people complete a work item, have them send an alert card or email to the "control" person (such as Kanban cards you often find in manufacturing)
- Train people in the new procedures
- Develop a plan to cover the transition period from the current high-WIP state to future WIP cap state
- Implement and monitor results; adjust as needed

Replenishment Pull Systems

Purpose

To eliminate shortages or overstocking of supplies by creating a system where items are automatically replaced as they are used up.

When to use a Replenishment Pull System

Use a replenishment pull system for in-process or end-item products, supplies, consumables (or any other item for which shortages and stockouts are not acceptable), which meet the following criteria:

- Usage on the item is repetitive
- Demand for the item is relatively consistent (low variability)
- Stocking shortages have a significant impact on service levels to the customer (internal or external)

A replenishment pull system should never be installed without a Generic Pull System already in place.

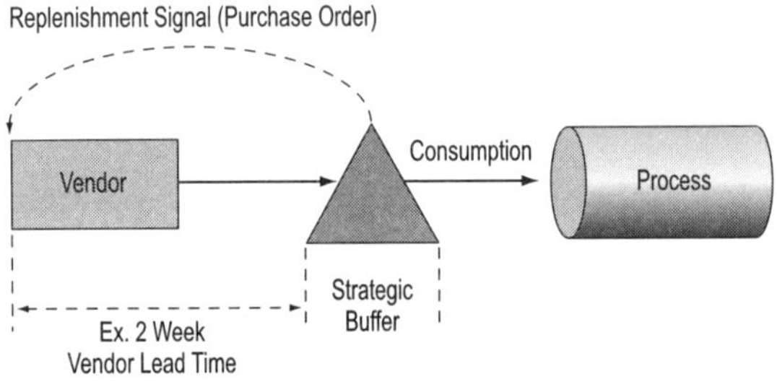

How to create a replenishment pull system

1. Determine work demand rate (DMD):

- Average weekly or average daily usage
  - Base on history, forecast (backlog) or a combination
  - Warning: historical usage may not reflect coming changes in the business (product or service mix, volume increases, etc.) So often a combination of factors should be considered.
- Recalculate frequently in order to capture changes

Handling seasonality

- Resize monthly if demand changes passes a "hurdle rate" (such as if demand changes > 20%)
- Use historical data or forecasts to determine signals that mean a resizing is necessary
- Forecast window should be at least the average Lag Time *weighted by volume* to account for lag times between demand and order receipt
- Use historical/future demand weighting tools to smooth ramp-ups/downs
  - Larger upswings >> higher weighting in forecast
  - Smaller upswings >> lower weighting on forecast

2. Determine Replenishment Lead Time (LT) and Order interval (OI)

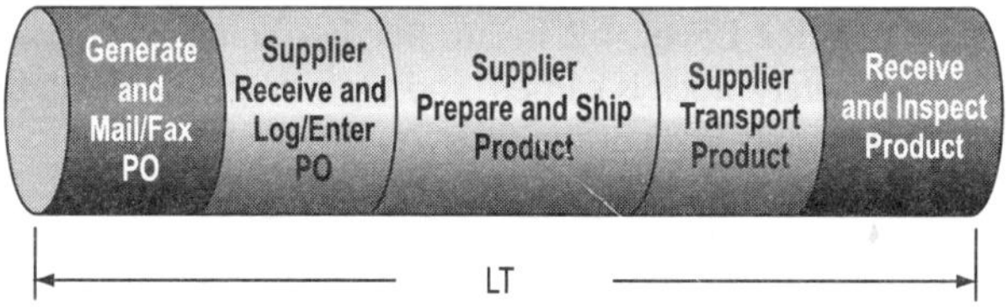

- **Replenishment lead time (LT):** the time from when a part or supply has been consumed until new supplies are received (replenishment time)
  - For purchased items such as supplies, etc., add together: (1) Time to generate a purchase order, (2) Supplier lead time, (3) Transportation time, and (4) Receiving/inspection/stocking time
  - For manufactured items, add together: (1) time to generate the Work Order, (2) Total process lead time, and (3) Receiving/inspection time
- **Order interval (OI):** Can be expressed as either the interval between orders (days, weeks) or the order quantity (items) to be purchased
  - Changing OI allows trade-offs between transactions, capacity and inventory

3. Determine optimal Safety Stock (SS) level

There are many ways to calculate safety stock. This method is based on empirical computations and experience.

- **Key Assumption:** The demand profile is normally distributed.

$$\textbf{Safety Stock} = \sigma\textbf{*service level*(LT)}^{\beta}$$

Where...

- Demand variability = **standard deviation** (σ). *See* p. 108 for formulas for calculating standard deviation.
- Desired service level (stockout coverage) = the number of standard deviations, relative to the mean, carried as safety stock. For example:

  Service Level = 1 means that one standard deviation of safety stock is carried, and on average there will be no stockouts 84% of the time

  Service Level = 2 means that two standard deviations of safety stock is carried, and on average there will be no stockouts 98% of the time
- Lead Time (LT) = Replenishment lead time
- β = a standard lead time reduction factor (set at 0.7)
- The coefficient of variation = σ/Xbar

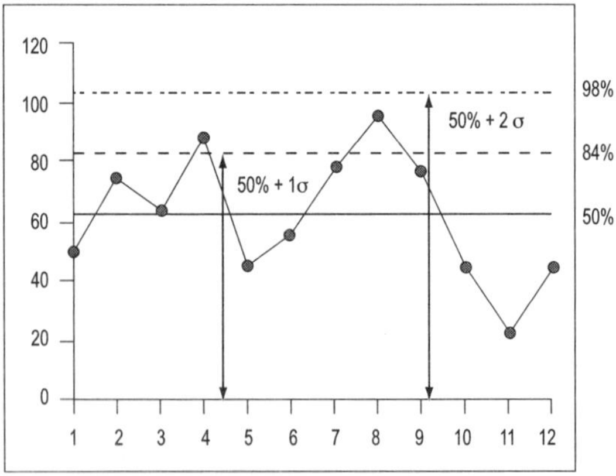

Coefficient Variation = s/x

Other useful formulas

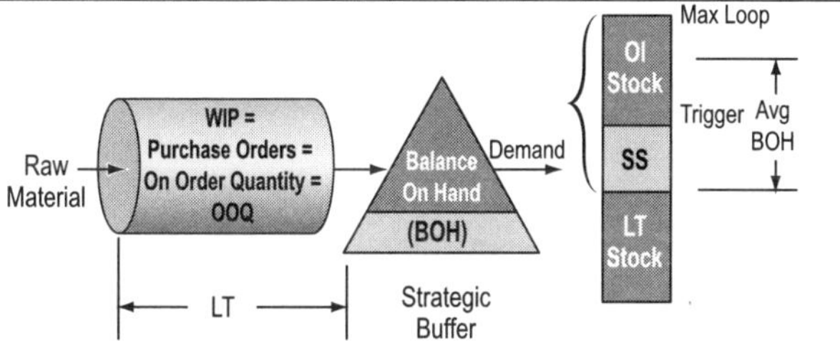

1. **Max Loop = [(LT * DMD) + (OI * DMD) + SS]**
   Maximum inventory in the pull system loop
2. **Loop Trigger Point = [(LT * DMD) + SS]**
   Minimum expected BOH inventory in the pull system loop
3. **Order if: (BOH + OOQ) < Trigger Point**
   Defining whether or not to order
4. **OQ = Order Quantity = [Max Loop – (BOH + OOQ)]**
   Order quantity if necessary (ROUND UP to nearest recommended multiple order quantity)
5. **Avg OH = Avg On Hand = [0.5 * (OI * DMD) + SS]**
   Average On Hand inventory

Where: BOH = Balance on Hand, the quantity of inventory in the strategic buffer
Where: OOQ = the number of items on order at any given time

Two-Bin Replenishment System

Highlights

A 2-Bin Replenishment Pull System is a simplified version of a standard replenishment pull system that uses just two bins of the stock item being replenished.

- Bin 1 has enough items to cover a calculated period of usage at the point-of-use
- When the bin runs out, Bin 2 is there to take its place while Bin 1 is being refilled/replenished
- The bins can be "Line-Side" (off to the side of the production line/work process) or "Point of Use" (immediately at hand on the production line or workspace—*see* diagrams, p. 221

When to use a 2-Bin system

- Items used repeatedly
- Relatively consistent demand/volume (low variability)
- Stocking shortages have a significant impact on service levels
- Supply costs are not in statistical control due to:
  - Lost or misplaced items/supplies
  - Lack of discipline or control over item dispersal

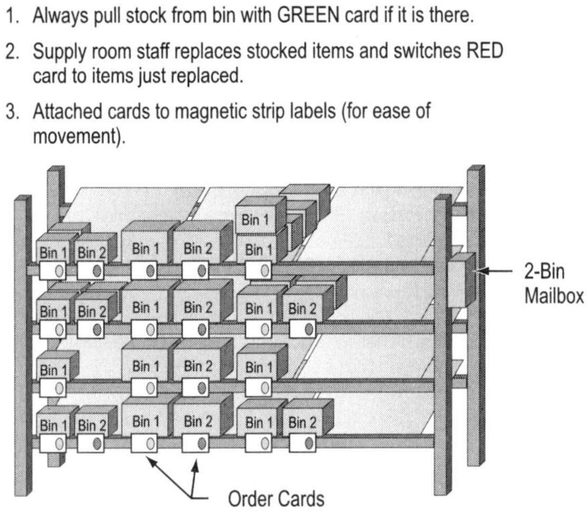

To use a 2-Bin Replenishment Pull System

- Same elements as basic replenishment pull system)– demand (DMD), replenishment lead time (LT), and order interval (OI).
- Safety stock typically set at 1/2 the max of [σ *Service Level * $(LT)^{0.7}$], or otherwise is dependent on individual conditions
- In addition, determine Box/Container Quantity

$$\text{Bin Quantity} = \max(LT, OI) * DMD + SS/2$$

- The bin doesn't necessarily look like a "bin"
  - Can be a standard plastic bin or tray, or the "standard pack" (the container an item is shipped in)
  - For larger items, a "bin" can be represented by a card attached to the item (the card is returned to the supplier when the item is consumed)

- If stock/supply room or vendor cannot divide shipping quantity, set bin quantity at some multiple of the box/container quantity

Option 1: Line-Side replenishment

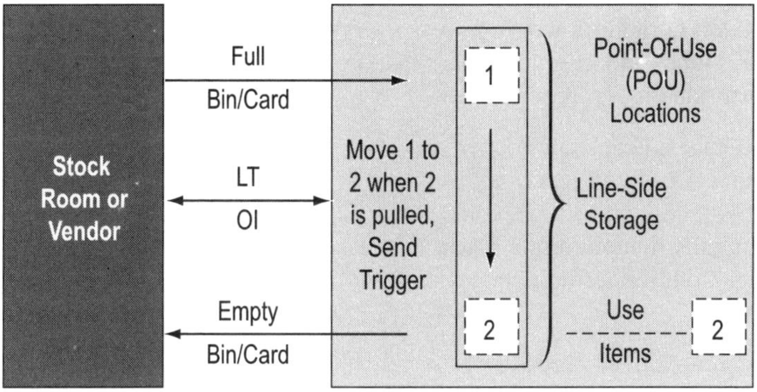

Option 2: Point-of-use stocking

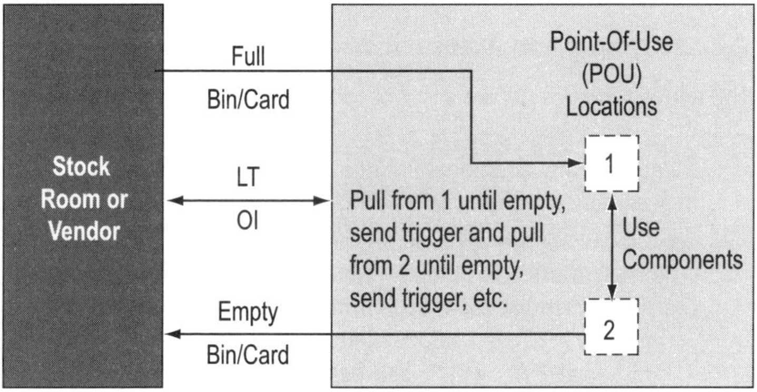

Bin Quantity = max (LT, OI) * DMD + SS/2

2-Bin POU stocking is used when restocking is not an issue

Quick Take

Computing minimum safe batch sizes

Note on Management Policy: the batch size is often set by management based on the EOQ formula or the demand for a fixed time period (a month's worth, a week's worth, etc.). Both methods result in lead times and inventory levels that are generally 30% to 80% larger than the process requires.

To have a Lean system operating at peak efficiency with lowest cost, you should compute the minimum safe batch size from the formula shown here.

Assumption: all products have the same demand and process parameters.

$$\text{Min Batch Size} = B = \frac{S\lambda}{2(1 - X - P\lambda)}$$

S = Setup time

λ = demand rate

X = defect%

P = processing time per unit

There is a more sophisticated version of the equation (protected by U.S. patents) that you can find in *Lean Six Sigma,* McGraw-Hill, 2001.

Accounting for Variation in Demand

The above formulas do not account for variation in demand, which is addressed two ways:

- Manufacturing: additional finished goods inventory must be built in accordance with the safety stock formula, p. 218
- Service: For service applications, safety stock is not possible and customers must wait in queue to receive their value add service time. The formula* for Queue time is:

$$\text{Queue Time} \cong \left(\frac{\text{Service Time}}{\text{Number of Cross-trained Servers}}\right)\left(\frac{\tilde{n}}{1-\tilde{n}}\right)$$

Where $\tilde{n}$ = % capacity at which servers are operating

**This formula assumes an exponential distribution of arrivals and service times which is adequate to guide the improvement process.*

Quick Take

Four Step Rapid Setup Method

Purpose

- To eliminate wasted time and non-value-add cost in a process
- To improve productivity rates

When to use setup reduction

- Use on any process step where there is a significant lag (setup or changeover time) between the completion of one task and full productivity on the next task

Step 1: Document setup procedures and label each as internal or external

Document all the setup activities and identify them as either:

- **Internal setup,** an activity that must be performed by the process operator even if it interrupts value-add work
  - Manufacturing example: exchanging dies/fixtures in the machine
  - Transactional example: Logging into a computer program

- **External setup,** an activity that could be performed while the equipment is producing parts or the process operator is conducting other value-add work
  - Manufacturing example: retrieving tools and hardware
  - Transactional examples: Preparing figures to enter into a service quote, loading software

Tool #1: Setup documentation worksheet

MACHINE: ______________ DOCUMENTOR: ______________

DATE: ______________ Page 1 of __

SEQ #	START TIME	EVENT	ELAPSED TIME	INT	EXT
1	0	Shut down machine	:30	:30	
2	0:30	Get change parts	3:00		3:00
3	3:30	Remove change parts from machine	3:30	3:30	
4	7:00	Place new change parts on machine	3:30	3:30	
5	10:30	Return change parts to storage	3:00		3:00
6	13:30	Load material onto machine	1:0	1:00	
7	14:30	Generate test piece	:30	:30	
8	15:00	Measure and inspect	2:00	2:00	
9	17:00	Adjust dies	1:00	1:00	
10	18:00	Generate test piece	:30	:30	
11	18:30	Measure and inspect	1:30	1:30	
12	20:00	Generate first good piece	1:00	1:00	
		TOTAL TIME THIS PAGE:	21:00		
		TOTAL TIME ALL PAGES:	21:00		

Tool #2: Area Layout

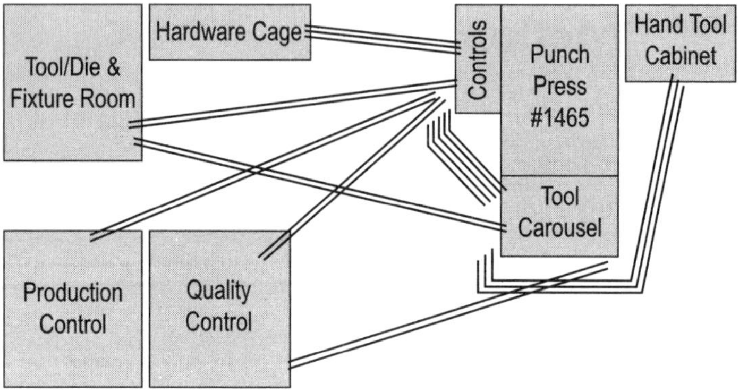

- Helps you understand what movement and motions are required by setup personnel

  Tip: You may discover inefficiencies in layout that can be solved with a 5S effort (*see* p. 206)
- Use the diagram to track pathways of operators/setup personnel to determine the total distance traveled during the operation
  - This information can be used to compare to "after" foot traffic patterns to gain support for workplace changes

Tool #3. The "before" timeline

Used to graphically show each event within the setup and highlight which take the longest. Leave room for the "after." *See the end of this section for an example that includes both before and after data.*

Tool #4. Improvements worksheet

- Number the setup activities in sequence, then enter those numbers on a worksheet

SEQ #	IMPROVEMENT	STEP 1	STEPS 2, 3, & 4
1	Moving "get change parts" to external	3:00	
2	Moving "return change parts" to external	3:00	
	SETUP REDUCTION BY STEP	6:00	
	TOTAL SETUP REDUCTION (STEP 1 and 2, 3, & 4)		
	(BST) BEGINNING SETUP TIME		
	% SETUP REDUCTION		(TSR/BST) 100

- Brainstorm and list improvement opportunities
- Estimate the net reduction in setup time from the improvement

STEP 2: Offload internal setup to external setup wherever possible

- Focus on any activity or task that causes you to stop the process. Then ask why you have to stop, and figure out how to eliminate that source of delays or interruptions.
- Brainstorm ways to convert internal setup to external setup
  - What could you to do make the information, equipment, materials, etc., available to the process operator without requiring him or her to interrupt value-add work?

    Ex: Have computer programs compile orders every evening so all that all the information is waiting for order processors the next morning

    Ex: Use Replenishment Pull systems (p. 216) that will automatically deliver required materials the workstation before the operator runs out

STEP 3: Streamline internal setup

Look for ways to make any setup that must be done by the process operator more efficient.

Ex: Redesign the workplace to simplify, reduce, or eliminate movement (put manuals or tools within arm's reach, for example)

Ex: Link databases so complete customer information is automatically filled in when an operator enters a name or address

STEP 4: Eliminate adjustments required as part of setup routines

- Adjustments and test runs are used in manufacturing to fix inaccurate centering, settings, or dimensioning
- Use mistake-proofing (p. 233), visual controls (p. 237), process document, and any other means you can think of to make sure that equipment settings, part placements, etc., can be performed perfectly every time
  - Abandon reliance on intuition. Do studies to get data on what settings are best under what conditions, what procedures result in most accurate part placement, etc.

Document results

Highlight conversion to external setup

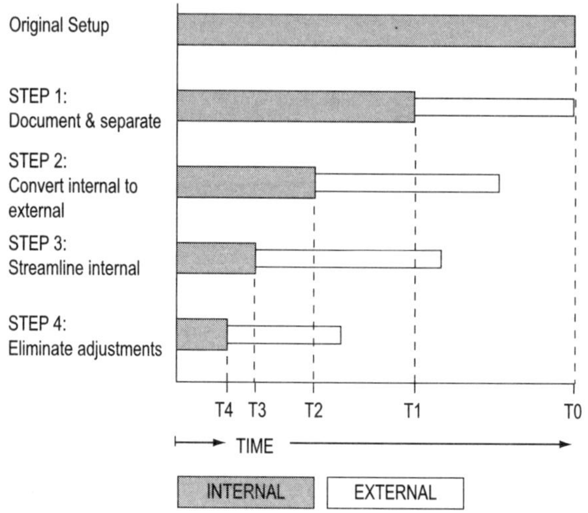

Before/After chart

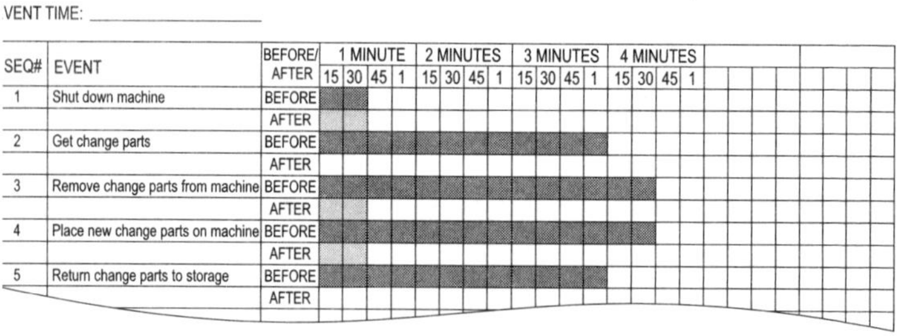

Quick Take

Adapting Four Step Rapid Setup for service processes

(*See* p. 223 for background on setup reduction)

The underlying principle is the same for reducing setup in transactional processes as it is for manufacturing processes: you want to reduce interruptions to value-add work. The language is a bit different, however.

Step 1. Document and differentiate serial from parallel setup activities

Serial events are activities that cannot (or should not) be performed while any other task is being completed

Ex: All activities by a Teller when dealing with a customer face to face or over the phone (don't want to make customers wait)

Parallel events are activities that **could** be performed while another task is being completed

Ex: Loading software programs, processing data

Step 2. Convert serial setup activities to parallel setup activities

- Goal: Offload setup activities to some other person, activity, or process (so they no longer disrupt value-add work)
- Use brainstorming and multivoting techniques to identify and select improvement ideas
- Include Impact/Effort (p. 264) to help you prioritize which ideas to test first
- Re-examine serial events from Step 1 and verify they are actually serial (put on your creative thinking hat and see if there are any activities you classified as serial that could be done in parallel)

3. Streamline remaining serial activities

- Simplify, reduce, eliminate movement
  Ex: Moving printers/copiers vs. walking to pick up hard outputs

- Use electronic aids where possible
  Ex: Barcoding vs. typing/writing, electronic notepads (that can be hooked into master databases) vs. handwritten notes
- Manage system/network needs:
  Ex: Computing equipment to sort disparate requirements offline (*see Lean Six Sigma for Service*, McGraw-Hill, 2003)

4. Eliminate adjustments/standardize work

- Examine the "ramp up" time in serial setup work—any time of reduced output
- Ask what prevents the process from operating at full speed during those time periods
- Be creative in finding ways to address those issues
  Ex: if people need to look up information, have it available through linked databases and keyword searches

Total Productive Maintenance (TPM)

Purpose

To reduce scheduled and unscheduled downtime from typical levels of 30% to below 5%.

Useful definitions

Preventive Maintenance: maintenance that occurs at regular intervals determined by time (Ex: every month) or usage (Ex: every 1000 units)

Predictive Maintenance: maintenance performed on equipment based on signals or diagnostic techniques that indicate deterioration in equipment

Both are common sense approaches for proactively maintaining equipment, eliminating unscheduled downtime, and improving the level of cooperation between Operations and Maintenance.

When to use TPM

- Use when planned and unscheduled downtime are contributing to poor Process Cycle Efficiency

How to do TPM

Prework: Assess current operating conditions

- Evaluate machine utilization, productivity, etc. (*see* form below)
- Tally maintenance repair costs (parts and labor)

Availability
A. Total time available _____ min
B. Planned down time (Breaks, meeting, Prev. Maint. ...) _____ min
C. Run time A-B _____ min
D. Unplanned Downtime 1+2+3= _____ min
1. Breakdown minutes _____
2. Change over minutes _____
3. Minor stoppages _____
E. Net operating time C-D _____ min
F. Available Percentage E/C x 100 _____ %

Performance
G. Processed Amount (total good and bad) _____ units
H. Design lead time (ideal) _____ min/unit
I. Performance percentage [(HxG)/E]x100 _____ %

Quality
J. Total Rejects _____ units
K. Quality Percent [(G-J/G)]x100 _____ %

OEE
Overall Equipment Effectiveness FxIxK= _____ %

Solution Phase #1: Return equipment to reliable condition

Inspect and clean machine, identify needed repairs, and tag defects that need attention.

1. **Clean machine thoroughly** (done by all team members)
   - Remove debris and fix physical imperfections
   - Thoroughly degrease
   - Use compressed air for controls
   - Change filters, lubricants, etc.

- Lubricate moving parts and joints
- Remove unnecessary tooling, hardware, supplies, etc.

2. Place a color-coded tag or note on areas requiring repair. Record all needed repairs in a project notebook.

Information Needed on Tags

- Asset number of machine
- Location and relative position of defect on machine
- Name of originator and date

Color coding of tags

- Oil Leaks - Orange
- Coolant Leaks - Green
- Air Leaks - Yellow
- Machine Defects - Pink
- Electrical Problems – Blue

3. Perform repairs

- Production Supervisor has to make machine available
- Manager/sponsor has responsibility to make sure tagged problems are fixed (by assigning individuals or teams, for example)
- Actual repairs can be done by any qualified person

Solution Phase #2: Eliminate breakdowns

1. Review defect tags from Phase 1
2. Eliminate factors contributing to failure:
    - Secure and tighten all fasteners, fittings, bolts and screws
    - Replace any missing parts
    - Replace any damaged, worn or wrong size parts
    - Resolve all causes of leaks, spillage, spray and splatter
3. Improve accessibility to the part or area so you can regularly clean, lubricate, adjust, inspect

Solution Phase #3: Develop TPM information database

- Document all preventive and predictive maintenance procedures
  - Often done by a team
  - Documentation should include who has the responsibility for performing each task, and frequency of the task

Solution Phase #4: Eliminate defects

1. Provide for early detection of problems by training operators in preventive and predictive maintenance techniques (PMs)
   - Operators must be trained on all prescribed PMs
   - Operator is responsible to perform PMs as documented
   - Production Supervisor to insure PMs are effective

2. Install visual controls (*see* p. 237 for details)

   Ex: Lubrication placards in place

   Ex: All air, water, gas, and coolant lines are labeled

   Ex: 5S Audit scores posted

3. Help prevent future failures by training maintenance staff in proper techniques
   - Preventive/Predictive maintenance procedures usually scheduled jointly by maintenance and production

4. Implement 5S housekeeping and organization (*see* p. 210)

5. Regularly review and improve machine performance
   - Hold regular, joint TPM reviews with both Maintenance and Production representatives
   - Track progress of ongoing activities
   - Identify areas for future improvements
   - Initiate corrective action when needed
   - Use TPM metrics (below)

6. Improve safety
   - Use any safety procedures standard for your business (lockout/tagout procedures, proper lifting techniques, use of personal protective equipment)

TPM Metrics

As with any process, metrics are needed to both monitor process performance and understand gains made from the TPM effort

Operation Equipment Effectiveness (OEE)
OEE = Availability Level x Operating Level x Quality Level

Mean Time Between Failure (MTBF)

Mean Time To Repair (MTTR)

Mistake proofing & prevention (Poka-yoke)

Purpose

Mistake prevention is the ability to stop mistakes before they occur.

Ex: Machine operations that make it very difficult or impossible to produce a defective product. Does not require human assistance.

Ex: Electronic checklist built into a process

Mistake proofing is making it impossible for errors to be passed to the next step in the process.

Ex: Devices or systems that either prevent the defects or inexpensively inspect each item to determine whether it is defective

Ex: Software programming that makes is impossible to move onto the next step until all information is entered into a form

When to use mistake prevention and mistake proofing

Use when rework to correct errors or process delays downstream (perhaps caused by a lack of material or information) are hurting Process Cycle Efficiency.

Two mistake-proofing systems

A. Control/Warning Approach

- Shuts down the process or signals personnel when an error occurs
- Dials, lights, and sounds bring attention to the error
- Prevents the suspect work from moving on until the process step is complete
- Process stops when irregularity is detected (may be necessary if too costly to implement mistake proofing)
- High capability of achieving zero defects

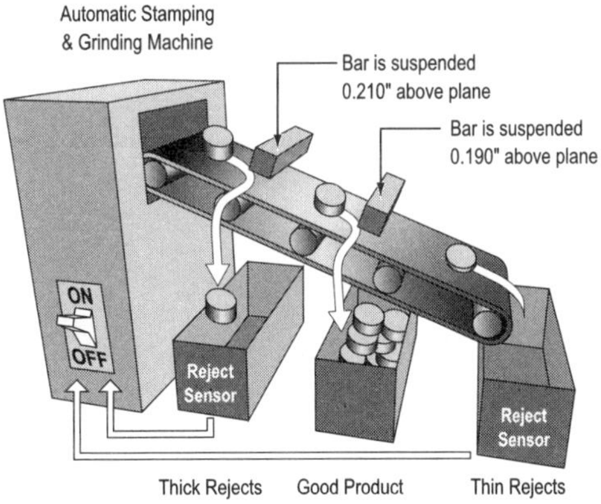

B. Prevention Approach

- Employs methods that DO NOT ALLOW an error to be produced
- 100% elimination of mistakes (100% zero defects)

7 Steps to mistake proofing

1. Describe the defect and its impact on customers
2. Identify the process step where the defect is discovered and the step where it is created
3. Detail the standard procedures where the defect is created
4. Identify errors in or deviation from the standard procedure

5. Investigate and analyze the root cause for each deviation
6. Brainstorm ideas to eliminate or detect the deviation early
7. Create, test, validate, and implement mistake-proofing device

Quick Take

Process balancing design principles

If overall lead time suffers because work is improperly balanced (*see* takt time chart on p. 53), use these principles to help you identify improvements.

- Minimize movement
- Stabilize lead time first before trying to minimize it
- Maximize resource efficiency
- Minimize number of process steps
- Balance tasks/labor across process steps
- Maximize space utilization
- Minimize takt variance
- Minimize NVA (conveyance, standby, and motion wastes)
- Minimize the need to rebalance as demand requirements change
- Minimize volume variability (combine product category demand)
- Maximize flexibility to allow for product introductions and discontinuations
- Use training and continual reinforcement to maintain gains

Work cell optimization

Purpose

To reduce the time needed to complete a task or set of tasks and eliminate opportunity for mistakes.

When to use work cell optimization

Whenever you have inefficient workflow (too much movement of people or materials).

Cell design principles

- Co-locate related work, use cellular layouts
- Cross-train employees for multiple jobs to create a flexible workforce
- Machine & resource layout follows process sequence
- Small and inexpensive equipment
- One-piece flow processing
- Easy moving/standing operations
- Production paced to takt (rate at which the customer buys the product)
- Standard operations defined
- Remove authorization barriers

How to optimize work cell design

You will never get the design perfect the first time around–get it in place, then use operator feedback and process performance to tweak the layout/design,

Phase 1: Prework

- Stabilize lead times throughout the entire process
- Eliminate part shortages
- Make sure the process AS A WHOLE is meeting customer requirements (demand, quality)

Phase 2: Redesign a work cell

1. Design (layout, flow) for multiple machines or multiple steps per operator, but typically overstaff at first (don't sacrifice CTQs)
2. Decide where raw materials and WIP inventory will be located
3. Select a cell design (*see* options below) and put into place
4. Apply operational improvements to reduce batch sizes
5. Apply line balancing principles (*see* p. 235) to smooth task times
    - End goal is a batch size of one (known as continuous flow manufacturing/one-piece flow)

Work cell optimization: Design options

U cell

- Easy to see entire product path
- Easy for operators to operate multiple machines
- Material handling to/from cell typically at single location
- Facilitates ownership of process

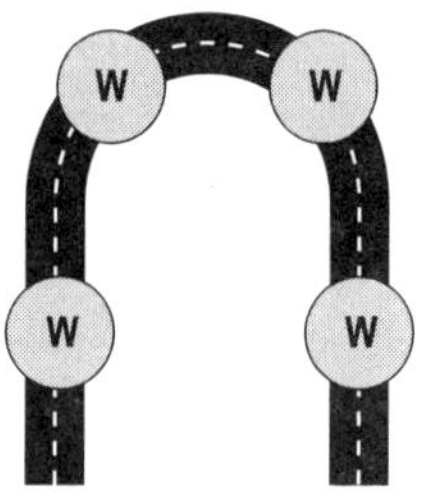

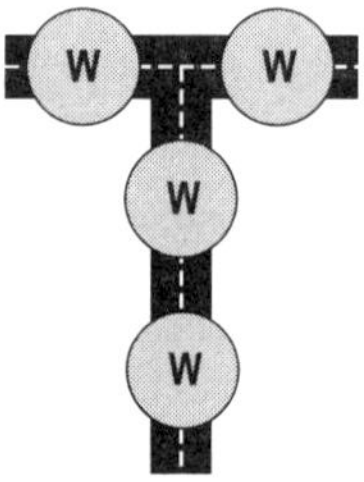

T Line

- Good for products requiring two or more sources of input (other cells?)
- Also good for cells that run two (or more) different end products with some operations in common

Z cell

- Good for building around monuments (structural beams, oven and machining centers, etc.) or other capacity constraints (receiving, shipping, etc.)
- Still allows operators to manage more than one machine/operation

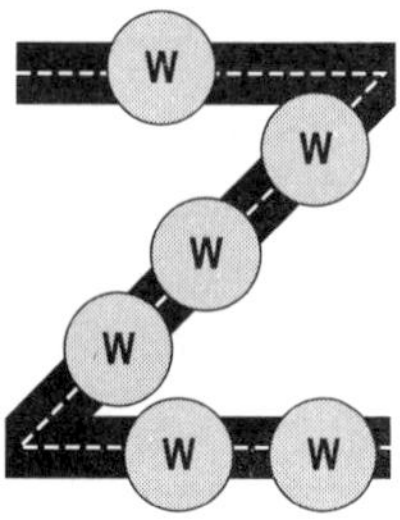

Quick Take

Visual Process Controls

Highlights

Visual controls include a variety of displays and visual markers in the workplace that help you:

- Establish and post work priorities
- Visually display whether expected daily performance was met: "Was today a good day or a bad day?"
- Better understand the flow of inputs and production
- Quickly identify abnormal conditions
- Display standardized methods in use
- Communicate performance measures
- Display the status of all elements critical to safe and effective operations
- Provide feedback to/from team members, supervisors, and managers
- Eliminate the need for meetings!

Safety Indicators

Takt boards/Production Summary Boards

- Takt boards monitor the output of a process or process step so you can judge if it is meeting customer demand
- Takt boards should provide at least three key pieces of information:
  - The work being done (be specific)
  - The desired speed (completion rate)
  - Actual completion rate

Takt Board: Order Entry Department				
Yesterday:		443 Orders		1.61 Orders/Hr
Today		**440 Orders**		**1.66 Units/Hr**
Hour	Scheduled	Actual +-	Cum Diff	Comments
7-8 AM	60	53	-7	System down f/5 min
8-9 AM	60	59	-8	
9-10 AM	45	48	-5	
10-11 AM	60	61	-4	
11-12 PM	30	34	0	Took late lunch
12-1 PM	60	59	-1	
1-2 PM	50	50	-1	
2-3 PM	40	41	0	
3-4 PM	35	35	0	Over 7 min: Software issue
Totals	440	440		

Production/process boards

Issue boards are used to communicate information about the improvement project or ongoing process management.

Process summary

Lists information relevant to your workplace:

- Jobs in process
- Amount of WIP and its dollar value (cost or potential revenue)
- Daily takt rate
- Productivity rates
- Actual vs. desired output, lead time

- Unresolved issues–divided between those the work team can handle and those where they need help from someone with particular expertise (an engineer, lawyer, etc.) or authority (a sponsor or manager)

Dashboard Metrics

- Rolled throughput yield
- On-time delivery
- Weekly takt rate average
- Equipment uptime/downtime (unscheduled maintenance)
- Productivity
- Sigma level

Personnel Skill & Training boards

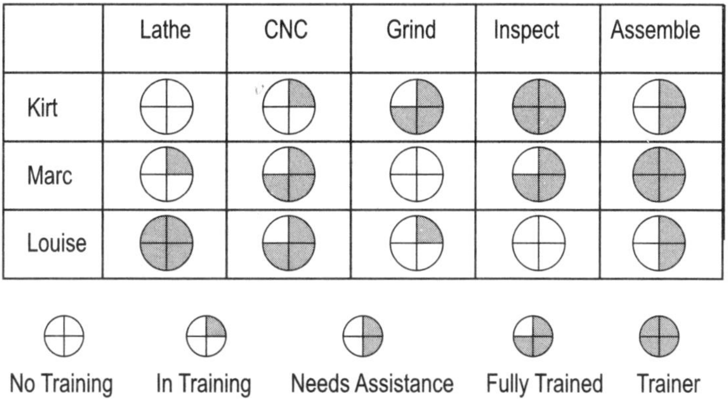

A posted board that lists individuals and summarizes their status with respect to desired training. Can help set priorities for training and help staff know whom to consult with a particular question.

5S boards

Displays status of 5S Project

- Set-in-order maps
- Standardize checklists
- 5S audit results (checklist)
- 5S audit results (spider graph)
- Action plan for improvement
- Before/After photos

CHAPTER 10

Complexity Value Stream Mapping and Complexity Analysis

Purpose of these tools

Lean and Six Sigma tools are most often used to investigate problems with only one product or service. For example, the value stream map of page 45 followed only one high-volume product family down the process flow. But often the biggest contributor to non-value-add time and costs is the *variety* of products and services (and especially the impact of low-volume offerings).

The purpose of these tools is to help you diagnose and quantify complexity opportunities in your business unit or value stream. (For more information on complexity analysis, and for the strategic corporate-wide approach, refer to *Conquering Complexity in Your Business*, McGraw-Hill, 2004.)

Overview of Complexity tools

1) **Product/Service Family grid,** p. 242–sorts your products or services into families based on which process steps they use and their costs. Use as prework for a complexity value stream map (to allow you to represent full diversity without mapping every single product or service through every process step).
2) **Complexity value stream map,** p. 243–visually depicts the combined flow of multiple products or services through a process, which can highlight where complexity has its biggest impact.
3) **Complexity Equation for assessing the impact of complexity on Process Cycle Efficiency (PCE),** p. 245–use to diagnose what process factors are contributing to low PCE.
4) **Complexity Matrix (including calculations of PCE destruction),** p. 246 to 247–a table that allows you to compare the amount of process efficiency "eaten up" by products or services at each major process step. The goal is to answer the question: is what we're experiencing a process problem or a product/service problem?

5) **Substructure analysis,** p. 248–illustrates opportunities to reduce complexity by exploiting common parts, procedures, etc., between products or services. Done as a check to prevent eliminating products or services that can be made less complex with little effort.

6) **"What if" analyses,** p. 250–allows you to quantify the impact of the options you propose taking to reduce complexity.

Product/service family grid

Purpose

- To help you determine where to focus limited resources on data collection and observation so you can create a complete complexity value stream map with the least time and effort

			PROCESS STEPS						
Extended Volume (thousands)	Margin	Service	Application	Processing	Credit Check	Appraisal	Inspection	Close	Family Class
$1,040	2.0%	Refinance ARM	X	X	X	X		X	A
$5,200	2.5%	Refinance Fixed	X	X	X	X		X	A
$1,560	1.8%	New Home ARM	X	X	X	X	X	X	B
$2,600	2.2%	New Home Fixed	X	X	X	X	X	X	B
$520	1.5%	Home Equity	X	X	X	X		X	C
$780	1.4%	Line Of Credit	X	X	X			X	D

When to use a product/service family grid

- Prior to creating a complexity value stream map to identify representative products or services to include in the map

How to create a product/service family grid

1. **List the subprocesses in a business unit, or within your project value stream, across the top of a matrix**
2. **List each product or service down the side**
3. **Mark which products/services use which processes**
4. **Sort your products or services into families based on the similarity of process flow**
   - You can also include other factors such as processing time per unit

– The grid on the previous page from a financial services company identified four separate families of services. In theory, they could have clustered "Home Equity" loans (Family C) with the two Refinance options that comprise Family A. But they decided to keep the equity loans as a separate family because the volume is so much lower than either Family A offering. Family B options all require Inspections; Family D is the only offering that does not require an Appraisal.

Tips

- Low-volume offerings have a disproportionate impact on complexity. While you can cluster several low-volume offerings into a single family do NOT cluster them with higher-volume offerings.
- Aim to group the products/services into 3 to 10 families.

Complexity Value Stream Map (CVSM)

Purpose

- To visually capture the process impact of having multiple products/services flowing through the same process.
- To capture key process data that help diagnose complexity. These data are inputs to the Complexity Equation.

When to use a complexity value stream map

- When performing complexity analysis or any time your processes handle multiple products or services

How to create a complexity value stream map

The beginning instructions are the same as for a VSM (see p. 45).

1. **Select one representative product/service from each family (based on a family grid, p. 242).**
2. **Walk the process as if you were each product or service and gather the following data:**
   - **Estimated cost per activity:** This is the total cost, not the cost per offering

- **Process time (P/T):** Total amount of time spent, broken out into value-add and non-value-add time per unit for each type of service or product
- **Changeover (setup) time:** Any time that lapses between changing from one service or product to another, including the time it takes someone to get up to full speed after switching tasks (a learning curve cost)
- **Queue time:** The time that items spend waiting to be processed
- **Defects and rework:** Raw counts (and/or percentages) of process yields and the time and cost needed to "fix" defective services or products at each activity
- **Demand rate (also called takt time):** The rate of customers demand for each type of service or product
- **Number of offerings:** Number of different services or products processed at the activity
- **Uptime:** Time worked per day minus breaks and interruptions
- **Things-in-process or work-in-process:** The number of items (physical, paper, or electronic) at each process step

3. **Use the instructions for creating a value stream map (see p. 45).** Use a unique symbol to represent each product or service family. The example below shows three families from the financial services company.

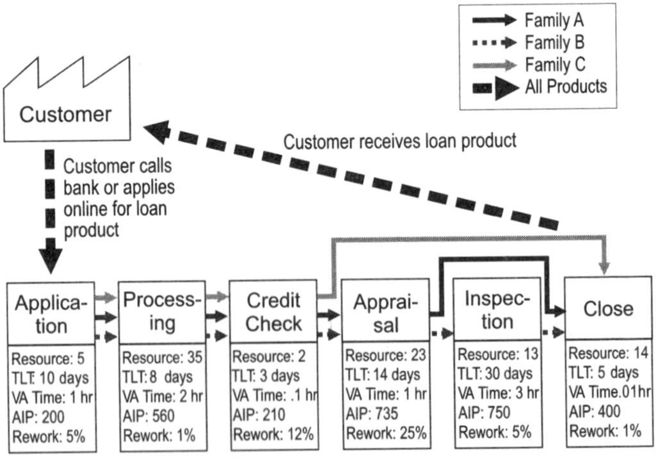

AIP = Applications in Process (WIP)
TLT = Total Lead Time

Quick Take

Process Cycle Efficiency (PCE)

Process Cycle Efficiency (PCE) is one of the most useful metrics for evaluating how well any process operates and for comparing different processes.

$$\text{Process Cycle Efficiency} = \frac{\text{Value-add Time}}{\text{Process Lead Time}}$$

Quick Take

The Complexity Equation

The Complexity Equation breaks down the PCE equation into its component parts. It should be used to determine what factors are contributing to low PCE levels.

$$\text{PCE} = \frac{2V(1-X-PD)}{N(2A+1)S}$$

V = Total value-add time in the process (Note: In many cases, it's OK to use processing time as a proxy for value-add time, so V= AP)

X = Percent of products or services with quality defects

P = Processing time per unit

D = Total demand of products or services

N = Number of different tasks performed at an activity

A = Number of activities or steps in the process

S = Longest setup time in the process

Note

- The equation above is a simplified version of the full complexity equation. For example, it assumes no variation in demand or processing times. In this form, it is fully adequate to provide useful insight. A much more sophisticated version can be built using the full equations to simulate the more complex case: *see Conquering Complexity in your Business* (McGraw-Hill, 2004) for more details.

Complexity matrix

Purpose

To uncover patterns and understand whether the biggest issue relates to a particular product or service family, or to the process through which a product or service flows.

Service	Process Step 1	Process Step 2	Process Step 3	Process Step 4	Total for each family
A	1.9%	2.3%	1.4%	5.9%	11.5 %
B	4.3%	2.8%	6.0%	6.0%	19.1%
C	12.8%	12.7%	14.4%	31.0%	70.9%
D	38.2%	47.6%	18.3%	17.5%	121.6%

PCE destruction figures

When to use a complexity matrix

Use a Complexity Matrix after complexity value stream mapping to analyze the nature and degree of PCE destruction.

How to create a complexity matrix

1. Calculate PCE Destruction (*see* next page) for each offering
2. Enter the data into a matrix like that shown below.

Interpreting the results

Matrix with a process problem

If a process problem is indicated, corrective actions may include traditional Lean Six Sigma actions, such as improving quality, reducing lead time or WIP, etc.

Service Family	Process Step 1	Process Step 2	Process Step 3	Process Step 4	Total for each family
A	1.9%	2.3%	1.4%	5.9%	11.5 %
B	4.3%	2.8%	6.0%	6.0%	19.1%
C	12.8%	12.7%	14.4%	31.0%	70.9%
D	38.2%	47.6%	18.3%	17.5%	121.6%

Step 4 generally has the highest PCE destruction levels

Matrix with a product/service problem

Service Family	Process Step 1	Process Step 2	Process Step 3	Process Step 4	Total for each family
A	1.9%	2.3%	1.4%	5.9%	11.5 %
B	4.3%	2.8%	6.0%	6.0%	19.1%
C	12.8%	12.7%	14.4%	31.0%	70.9%
D	38.2%	47.6%	18.3%	17.5%	121.6%

Families C and D have much higher PCE Destruction levels than Families A and B

If a product/service problem is indicated, traditional Lean Six Sigma approaches may be less effective, since the cause of poor PCE is not a process step but the product itself. Options include stratifying the offering or increasing commonality (reducing the number of parts, assemblies, suppliers, forms, etc.). Other options include diverting products through a different (and lower-cost or separate) delivery channel; improving the design or configuration; or potentially outsourcing or eliminating the offering.

Quick Take

PCE destruction calculations (for a Complexity Matrix)

The heart of the Complexity Matrix a figure called PCE Destruction (PCED).

$$\text{PCED} = \frac{\left(\dfrac{(\text{PCE of all steps except Target}) - (\text{PCE Baseline})}{\text{PCE Baseline}}\right) * 100}{\text{Demand}}$$

The PCED equation has three important aspects:

1) You're comparing the process with and without the particular step for each family of offerings—that's the "all steps except target minus baseline" part of the equation. It's like asking "what would PCE be if we removed this step for this offering?"
2) The impact is being expressed as a ratio or percentage of the "with" and "without" figures compared to the baseline. That

means you may get numbers bigger than 1 (equivalent to 100%).

- Ex: if PCE rose from 1% to 4% when an offering was eliminated, then that offering was destroying 3% of PCE or three times the amount of the baseline PCE

3) The ratio is adjusted for demand so the final PCED number is a "per unit" figure.
   - Ex: Suppose you got the numbers used in item 2 (an increase from 1% to 4% PCE) for both a low-volume (say, 10 unit) offering and a high-volume (say, 100 unit) offering. PCED is 30 for the low-volume offering vs. 3 for the high-volume offering.
   - Focusing on "per unit" PCED reinforces the message that low-volume offerings have a proportionately greater impact on PCE than high-volume offerings

Higher PCED numbers are always worse than lower PCED numbers. What's "high" and what's "low" depends on your situation, but higher numbers mean that a particular combination of offering and process task consumes more PCE than combinations with lower numbers.

Quick Take

Substructure analysis

Highlights

- A substructure analysis looks at the commonality between the components of the offerings in a given value stream
- More easily done in manufacturing operations where there is better documentation of part numbers used in various end products, but can be applied in services as well
- The purpose is to expose duplicate or near-duplicate components that could be combined in order to reduce the complexity of the product/service design and delivery

In manufacturing

1. **Locate and compare any documentation that lists parts, materials, process steps, etc., used by different products**
   - In manufacturing, this is most often in a Bill-of-Material (*see* next page)

2. **Look for hidden commonality between the different products**
3. **Identify ways to increase commonality (reducing part numbers, assemblies, suppliers, etc.)**

Segments of two Bill-of-Materials from Electric Generator Inc. for two frames that differ in only four parts

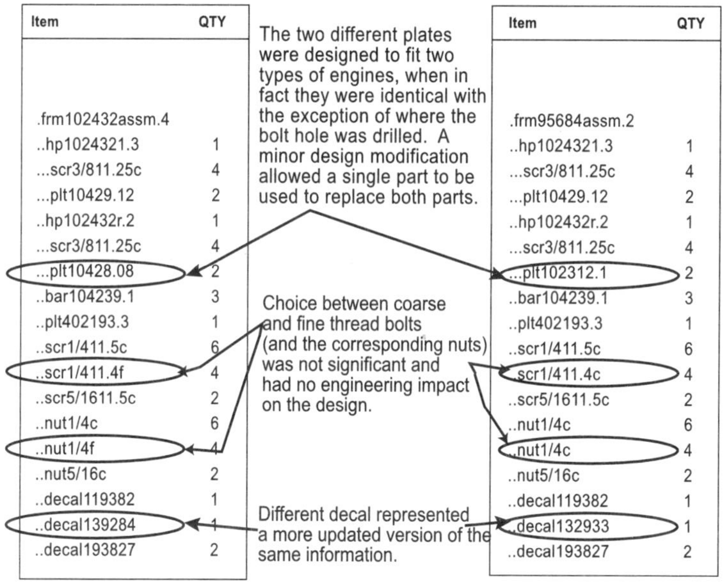

Item	QTY
.frm102432assm.4	
..hp1024321.3	1
...scr3/811.25c	4
...plt10429.12	2
..hp102432r.2	1
...scr3/811.25c	4
...plt10428.08	2
..bar104239.1	3
..plt402193.3	1
..scr1/411.5c	6
..scr1/411.4f	4
..scr5/1611.5c	2
..nut1/4c	6
..nut1/4f	4
..nut5/16c	2
..decal119382	1
..decal139284	1
..decal193827	2

Item	QTY
.frm95684assm.2	
..hp1024321.3	1
...scr3/811.25c	4
...plt10429.12	2
..hp102432r.2	1
...scr3/811.25c	4
...plt102312.1	2
..bar104239.1	3
..plt402193.3	1
..scr1/411.5c	6
..scr1/411.4c	4
..scr5/1611.5c	2
..nut1/4c	6
..nut1/4c	4
..nut5/16c	2
..decal119382	1
..decal132933	1
..decal193827	2

This company compared the bills-of-material for two frames that were treated as entirely separate assemblies. They discovered the two frames shared all but four parts, three of which added no form, function, or feature to the frame. The company found areas of commonality that could be exploited to simplify product design and manufacture (which reduces non-value-add work and will translate into improved PCE).

In services

- Comparative information is not as easy to come by in services, so you'll have to do more digging
- Try documenting the types of paperwork used in different processes, commonality in the software applications, common process steps (perhaps revealed in the value stream map), and so on

Quick Take

What-if analyses with Complexity Matrix data

Highlights

- Looks at the impact on PCE Destruction of proposed process or offering changes, such as substructure analysis or Lean Six Sigma improvements

To use what-if analyses...

1. Identify a likely course of action for attacking a specific complexity problem (addressing either a process issue or a product issue).
2. Determine how this change would affect the PCED numbers in the complexity matrix. What impact would you see if you improved quality by X%? Standardized components? Reduced setup time? Eliminated a product or redirected it through a different channel?

Example #1: The impact of removing a process step

Using CVSM data, a company decided to see what would happen if they removed a process step that injected a lot of non-value-add cost into the process. If everything else remained the same, the impact would be...

Steps in process = 9 (down from 10)

Setup time = 0.8 hr (down from 1 hr)

Processing time = 0.0009 hr/pc (down from.001)

From the Complexity Equation, we get...

New expected level of WIP = 40,366 pc

(Note: WIP has been adjusted to account for obsolete inventory in the process)

New Process Lead Time (PLT) = 40,366 / 467 = 86.4 hrs

PLT is reduced from 120 hours to 86.4 hrs

WIP is reduced from 56,000 to 40,366

To gauge overall impact, do the calculations quickly by going back to the basic version of the PCE equation:

PCE = Value-add time (VA) divided by Process Lead Time (PLT)

VA remains constant
(still producing the same number of the same parts)

PLT is now 86.4 hours

PCE_{new} = 2 hrs / 86.4 hrs = 2.3%

$PCE_{new} - PCE_{old}$ = 2.3% - 1.6% = 0.7% gain in PCE

The change in PCE shows that the eliminated step "destroyed" 0.7% of PCE. This represents an improvement of over 40% in the PCE of the process.

Example #2: The impact of removing an offering family

This company also identified one product family that consisted of only two products. They want to investigate the impact of simply stopping production of that family, thus simplifying their product portfolio. Here are the relevant data for the entire manufacturing process, fabrication through shipping, before changes are made…

Process Lead Time is 6 weeks (240 hrs)

Total VA = 192 minutes

PCE = VA/PLT = 192 min / 240 hr * 60 min/hr = 1.3%

WIP = $2.4M or 4800 equivalent finished generators (average cost of $500, sales price of $626 (GPM of 20%)

Exit rate = 4800/240 = 20 generators per hour output

Aggregate demand = 20 pc/hr

Steps in process = 25

Parts in process = 6

Cumulative setup times = 3 hr

Processing Time = 0.008 hr/pc (each unit takes more than 0.008 hrs, but this is scaled by the number of parallel assembly stations)

If the two-product family were dropped but everything else remained the same…

Aggregate demand = 18.6 pc/hr
(down from 20; volume decreased by 7%)

Parts in process = 4 (down from 6; removed two products)

New expected WIP is ~2480 equivalent pieces

New PLT = 2480 / 18.6 = 133 hrs (from 240 hours)

WIP-value is down from $2.4M to $2.14M, a $260,000 reduction in WIP

To gauge overall impact, go back to the basic PCE equation again:

New PCE = VA / PLT = 192 min / (130 hrs * 60 min/hr) = 2.4%

PCE consumed by the small contractor products = 2.4% – 1.3% = 1.1%

CHAPTER 11

Selecting and Testing Solutions

Purpose of these tools

- To generate solution ideas targeted at identified problems
- To select the best solution from among multiple options
- To successfully implement solutions

Deciding which tool to use

- **If you need help generating solution ideas…**
  - Review Sources of Solution Ideas (p. 254) and Benchmarking (p. 254)
- **If you want to compare alternative solutions…**
  - Tips on Solution Selection, p. 255
  - Developing and Using Evaluation Criteria, p. 256
  - Solution selection matrix, p. 258
  - Pairwise ranking, p. 261
  - Cost Evaluation, p. 264
  - Impact/Effort Matrix, p. 264
  - Pugh Matrix, p. 265
  - Other evaluation techniques, p. 268
- **If you want to identify and counteract risks for likely solutions …**

  These tools are generally used on solution ideas that have made it through the initial assessments:
  - Controls Assessment Matrix, p. 269
  - Failure Modes and Effects Analysis (FMEA), p. 270
- **If you want to plan and test solutions…**
  - Piloting testing, p. 273

Quick Take

Sources of solution ideas

- Always start with a confirmed **root cause**, verified by data collection, process observation, and/or experimentation
- Look to the following for ideas on how to counteract the root cause:
  - Ideas sparked by discoveries made during process analysis
  - Best practices
  - Other projects that have faced similar or related challenges
  - Brainstorming (p. 27) (be sure to explore the many advanced creativity techniques published in many sources)
  - Performance targets
  - Benchmarks

Tips

- Focus on one root cause at a time
- Start with the root causes determined to have the biggest contribution to the problem statement

Quick Take

Benchmarking

Highlights

- Benchmarks are measures (of quality, time, or cost) that have already been achieved by some company, somewhere
- They tell you what's possible so you can set goals for your own operations
- Benchmarking can be very helpful to inject new ideas into the process and borrow the good ideas from other companies/industries

Sources of benchmarking data

- Surveys or interviews with industry experts
- Trade or professional organizations (check their databases, seminars, publications, websites, experts)
- Published articles (research, trade)

- Company tours
- Prior experience of current staff
- Conversations

Types of benchmarks

	Pros	Cons
Internal/ Company	Establishes a baseline for external benchmarking Identifies differences within the company Provides rapid and easy-to-adapt improvements	Opportunities for improvement are limited to the company's internal best practices
Direct Competition	Prioritizes areas of improvement according to competition Initial area of interest to most companies Best used for in-depth studies as supplement to competitive intelligence studies	Often a limited pool of participants Opportunities for improvement are limited to "known" competitive practices Potential antitrust issues
Industry	Provides industry trend information Provides management with a conventional basis for quantitative and process-based comparison	Opportunities for improvement may be limited by industry paradigms
Best-in-Class	Examines multiple industries Provides the best opportunity for identifying radically innovative practices and processes Provides a brand new perspective Free exchange of information more likely to occur	Often difficult to identify best-in-class companies Sometimes difficult to get best-in-class companies to participate

Quick Take

Tips on solution selection

1) **Generate potential solutions**: It is best to exhaust all ideas that the team can produce. Often, the best potential solutions emerge toward the end of intense creativity efforts, when everybody has many details fresh in mind related to the problem at hand.
   - The more potential solutions available to explore, the more opportunities for uncovering ideas for improvements

2) **Narrow the list and synthesize:** If you have more ideas than you can reasonably act on, use affinity diagrams (p. 30), multivoting (p. 31), or other techniques to identify themes and trim the list. Whenever possible, synthesize by combining the best characteristics from alternative options to generate a single stronger solution. (Be sure to develop and use evaluation criteria, *see below*.)
3) **Select the best solution:** Selection involves deciding which solution improvements to implement.

Tip

- The synthesis and selection process is iterative. Work through it once to generate some ideas, evaluate those ideas, then brainstorm off the best options or newer ideas to see if you can develop even better solutions.

Quick Take

Developing and using evaluation criteria

Highlights

- Identifying and documenting criteria takes the guesswork out of selecting solutions
- Use all sources of information to determine evaluation criteria
  - Talk to project sponsors, stakeholders, customers, process staff
  - Review your team charter and customer interview notes

Example criteria

- Customer requirements (CTQs)
  - Process or Output Impact–How well will this solve the problem?
  - Customer satisfaction
- Business needs
  - Alignment with strategy
  - Impact on time, operating costs, marketshare, etc.

   - Capital investment
   - Risk to implement
   - Penetration of new markets
   - Brand recognition or enhancement

- Regulatory/Other
   - Adherence to regulatory requirements
   - Safety
   - Environmental and political constraints

Weighting criteria

Not all criteria are created equal. When evaluating alternatives, it's best to weight the criteria by assigning numerical values that indicate relative importance.

1) Identify the criteria you want to use
2) Assign a numeric value to each criteria that indicates its relative contribution towards achieving your goals
   - You can use pairwise comparisons (p. 261) to develop weights if you want
   - Make sure there is enough spread in the values to allow you to distinguish between truly good and truly poor ideas
     Ex: If "Providing on-time delivery" is a lot more important than "using existing software," give delivery a value of 10 and software a 3 or 4
     Ex: If on-time delivery is only slightly more important than using existing software, give delivery a 10 and software a 7 or 8

Tips

Questions to help determine the evaluation criteria:

- What will the best solutions look like?
- What are the barriers to implementation?
- Which type of solutions will be the cheapest to implement?
- Which type of solutions will be the most dramatic? The most visible?
- Which type will show the fastest results and deliver the most "bang for the buck"?

- Which type will meet the least resistance and be the easiest to put in place?
- What factors are most likely to affect your department and other departments?

Solution selection matrix

Purpose

- To document the solution selection process and criteria
- To make sure the solution selected for implementation provides the best chance for meeting the project goals

When to use a solution selection matrix

- Use a solution selection matrix whenever you have two or more alternative solutions to compare (which will be most of the time)

How to create and use a solution selection matrix

1. **Remove show stoppers from your list of alternative solutions.** Solutions with components that would prohibit their implementation should be removed prior to performing additional analysis.

   Ex: addresses a defect but results in a large adverse impact on customers

   Ex: directly conflicts with the organization's strategy

   Ex: goes beyond the scope of the charter

2. **Consider organization fit for each remaining idea.** The solution must be capable of obtaining management commitment, and fit with customer needs, strategic objectives, organizational values, and the organization culture. Eliminate any options that do poorly on questions such as:

   Management commitment—can you develop support for this idea?

Strategic factors and organizational values–is this idea consistent with our one- and two-year goals? five-year goals?

Operating and management systems–does the potential solution complement or conflict with our decision-making, accounting, communication, and reward systems?

3. **Determine project goal impact for each remaining idea.** Each potential solution must be evaluated on its ability **to reduce and eliminate the root causes of poor performance**. The solution must have a sufficient impact on the process to achieve the desired performance levels. Solutions that can't produce the desired results must either be altered to meet the goals or removed from consideration.

   - **Standalone (independent) solution ideas:** These are solutions that by themselves are capable of satisfying the project goals or, due to their uniqueness, can't be combined with other solutions
   - **Coupled solutions** These are solutions that in isolation are not capable of satisfying the project goals, but are capable of being combined with other solutions

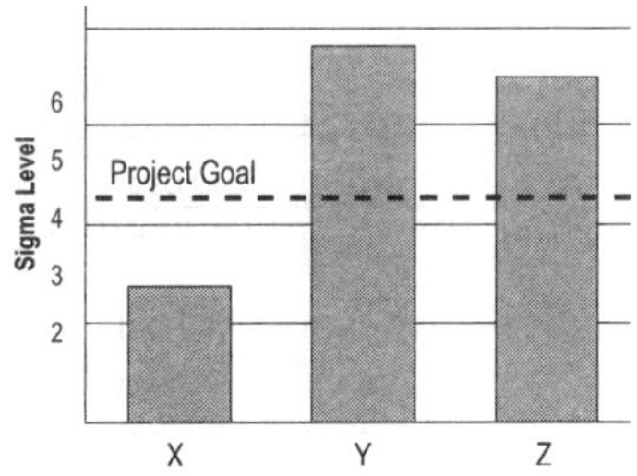

Idea X is removed from consideration because it cannot meet the sigma goal

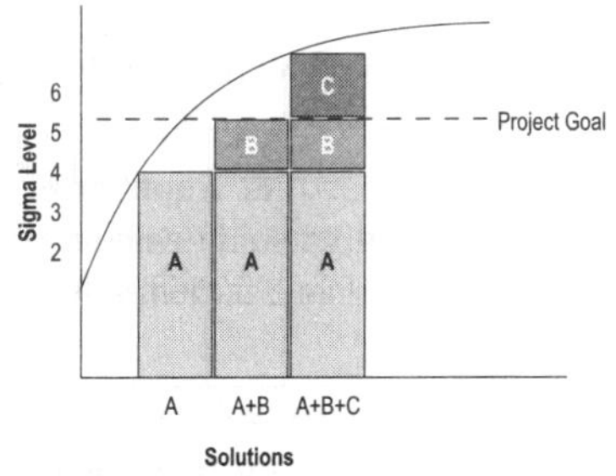

4. **Narrow the list.** Alternative techniques include:

Multivoting–Use to trim a list down to a manageable number (4 to 7). *See* p. 31 for instructions.

CDAM–Evaluate the alternatives and see if you can Combine, Delete, Add, or Modify them.

Pairwise Ranking–Qualitatively rank solutions against each other. *See* p. 261 for instructions.

Force Field Analysis–Evaluate forces working for and against the various alternatives.

5. Enter criteria and top solution alternatives into a solution selection matrix

	Process Impact	Time	Cost vs. Benefit	Other	Total Score	Rank
Weight	2	2	3	1		
Opt 1	8	8	10.5	4	**26.5**	3
Opt 2	14	18	22.5	7	**32.5**	1
Opt 3	2	4	21.0	1	**28**	2

= Raw score (7) times weight (2)

The Option ratings in the chart are calculated by multiplying the base score times the criteria weighting.

6. Score alternatives on each criteria

Process impact: Score the impact the solution will have on the problem (the 'Y'), versus the other solutions.

Evaluate time impact: Decide whether it's important to understand (a) The total amount of time needed to design and implement the solution, or (b) How long it will be before a process is actually performing at desired levels (weeks, months, etc.). Rank or score accordingly. An alternative is to express time impact in terms of the expected full-time resources (FTEs) necessary to implement the solution.

Evaluate cost/benefit impact–What is the relationship between the total costs and the expected benefits the business will realize as a result of the implementation?

Evaluate other impacts–What impacts does the organization want to keep visible during the decision-making process? Common examples include safety, business risk, and morale.

7. Use FMEA (p. 270) or any risk-evaluation technique commonly used in your company, as appropriate

Tips

- After discussing all solutions, team members may find themselves gravitating toward one or two favorites. Remaining objective is important–a bias or uninformed preference may cause the team to overlook excellent cost-beneficial solutions.

- Remember, nothing gets thrown away. These tools help the team focus on likely solutions–but later you may find it helpful to revisit ideas that were set aside previously in order to spark more creative thinking.

Quick Take

Pairwise ranking

Highlights

- Pairwise ranking techniques can be used by individuals or teams to prioritize a list of items qualitatively.
- While there are many different variations of this technique, all of them force you to rank items against each other. The combined results of these paired rankings help to clarify priorities.

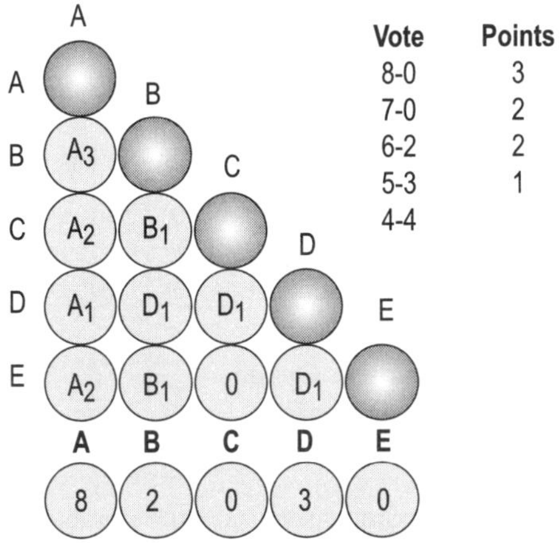

To use pairwise ranking to select solutions...

1. Identify the solution ideas you want to compare
    - List them on a flip chart or white board so that everyone can see them
    - Label them with numbers or letters (Ex: A to E if you have five options)

2. Draw a matrix with as many columns and rows as there are items (Ex: five rows and five columns if you have five items)
    - This matrix will be used to record the results, so it should be visible to everyone (on a flip chart, white board, overhead projector, etc.)
    - Label the columns and rows with the assigned numbers or letters
    - Color in or otherwise mark off the diagonal boxes that represent comparing an item to itself

3. Review or develop criteria
    - During the comparison, you'll be asking how one solution compares to another, which means you all need to agree on what criteria will be used

4. Compare each item to every other item, one at a time, until you've filled out the upper or lower half the matrix (doing both sides would be repetitive)
    - For each comparison, ask which solution is better
    - Use a show of hands or other voting method to select which is better

5. Record the results
    - Simply put the letter or number of the preferred option in the box

      Ex: In one comparison, Option A was voted as being better than option B

	A	B	C	D	E
A		A	A	D	A
B			B	D	E
C				D	E
D					D
E					

6. After completing all comparisons, tally the number of times each option won out. Interpret the results.
    - In the example above, A = 3, B = 1, C = 0, D = 4, and E = 2
    - This would indicate an overall preference for item D.
    - Explore ways to improve option D by incorporating elements of the other strong options. Here, for example, ask why Options A and E are stronger than B or C. Can you work elements of A and E into the solution?

7. OPTIONAL: Sometimes the interpretation is easier if you tally the number of votes each item gets instead of the number of times it "won." Here's a portion of the above example, this time with the number of votes recorded:

	A	B	C
A		A 3	A 4
B			B 5

   - This increases the spread between items, emphasizing strong differences and giving added weight to items that people feel strongly about
   - In this example, the tally might end up something like: A = 12, B = 5, C = 0, D = 18, E = 8

Using pairwise ranking to weight criteria

Uses the same method above except compares potential criteria for evaluating solutions, not the solutions themselves.

1. Identify and label (letter or number) the criteria.
2. Create a table and compare each criterion against each other criterion. In this case you're asking "Which of these criteria is more important?"
3. Tally the number of times each criterion "wins" then add one point (to make sure there are no 0s in the table).
4. Tally the total number of points.
5. Determine the % of points each criterion received.
6. Assign weights (usually on a scale of 1 to 5 or 1 to 10, with higher numbers being better)

Cost evaluation

Most solutions will need to be evaluated based on the cost of implementation.

- Sources of costs: direct vs. indirect, one-time vs. ongoing
- Timing of cost and benefits
- Financial analysis using company-preferred measures (talk to your financial experts to find out which of these are used in your company):
  - Economic Profit (EP)
  - Return on Invested Capitol (ROIC)
  - Working Capital
  - Type I, II & III Savings
- Sensitivity analysis of involved factors
- Qualitative factors (cultural fit, potential shifts in jobs, etc.)

Impact/effort matrix

Quantified Impact on Goal — Final Ranking Priority

Solution	Sec Saving	Final Ranking	Responsible
Close Gap 56', Quick software change, Move Light Downstream	40	1.0	Gary
Formalization of Daily Feedback for Corrective Action	120	1.1	Nate, Mary, Ed
Autowidth Water Jet	30	1.1	Dave Sw.
Shift Standardization, Specified Tasks, Training, Best Practices, Change Matrix	30	1.1	Francis, Mary, Gary
Scale Fix – Power Source	1	1.2	Dave Sw
Fix Top & Bottom Weight Issues (DOE) Change Software for Zone 1& 2 for DP	30	1.2	Nate, Mary, Ed, Dave
Improve Communication (Headsets and Procedures)	20	1.3	Francis, Jordan

Impacts to consider

- Anticipated changes to the overall flow of the work
- Changes in job responsibilities

- New ways to accomplish key tasks–Do you have access to new technology? Can you outsource?
- New ways required to deliver on customer needs
- How will you avoid problems/defects?
- How will you reduce cycle time?
  - Reduce or eliminate rework, sequential processing, batch work, handoffs, approvals/inspections, delays or bottlenecks
  - Increase or improve customer involvement, employee skills/knowledge, parallel processing, one-at-a-time processing (start to finish), non-stop processing, appreciation/accountability for entire job

Pugh matrix

Purpose

A decision-making tool to formally compare concepts (processes, services, products) based on customer needs and functional criteria.

- It quickly identifies strengths and weaknesses for each potential solution so that the strengths can be preserved and the weaknesses corrected or at least addressed
- The objective is to improve upon the initial ideas and eventually converge on an optimal solution

When to use a Pugh matrix

- Primarily used when designing or redesigning products, services, or processes

How to create a Pugh matrix

NOTE: A Pugh matrix analysis is performed iteratively, with each time through called a "run." The first time through ("first run") you want to develop a small number of strong solutions. Then you repeat the full analysis to confirm the initial results.

1. Develop potential solutions (alternative concepts). Capture each, as appropriate, in...
   - Drawings

- Word descriptions
- Other characterizations of potential solutions

2. Identify criteria
   - *See* p. 256 for general instructions. Focus on those most relevant to the purpose of your current effort (customer requirements, design parameters, project goals, etc.)
3. Weight the criteria (*see* p. 257)
4. Select one alternative as the **baseline**
   - Often the current method or model, but could be any of the alternatives
5. Prepare an evaluation matrix
   - List alternative solutions across top of matrix
   - List criteria in first column
   - Importance ratings in second column or in last column
   - Enter "B" in all cells under the Baseline alternative

Pugh Matrix															
Key Criteria	Concepts														Importance Rating
Sum of Positives															
Sum of Negatives															
Sum of Sames															
Weighted Sum of Positives															
Weighted Sum of Negatives															

Concept Selection Legend
Better +
Same S
Worse -

6. Score each of the alternative solutions against the baseline:

   + or ++ means better or significantly better than baseline

   – or – – means worse or significantly worse than baseline

   S means about the same

7. Sum the pluses (+), negatives (–), and "sames" (S)
8. Multiply the counts of the +'s, –'s, and S's by the Importance Rating (weights) and sum vertically to compute the Weighted Total for each concept
   - Do not treat the numbers as absolute
9. Focus first on the alternative(s) with the most pluses and the fewest minuses
10. Look for strengths and weaknesses and determine how to attack the weaknesses
    - What is needed to reverse the negatives?
    - Does the change reverse any of the positives?
    - Can strengths of other alternatives be incorporated to address or reverse the negatives?
    - If another alternative is "S" or "+", perhaps that alternative contains an idea (solution) that could improve the selected alternative
    - If a modified solution emerges, enter it into the matrix
    - Eliminate truly weak concepts from the matrix
11. Examine positives
    - If you find a uniform strength exhibited across a number of solutions, either (a) the criteria are too ambiguous to discriminate between solutions or (b) some solutions are strongly related (are subsets) to the others
      - In the first case, **decompose the criteria** (divide them into subcomponents)
      - In the second case, **decompose the solutions**, then look for ways to recombine them
12. Identify the strongest possible solutions and repeat analysis to confirm first-run results
    - If the first run is not confirmed, continue to analyze and improve the alternatives until a strong solution emerges
    - Conduct a confirmation run using the strongest solution as the baseline

- If the second run confirms the first, proceed to Controlled Convergence

13. Perform Controlled Convergence analysis: enhance positives and eliminate negatives to get a better solution than any of the original ideas
    - List product service and process attributes
    - List alternative solutions
    - Pick strong solution as baseline
    - Evaluate solutions against defined criteria
    - Evaluate solutions as better (+), worse (-), or same (S) compared to baseline
    - Assess the individual solution scores
    - Identify strong and weak solutions
    - Attack the negatives and enhance the positives
      - Attempt to reverse the negatives by improving designs
    - Enhance the positives of the weaker solutions
      - Attempt to improve the solution designs. Strengthen strong solutions with strong aspects of the weaker solutions
    - Abandon solutions that remain weak
      - Add new Solutions if warranted. Matrix should get smaller.
    - Rerun the matrix using the strongest Solution as a new baseline
    - Repeat the process until strong solutions persist through several runs

14. Perform product and process design work if necessary

Tips: Pitfalls that often occur in the first run

- Desire to cut-and-run prematurely terminates process
- Doubts about the validity of process arise, especially as strong solutions emerge and stay strong
- Disruptions by those who see the process as a competitive win-lose contest, rather than a collaborative win-win effort

Other evaluation techniques

Simulation models–Ask for help from experts to develop computer simulations that model the current process and demonstrate how an improved process might operate.

Benchmarking–Identify the "Best-in-Class" organization in any process or capability you're studying, regardless of what industry that company is in. For example, Memorial Hospital might look at Hilton Hotel's guest registration process when evaluating its patient admission process. (*See* more on benchmarking on p. 254.)

Industry standards–Research organizations conduct comparative studies of industries and publish performance data. A project team at a refinery might reference research data on refinery capacities to assist their decision.

Internet research–Using the numerous search engines, teams can conduct competitive analysis or benchmarking with organizations worldwide.

Conducting a limited pilot–The team may elect to implement the solution through a limited pilot. Before and after measurements may be used to extrapolate the value if implemented on a larger scale. Consider the time to implement as well as the associated risks to the normal operation.

Controls assessment matrix

Project Objective: Accurate receipt of contracts via EDI

Risk: Information is lost in transaction

Sufficiency of Control: (x = excessive, a = adequate, i = inadequate)

Controls	Existing Y/N	Is it sufficient? If not, why?	Next Steps
a) Training	Y	a – Training conducted	What? Who? When?
b) Procedures not specific	N	a – Configured to prevent submission of transactions without required data	
c) No Process for customer master	N	i – Customer master verification	

Date: _____ Prepared by: _____ Reviewed by: _____ Next Update: _____

Highlights

- Helps identify the activities designed to protect you and your business unit from high-priority risks

To create a controls assessment matrix...

1. List your highest priority risk
2. List the controls that would help mitigate or eliminate the risk
3. Determine if those controls exist
4. Discuss the appropriateness and sufficiency of each control
5. Identify actions needed to address any control deficiencies

Tips

- Use the results as an input to the Process Control Plan

Failure Modes and Effects Analysis (FMEA)

Purpose

A structured approach to:

- Identify the ways in which a product, service, or process can fail
- Estimate risk associated with specific failure causes
- Prioritize the actions to reduce risk of failure
- Evaluate design validation plan (product/service) or current control plan (process)

When to use FMEA

- When designing new systems, products, and processes
- When changing existing designs or processes
- When carry-over designs are used in new applications
- After system, product, or process functions are defined, but before beginning detailed final design
- In Define: To understand the risks of a project
- In Measure: To understand how process steps or KPIVs relate to risk, and to prioritize KPIVs

- In Analyze: To understand the improvement implementation risks
- In Improve: To assess the effectiveness of a Control Plan

Types of FMEA

1. **Design FMEA:** Analyzes a new process, product, or service design before rollout to understand how it could fail once released. Exposes problems that may result in safety hazards, malfunctions, shortened product life, or decreased satisfaction.
2. **Process FMEA:** Used to improve existing transactional and operational processes to understand how people, materials, equipment, methods, and environment cause process problems. Exposes process problems that may result in safety hazards, defects in product or service production processes, or reduced process efficiency.
3. **System FMEA:** Analyzes systems and subsystems in the early stages of concept and design.

Process or Product Name:	Prepared by:
Responsible:	FMEA Date (Orig) ____________ (Rev)

Process Step / Input	Potential Failure Mode	Potential Failure Effects	SEVERITY	Potential Causes	OCCURRENCE	Current Controls	DETECTION	RPN
What is the process step and Input under investigation?	In what ways does the Key Input go wrong?	What is the impact on the Key Output Variables (Customer Requirements)		What causes the Key Input to go wrong?		What are the existing controls & procedures (inspection and test) that prevent the cause of the Failure Mode?		
								0
								0

How to perform FMEA

1. Review the product, service or process
    - If working on a process, start with the steps that contribute the most value
2. Brainstorm then sort possible failure modes
    - A failure mode is the way in which the component, subassembly, product, input, or process could fail to perform its intended function. They may be the result of upstream operations or may cause downstream operations to fail.

3. List one or more potential effects for each failure mode
   - Answer the question: If the failure occurs, what are the consequences?

4. Assign ratings for severity and occurrence

   Severity of failure: 1-10, with 10 representing *most severe impact on customers*

   Likeliness a failure will occur: 1-10, with 10 representing *most likely to occur*

5. List current monitoring and controls for each failure then assign a detection rating to each

   Detectability of failure: 1-10, with 10 representing least likely to be noticed given your current control methods

6. Calculate a risk priority number (RPN) for each effect by multiplying the three numbers (severity * occurrence * detection)

7. Use the RPNs to select high-priority failure modes
   - Prioritize actions so the highest RPNs are attended to first
   - Exception: Any failure with a severity rating of 10 must be worked on immediately because of impact on customers, even if it does not score a high RPN overall

8. Plan to reduce or eliminate the risk associated with high-priority failure modes
   - Identify potential causes of the selected failure modes
   - Develop recommended actions, assign responsible persons
   - Look for both:
     - Preventive action: Steps that reduce the likelihood of a problem occurring at all, focused on reducing/eliminating root causes prior to occurrence
     - Contingent action: Measures implemented to limit the damage caused by a potential problem should it occur; focused on achieving the goal in spite of difficulties

9. Carry out the plans. Document actions taken

10. Recompute RPN

Process or Product Name:	Prepared by Page ___ of: ___	Process/Product FMEA Form
Responsible:	FMEA Date (Orig) ________ (Rev)	

Process Step / Input	Potential Failure Mode	Potential Failure Effects	SEVERITY	Potential Causes	OCCURRENCE	Current Controls	DETECTION	RPN	Actions Recommended	Resp.	Actions Taken	SEVERITY	OCCURRENCE	DETECTION	RPN
What is the process step and Input under investigation?	In what ways does the Key Input go wrong?	What is the impact on the Key Output Variables (Customer Requirements)		What causes the Key Input to go wrong?		What are the existing controls & procedures (inspection and test) that prevent either the cause of the Failure Mode?			What are the actions for reducing the occurrence of the cause, or improving detection?		What are the completed actions taken with the recalculated RPN?				
Fill carafe with water	Wrong amount of water	Coffee too strong or too weak	8	Faded level marks on carafe	4	Visual inspection	4	128	Replace Carafe	Mel	Carafe replaced	8	1	3	24
			8	Water spilled from carafe	5	None	9	360	Train employees	Flo	Employees trained	8	2	7	112
	Water too warm	Coffee too strong	8	Faucet not allowed to run and cool	8	Finger	4	256	Train employees	Flo	Employees trained	8	2	6	96
			8	Employee not aware of new need for cool water	7	None	10	560	Train employees	Flo	Employees trained	8	1	8	64
	Carafe not clean	Foreign objects in coffee	10	Carafe not washed	4	Visual inspection	4	160	Appoint inspector before storage	Alice	Vera is the new inspector	10	1	4	40
		Bad taste	10	Carafe stored improperly	7	training	5	350	Create storage bin & train employees	Alice	New storage bin & employees trained	10	2	3	60

Tips on scoring systems

- There are a wide variety of quantitative and qualitative scoring "anchors" that can form the basis for your rating scales. If you have difficulty, ask data experts to help you find examples you can use as models.
- Two rating scales typically used:
  - 1 to 5 scale makes it easier for the teams to decide on scores
  - 1 to 10 scale allows for better precision in estimates and a wider variation in scores; it is more commonly used

Pilot testing

Purpose

To identify practical problems and failures in a chosen solution so those can be addressed before full-scale implementation

Key characteristics of a pilot test

A pilot is a **test** of a **selected solution**. This type of test has the following properties:

- Performed on a small scale (limited in scope, budget, and/or time)
- Used to evaluate both the solution and the implementation of the solution

- Used to make full-scale implementation more effective
- Gives data about expected results and exposes issues in the implementation plan

The pilot should test if the process meets both the design specifications and customer expectations.

How to pilot a solution

Phase 1: Plan

What needs to be piloted

Where will the pilots be run

Who will be involved

When and **for how long** will the pilots run

How will the pilots be conducted

Phase 2: Review design

Before conducting the pilot, review your plans to ...

- Make sure all the elements of the design are complete
- Make sure all the elements are well integrated and that interfaces between different parts of the design are tight
- Identify possible failure points and areas of vulnerability to be tested in the pilot
- Evaluate predicted design capability (sigma or capability level)
- Review the pilot and implementation plans

Tips

- Establish review objectives and agenda in advance
- Complete all prework in preparatory meetings
- Keep documentation clear and consistent
- Index documentation to make it easy to find and reference
- Distribute documentation in advance of the meeting
- Set follow-up procedures to confirm completion of action items

Outcomes

- List of key issues raised, identifying who raised them
- List of proposed actions for modifying the pilot, including who is responsible for making the changes
- List of changes needed in documentation
- Schedule of future meetings to assess completion of proposed actions
- Schedule of future design review meetings as appropriate

Phase 3: Finalize design and implement

- Implement design changes identified in Phase 2. If necessary, perform another design review.
- Move to pilot testing and implementation.

Tips

- Carefully observe all activities, effects, and interactions during the pilot
- Actively manage the implementation plan
- Manage expectations and perceptions of customers, management, and staff
- Continue the pilot long enough to establish reliable baseline performance data
- Check for ripple effects and unintended consequences

Phase 4: Evaluate the test and verify results

- Use applicable statistical tools to properly evaluate design predictions, process control, and capabilities
- Celebrate success
  - Communicate small victories
  - Celebrate initial successes
  - Celebrate final results
- Improve on the design if the pilot demonstrates any weaknesses

Tips

- People get impatient to implement solutions so they can have results to show their sponsors, but don't skip the pilot!

- Define success criteria before testing the pilot
- Document all test results and control procedures
- Train all process participants
- Use the tools to help identify project risks
- Identify risks early–evaluate their likelihood and impact
- Create a comprehensive plan to reduce risk exposure

Index

D

F

G

H

I

K

L